# HOW TO SAVE
# FREE ENTERPRISE

# HOW TO SAVE FREE ENTERPRISE

By

## ARTHUR DAHLBERG

*Director, Visual Economics Laboratory,*
*Columbia University*

*Foreword by* Richard Stanton Rimanoczy

*Introduction by* John Chamberlain

THE DEVIN-ADAIR COMPANY / *Old Greenwich,*
Connecticut

*In gratitude*
*To the memory of my parents,*
*Olaf August and Christina Nelson Dahlberg*

# Foreword

MOST ECONOMISTS have resigned themselves to the recurrence of periods of low economic activity known as slumps, recessions, depressions, etc. There is one, however, who has not. He is Dr. Arthur O. Dahlberg, who has a distinguished professional background in predicting business activity, and has published five books on basic economic issues.

Everybody knows *why* slumps occur; people who could be buying stop buying. But why is it feasible for them to defer their buying? Dr. Dahlberg believes that he has the answer.

Money—in its broadest meaning of being a claim to goods—is concurrently produced when the goods are produced. In our economic system the production of goods and of the claims to the goods go on concurrently. The two are synchronized. But in our modern monetary system the use—the exercising of the claims to the goods in the markets —is not designed to be synchronized with the rate of production.

Dahlberg's major premise is that, unlike primitive commodity moneys which, if held off the market, involved a cost of storing and protecting them, modern money—under our commercial banking system—is so backstopped with borrowers' collateral that it can be sluggishly used by both savings banks and individuals without costs. Such sluggishness depresses prices, reduces production and employment and gives the savers a bargaining advantage against workers in the market that attacks the very functioning of limited government.

Dr. Dahlberg's proposed solution is to nudge savings into continuous action by designing a demand deposit money with a demurrage cost.

The author's premise for a continuously balanced economy is sound. Every productive process creates exactly the right amount of purchasing power to buy what is produced because the selling price (under normal conditions) is the total of the payroll, taxes, material costs and profit. Enough is paid out to promptly take the goods off the market. When spending falls below normal, goods accumulate and must be sold for less and unspent money begins to slow down. If this money diminished in purchasing power, Dr. Dahlberg reasons, it would be spent for *something*. What that something might be would not matter; the money would be at work.

We like what he says about his projected methodology: "There are two superior methods of properly attuning a carrying charge on money with the built-in carrying charge that bears on all physical goods. And neither of these ways involves the imposition of any tax whatsoever. Nor does either of them call for any governmental bookkeeping or administrative effort whatsoever. Neither, moreover, would confront the government with additional problems of enforcement, surveillance or compliance."

The enormous importance of Dr. Dahlberg's objective is too obvious to need any supporting comments by us. Depressions start when people begin to cut back on spending, not for lack of money, but for the unwillingness to spend.

In originality, profundity, lucidity, mastery of the analytical method, and freshness of approach this book will find few equals in economic literature. It is an explosive breakthrough into overlooked economic areas.

"How To Save Free Enterprise" could well turn out to be the base book from which the libertarians of the world proceed to counterattack excessive governmentalism in its many forms.

RICHARD STANTON RIMANOCZY

# Introduction

JOSEPH CONRAD once said that the business of the writer is, above all, to make you see. This may explain why economists, who are writers too, indulge in a predilection for making models. You can see a model. But what if you are seeing something static? Arthur Dahlberg, an economist with a difference, concentrates in his own superior model-making on the dynamic relationships between the various factors of production. An hour's experience in following the flow of purchasing power through the stop-and-go conduits of his "visual economics laboratory" is a revelation.

Dahlberg has the seeing mind par excellence. And, unlike most of our economists, he knows something about the history of production over the entire Christian millenia. He notices the power of the adventitious, the role of accident, in the economic process. It was Arthur Dahlberg who called attention to the part played by the Black Death in raising the wages of the suddenly scarce medieval laborer and emancipating men from serfdom.

A student of John Maynard Keynes, who can both appreciate and see beyond the master, Dahlberg accepts the Keynesian proposition that depressions result when the savings-investment ratio gets out of whack. "Idle money, idle men," as Stuart Chase once put it. But where Chase, along with other Keynesians, jumped to the conclusion that "government investment" was a suitable answer to the problem of putting money into motion, Dahlberg considered the side effects: government investment must be paid out of taxes and/or inflation, and it serves as a damper on the very enterprise that must pay the taxes.

How to tickle savings into productive motion without invoking the heavy hand of the state? Combing over a few thousand years of history, Dahlberg noticed that when money takes an unhoardable form, the result is an evenly-rotating productive system. When the money medium consisted of commodities such as furs or tobacco or of warehouse receipts for precious metal, there was always a wastage factor or a storage charge. Modern checkbook money incurs no such wastage — our modern medium of exchange involves no ownership costs. The owner of potential investment funds can always sit the hurricane out.

With his special knowledge Arthur Dahlberg went back to the "Age of the Gothic," that three-century span in which medieval Europe, emerging from the Dark Ages, went on a building spree. The splendid city halls, elaborate castles, beautiful private mansions and soaring cathedrals all testify to investment money in motion. What made the money move? Christian faith, say the ecclesiastics. But author Hugo Fack noticed that medieval Europe had an unhoardable currency. The rulers of the time had a habit of recalling the money-issue of their predecessors for a re-minting charge or seigniorage fee, sometimes amounting to twenty percent. Eventually the princes, both secular and clerical, started to recall the money-issue every year. Nobody among the common folk wanted to get caught with unused money, so it went into capital forms — sumptuous buildings, beautiful silver shoe buckles, etc. — that eluded the grasp of the re-minter.

Dahlberg's deduction from history prompts him to suggest that the state enforce only those agreements between bankers and borrowers — when borrowers swap their notes and mortgages for newly created demand deposits — which provide that the deposits created shall decline in value by, say, two percent a year. There would be no tax involved; the government would be kept out of it. Big borrowers, faced with a slow erosion of the funds they assemble to carry the costs of business or to engage in new projects would be eager to get the last possible bit of mileage out of their money. Spending would cease to be deferred.

As a second proposition Dahlberg would set the Treasury price for gold at the prevailing free market price, or even above it, and then lower the support price gradually. This would make gold an unhoardable medium along with check money. But Dahlberg doesn't insist on his second proposition; the built-in demurrage of maintaining demand deposit money in idleness would be enough, he thinks, to eradicate the one big flaw in the capitalist system.

There is much more than a cure for "postponable investment money" in Dahlberg's book. Even those who reject his built-in demurrage proposal will find its general analysis of the way money works fascinating. "How To Save Free Enterprise" is a profoundly interesting and thought-provoking book. The analysis in the book is superb. The historical sweep of the book is magnificent, and is alone worth the price of admission.

JOHN CHAMBERLAIN

# Contents

## PART THREE – INTERNATIONAL EXCHANGE PROBLEMS

## PART FOUR – SOCIOECONOMIC PROBLEMS BROUGHT ON BY UNRELIABLE MONETARY DEMAND

## PART FIVE – SUPPLEMENTS

# Charts, Diagrams and Tables

COLOR CHART FOLDOUT ON PAGE 92

# Acknowledgements

THE CHAPTER, How Money Originates and Circulates, grew out of an exhibit which I was retained to devise for the American Economic Foundation (of which I am a trustee) for use in its exhibit building, The Hall of Free Enterprise, at the New York World's Fair. In particular I wish to express my thanks to Mr. Richard Rimanoczy, president of that foundation, for his critical reading of the section of this book dealing with inflation and other major portions of my work, as well as for his continuous and wise counseling.

For reading practically the entire manuscript critically and most helpfully, I wish to thank both my good friend, Mr. Alfred Litwak, and my son, Eric. My gratitude also goes out to my many friends who have encouraged me to continue with the writing of this book.

I also wish to thank the Alfred P. Sloan Foundation for its grant to Columbia University for funding the establishment there of the Visual Economics Laboratory, the purpose of which was to enable me, as the director, to visualize economic processes and arrangements graphically with my unique diagrammatic technique. It has been there that I have had the opportunity to diagram three or four major sectors of the economy, such as Money and Banking, and National Income Accounting, portions of which are included here.

Grateful thanks are also due the magazine, *Banking*, for permitting me to reprint, in my chapters on inflation, large portions of my article, "Why More Inflation Lies Ahead," from its November, 1970, issue; and to the magazine, *Finance*, for permitting me to reprint—in the same chapters—large portions of my article, "Why The Fight Against Inflation Will Fail," from its November, 1969, issue.

# Author's Note

SUPPOSE there were no gold, silver or precious metals in the earth, and that other metals and commodities could not feasibly be used as money. What then could we use as medium of exchange?

If the enforcement of contract agreements in a community could be relied upon—as, in the main, it is today—people could use one another's debt obligations as money. *For better or for worse, that is what the people of major countries have got around to doing.* Today, contract agreements—the mortgages, notes, and bonds of bank borrowers which have been transmuted by the borrowing process into the debt obligations of commercial banks—constitute the money of the world.

This book maintains that the form of contract agreements now used is slightly defective, and that it is in itself occasionally disruptive of the aggregate private monetary demand for goods. Moreover, this book maintains that it would be a relatively simple matter to modify the contract form so as to eliminate the defect, and outlines *two* easy remedies.

Commodity Monies of the eighteenth century, like furs and tobacco, had one of the characteristics of a hot potato—the proverbial item which we try to transfer quickly out of our hands. Because a small cost was involved in merely owning and protecting them, commodity monies carried within themselves a small inducement for their possessors to get rid of them promptly in the markets.

Credit Monies, however, like demand deposits and certificates of bank indebtedness (which constitute our paper currencies) involve no ownership costs, and possess no built-in inducements to their owners to use them promptly in the markets. I will show how, in the evolution of money, that inducement was accidentally removed.

I will point out how it would be easy and desirable to give our current money some of the quality of a hot potato. I will also bring out that such an innovation would cause such different economic behavior, and such far-reaching socio-logical effects, that the end result would essentially be a new social order.

Three highly different interpretations of economic life have had massive impact on governmental policies and man-kind's way of life. Adam Smith, Marx, and Keynes have each advanced observations and recommendations which to this day move millions of people into action in efforts to improve their lot.

In the light of the situations and institutional arrangements that have become dominant during this century, none of the three interpretations—in my opinion—are adequate today.

Since Smith wrote his *Wealth Of Nations,* his scarcity analysis has ceased to be relevant for the U.S. The American capacity to produce is no longer the key factor that limits our welfare. Rather it is the problem of how to induce those who have the power to command U.S. facilities to operate, to exercise their power steadily and continuously. Checkbook money—which I will show possesses a unique disruptive power—was also not in general use when Smith wrote, and thus did not constitute a problem for him to deal with.

Marx's view that all industries should be controlled by the state, and not by individuals, became the basic tenet of all communist movements. Complete government control of both production facilities and monetary demand naturally assures stability of consumer demand for whatever limited volume of goods and services a communistic system brings forth. But the means used sacrifices most human values.

Keynes faced up squarely to the problem of maintaining adequate and stable monetary demand for goods and services. But he advocated that when private demand falters, the government should throw public monetary demand into the breach. His governmentalist recommendations are currently being followed throughout the Western world.

This book points out the shortcoming of each of the above three interpretations, while it concurrently advances a fourth and wholly different presentation of what I term a New Social Order.

I will also show how the historic failure (or inability) to provide a small and steady pressure on the recipients of money to reuse it promptly caused the velocity of money in general to be anarchic, with the result that it generated occasional sags in overall monetary demand. I will furthermore show how the worldwide efforts to neutralize the sags, by "fine-tuned" compensatory increases in the money supply—through the price inflation that the efforts engender—necessarily imposes on the ownership of money an inflation cost more volatile, and in size far larger, than the stable cost proposed by this book: a cost of between five and ten percent that the Western world now bears versus one of about two percent.

Moreover, I will demonstrate that the efforts to stabilize monetary demand by means of compensatory increases in the money supply (rather than by forestalling decreases in money's velocity) necessarily—by requiring the administrative services of bureaucrats—extends the evil of excessive governmentalism, whereas the velocity approach does not.

I finally, will explain why, from a functional point of view, the very design of the free market system should logically call for the use of "hot potato" money as its medium of exchange, and that the market system is currently doomed to experience a multitude of troubles because it attempts to make use of a "sanctuary" money.

# Preface: A New Social Order

THERE is a cancer in the free market system that goes entirely undiscussed. That cancer is the *excessive* store of value of the banking system's demand deposit. That deposit, as it is designed, can be used at disruptively laggard rates without declining in value. The free market tries to operate with such money, but by doing so it weakens its otherwise fine operation. Fortunately, if a small change were made in the monetary instrument, malignant effects would be overcome.

Historically, all economists have premised that the kind of money that we use for medium of exchange is a neutral tool in influencing a nation's level of economic activity. The English economist, D. H. Robertson, in the concluding paragraph of his classic book *Money* puts it this way:

> The real economic evils of society — inadequate production and inequitable distribution — lie too deep for any purely monetary ointment to cure. An unwise monetary policy can wreak unmerited hardship and engender unnecessary confusion and waste; not even a wise one can turn a world which is unjust and poor into a world which is rich and just. The mending of the road over which the produce passes to market is no substitute for the digging and dunging of the fields themselves. No tinkering with counters will take us very far towards the discovery of an industrial system which shall supply both adequate incentives to those who venture and plan and peace of mind to those who sweat and endure.

I will try to show that Robertson's generalization was probably true when our money medium consisted of commodities like copper, furs, and tobacco, or of warehouse receipts like silver certificates — but that that view came to be disastrously in error when our money medium evolved to consist instead of bank debt obligations (that is, of demand deposits) which constitute the checkbook money of today. Bank debt obligations are now our dominant medium of exchange.

In every society which respects and protects private property, each worker who produces an article simultaneously produces a claim to that article. In societies which resort to a division of labor, it is a basic requirement that all specialists who receive claims to goods in payment for their own output turn around and use the received claims rather promptly in demanding the goods of other specialized producers. It is also a basic requirement that as a group they use their claims at the rate at which they are paid for their own output. If as a group they do not do so, then the aggregate monetary demand within the economy breaks down. The rate of use of claim checks in the aggregate must be synchronized with the rate of production of the goods to which the claims relate. Our gradual shift from the use of commodity money to checkbook money shattered that synchronization.

I take serious issue with Robertson's view on the neutral role of money. It is true that no amount of tinkering with the physical counters themselves will help us achieve a general well being. Still, I will show that one of the greatest opportunities for improving industrial conditions lies in the recourse of reducing a certain privilege that was unwittingly extended to the owners of checkbook money as money evolved from simple, tangible commodity forms to intangible agreements.

Most economists regard money merely as "counters" and "tokens." Some men have seen that modern money consists mainly of indirect claims against those bank borrowers' assets which have been converted into the generalized assets of the banking system. But no one of whom I know seems to have dealt with the behavioral privileges which attach to these claims. For modern credit money is far more than a "token." Basically it is a debt obligation—a contract—that has been modified by the handling which it receives by the banking system. It is a contract relating to wealth that exists between banks, borrowers (who are usually producers), and the owners of the credit tokens. And being a modified contract, money necessarily has attached to itself a bundle of legal rights and duties, powers, and privileges. It is the adequacy and appropriateness of this bundle of property privileges that this book challenges and seeks to change.

I shall therefore attempt to explain vividly in both words and diagrams how the world's gradual shift from commodity money to credit money operated subtly, accidentally, and unintentionally to remove all ownership costs from our medium of exchange, and—as later pages will bring out—how in the shifting process it has given to checkbook money an occasional disruptive role.

By highlighting the implications of this shift, I hope to force a long overdue revolution in monetary thinking. It may, for example, compel economists to examine the privilege of using modern money at anarchic rates, and to consider the disruptive business cycle implications caused by the big difference between the property content of the debt obligations constituting our checkbook money, and all other forms of property. Nowhere in economic literature can one find a concern with the unique delaying privileges that go with the ownership of checkbook money, despite the fact that such money is the only form of property that is uniquely free from ownership costs. I concern myself with the implications of that fact.

Because the whole matrix of my analysis and proposal lies outside the groove of today's monetary thinking I additionally submit abbreviated, graphic versions of my monetary analysis in what I believe to be a more vivid and effective form than before.

This book includes a clean-cut depiction of the subtle

defect that has periodically made the otherwise fine free market system subject to the unemployment and disruption that has provided the historic excuse for resorting more and more to the nostrum of governmentalism. No issue of our time is more urgent than the problem of pushing back the coercive power of government. Therefore, a proposal is advanced here to do it by correcting the flaw in the system which leftists of all stripes try to neutralize with new extensions of government power. That power has grown tremendously. In 1929, the federal, state, and local disbursements totaled 10.2 billion dollars. In 1973, they came to almost 447 billion dollars. They grew in 44 years from 10.1 percent of Gross National outpayments to 33 percent.

One may at first be puzzled by the proposal that a new money instrument that is costly to own could intensify and stabilize the aggregate private monetary demand for goods, introduce flexibility of exchange rates, and reduce imbalances in the balance of payments. Later pages, however, will show how that can be done.

My analysis and proposal may be very timely. In 1971 and 1973 dollars flooded into Germany, Japan, and Switzerland. The dollar went to a discount against most of the currencies of the world. Foreigners were holding over 50 billion dollars in liquid dollar claims, but would not use them promptly. Dollars kept piling up abroad, but were not respent at the rate at which they were received.

The following editorial in the June 1, 1971 issue of the *National Review* points to a pattern of transaction that should occur. My proposal is for a means that would insure the certainty of that pattern's occurrence.

> Over the past five years or so the European central bankers have wept under the load of their burden of absorbing billions of "unwanted" U.S. dollars. Simultaneously, continental politicians and publicists complain that these same dollars enable the giant multinational U.S. based corporations to build European factories and buy out locally owned firms, so that they more and more dominate European local markets.

But what is to prevent the Europeans themselves from using these dollars to buy into the very U.S. corporations about which they complain so tearfully, or any other U.S. corporations that happen to strike their fancy? If the German central bankers don't like having to absorb a billion U.S. dollars in a spring week, why don't they rouse themselves from their rentier-slumbers and finance a Volkswagen takeover of American Motors? Or help Lufthansa buy up TWA?

Unfortunately the Europeans need an institutionalized nudging to do this. I describe farther on how a very slight modification of our monetary instrument would provide such a nudging.

When the Arab nations imposed their oil embargo in 1973 and raised their petroleum prices, it became clear that they would experience huge export surpluses and enormous cash accumulations every year. Many people fear that the Arabs may so drastically delay the re-disbursement of their dollar accumulations that the U.S. will experience recession as a result. But if the petro-dollars paid to the Arabs were designed to carry an ownership cost of, say, 2% or 3% per year, that fear would disappear. The time is extremely propitious for the whole world to adopt a hot-potato money. The economic hammerlock that the Arab countries have on the world assures that the monetary issue of whether to use boomerang money or sanctuary money will be with us for many years to come.

The scope of this book is admittedly ambitious. It aims (1) to contribute a scientific method of communication for use by the social sciences and (2) by the help of this method to reveal a large part of how our economic system functions, and (3) how it can be made to function to eliminate many of our socio-economic maladjustments. It aims to present a revolutionary Wankel engine, so to speak, for the free market system.

This book is not an apology for the free market system. Far from it. I am familiar with and dislike its shortcomings as much as anyone. But unlike most critics of the free market, I believe that as a system of economy, it has not had a sensible trial. The trial has been long enough, true indeed; but it has almost always needlessly operated under an inadequate aggregate private monetary demand. And under such conditions, the free market system is necessarily in unstable equilibrium.

The subject matter of this book is obviously of an electric nature. Views bearing on the causes and cures of major social problems tend to entangle themselves deeply in our emotions; they tend to be held tenaciously and to be sponsored vigorously. Facts, relationships, emotions and cultural values necessarily enter in varying degree into the making of social judgments. Unfortunately, there is no calculus by which one can extract provable answers. For that reason, conviction regarding social action should perhaps always be tentative. Solutions are necessarily relative to one's changing time and culture. Social forces are too numerous and dynamic to warrant fanatical conviction. Any plan meeting with public approval, therefore, should probably be introduced gradually, cautiously, a little bit at a time, rather than impetuously and sweepingly.

Appendices B and C describe and illustrate how a new graphic symbolism can be used to show vividly many economic situations and processes, and how it can facilitate economic communication and understanding. I strongly recommend that those readers who like charts and diagrams begin their reading of this book by reading Appendix C, for it will provide a vivid frame of reference for comprehending easily many of the relationships dealt with in this book.

The American people are being plagued with expanding governmentalism, price inflation, increasing violence and breakdown of law and order. I hope that this book may provide a practical means for reversing these seemingly irresistible trends.

Columbia University　　　　　　　　ARTHUR O. DAHLBERG
New York City

# PART 1

## The Problem

# Chapter 1

## A Free Market Alternative to Governmentalism

THE thoughtful American senses that despite its many fine features, the free market system contains some subtle, baffling defect in its design. He is disturbed. He sees his country's technicians increase the nation's per capita output by about three percent per year and sees almost everyone move up the income scale to acquire automobiles, appliances, education and vacations. And yet he is heavy-hearted over his own and his children's future. The cloud of advancing authoritarianism saddens his outlook. And he is puzzled over how to combat it.

The informed people of the world know all about the relatively poor economic performance of communism in Eastern Europe and all about the doctrinaire cruelty of China. They know of the absence of freedom and civil liberties in Russia, of the cleverly organized dishonesty, and of the millions of refugees who flee her guarded borders. They know about the glumness and poverty that uniformly prevail wherever communism has taken over. And yet no fighting wave of opposition builds up against her. Why?

The reasons are many. But among them is a paralyzing one that restrains many who would otherwise defend their system wholeheartedly. It is the free market's chronic failure to learn how to maintain full employment and economic growth continuously without calling periodically for more and more spending by the State.

Today those who would emotionally fight for the free market system are forced to champion that system from an embarrassing posture. Economists, politicians, and voters in general know that their own free market system—as currently designed—desperately seeks the aid of the State from time to time. They know their system will run well for a period of years, but then it will almost certainly sag into recession. They also know that at such times even they themselves will probably, as humanitarians, call on the State "to do something" to overcome recession and the unbearable unemployment. Thus they feel that occasionally it is only the potentially tyrannical State that can provide them with the needed relief.

Spreading over the world in glacierlike fashion is governmentalism in its many forms. Nominally dedicated to "welfare," but often lawless in its drive for that welfare, it advances its economic power steadily while free enterprise sinks back. There is no dodging the portent. Either the free market system, which rests on private persuasion, must begin to function with increased coordination, rhythm, and widespread understanding of its design, or energetic men will before long begin to install, to an expanding degree, some overwhelming system of bureaucratic control.

The problem of stabilizing full employment and inducing rapid economic growth through private persuasion rather than state compulsion is with us still. After four decades of deficit financing and governmentalism, the basic problem of how to insure the growth of the U.S. economy in an atmosphere of freedom is an issue left largely untouched.

Unless we do repair the "aggregate private monetary demand mechanism" of capitalism, we Americans could conceivably suffer the dismal fate of being made into robots who labor, marry, kill, and cheer as dictators command. Quickly and fundamentally we must improve our market mechanism if it is not to give way bit by bit to one of those rationing economies which must snuff out personal liberty and other rights merely to turn its wheels of industry. It is not enough for people who dislike dictatorship to rant against governmentalism and communism. Capitalism had the field first, and if it is losing the field to governmentalism, it is doing so because an increasing number of people are willing to try desperate alternatives to a capitalism which seems destined always to be chronically in need of shoring up by government. Why does it periodically need such shoring up? This book will provide the answer.

There is no doubt that political interference — usually stupid interference — with the operation of a highly automatic market mechanism is itself very disruptive and destructive. But I will show that a subtle, unnoticed flaw that evolved in the design of our monetary instrument condemned the free market system to generate such a poor distribution of income, as well as periodic distress, that bumbling politicians were driven to tinker with a complex system in their amateurish efforts to extract a better performance from it. If capitalism is to survive, those key shortcomings within it which bring forth a clamor for government programs must be quickly uncovered and removed.

There are, of course, those who question the wisdom of repairing capitalism, who have given up all faith in the worthiness of bargaining economies. But I believe that a tremendous case can still be made for the potentialities of the competitive as against the administrative state.

I recognize the theoretical need for continuity of monetary demand. I do not, however, advocate governmental injection of new money into the economy when those who have the old money choose not to disburse it for goods or investment rapidly enough to maintain full employment. I advocate instead that, through the design of an improved monetary medium, savers (including the banks as their agents) be selfishly motivated to disburse it continuously at high and stable rates for goods, services, capital facilities, or other investments of their own choosing. No surveillance or monitoring of anyone's personal rate of disbursement would be contemplated or required. The higher and more stable disbursement rates would develop as a normal self-directed response to a slightly altered monetary instrument.*

One cannot highlight how our many economic ailments hang together unless one starts at the beginning with something as elementary as the processes of exchange that occur in simple societies that go in for a specialization of labor. Such a beginning will make clear that the steady use of one's claims to the goods of others, which one receives for one's own output, is a basic requirement of a viable social order.

In all societies that protect personal property, *money — in its broadest meaning of being a claim to goods — is concurrently produced when the goods are produced.* A farmer who

---

* You probably assume, when you deposit money in the bank which you yourself do not disburse, that your money is automatically invested. In a sense it is, even if the bank drags its feet and lengthens the interval between its investment decisions. (See Figure 6, page 20.)

For example, a bank makes loans and investments at the rate of ten million dollars per month, while an equal ten million dollars per month of deposits are coming in. But then its business borrowers may seek smaller loans, or the bank itself may not feel that it is safe to lend money at the old tempo — so that total loans and investments shrink from, say, a one hundred million level to eighty million (although ten million dollars of deposits per month continue to come in), it will nonetheless be true that even the new ten million dollars are *nominally* invested. What occurs is this:

Say, the bank is receiving an investment income of one million dollars per month from its prevailing loans and investments, and that it is able to pay four percent interest on its prevailing deposits. Then, if it slows its investment tempo and its investment revenue declines while its deposits continue to come in at the 10 million dollars per month rate, the bank simply allocates the available investment revenue over a larger deposit sum and lowers the interest rate that it pays on its deposits to something less than four percent. Meanwhile, all the depositors continue to feel that their deposits "are invested," and that they have not been slowing down the required prompt flow of savings into investment. Nonetheless, their agent, the bank to whom they as savers delegated their money for investment, has been guilty of laggard action. Figure 6 p. 20, shows how such laggard action has preceded all recent recessions.

raises wheat creates concurrently an ownership claim to that wheat which he can exchange for something else. The title or claim is the equivalent of money to him. Similarly when a U.S. corporation produces a million tons of steel, the stockholders concurrently own the title to that steel and possess claims which they can exchange for other things. *In our economic system the production of goods and of the claims to the goods go on concurrently. The two are synchronized. But in our modern monetary system the use — the exercising of the claims to the goods in the markets — is not designed to be synchronized with the rate of production. That, as we shall see, is the basic cancerous defect of our capitalistic system.* It is also the defect, as we shall also see, which can easily be corrected by either an entirely new governmental policy toward gold, or by a small limitation on the kind of monetary contracts that the courts may enforce. An illustration will highlight the serious problem that the lack of synchronization brings about.

In writing my *Analysis of Recovery Plans* for the Congressional Temporary National Economic Committee in 1940, I paraphrased an illustration of a weakness in our monetary system which Mr. Ralph Manuel, then president of the Marquette National Bank of Minneapolis, presented to the committee. In condensed form the illustration was this:

Let us suppose that a hundred families occupy a completely isolated island and undertake to raise their potatoes collectively and that each family is to receive its share of the crop in proportion to the contribution which it makes to the production thereof. Some families may contribute shovels, baskets and tools; others only their manual labor. Let us suppose that a manager from day to day delivers to each family the claim checks which evidence the contribution that each has made. When the crop has been harvested there might be a thousand bushels of potatoes in the pile and there might be a thousand claim checks outstanding.

If some families have acquired claim checks substantially out of proportion to their needs for potatoes, these families may choose to present only part of their claim checks and to save the remainder for use in some future season. The manager of the enterprise may then find that a hundred bushels of potatoes remain uncalled for. The less fortunate families will have received their full share of the crop, and the more fortunate families will have received all they can use; so the enterprise appears to have been a complete success.

But what about the hundred claim checks that are still outstanding? Shall the families who neglected or refused to claim their shares of this year's crop be permitted to claim shares of next year's crop instead — even though their claim checks do not evidence a contribution to the production of next year's crop and the whole of that crop will belong to those who produce it?

Having said this, the basic question arises: should claim checks that have been issued during previous seasons, and have not been presented at the tempo at which goods were produced, be fully honored against the crops of coming years? Again, should the value of claim checks to current production be embalmed without cost for use in future seasons against later production? Naturally when claim checks to current production sit inactive on the side lines, monetary demand sags and "recessions" occur. When the claims come back in a later season, the total demand expands. Booms and even inflations then tend to occur. Would Islanders be warranted in establishing community rules which would dampen to some degree the value of laggardly used claim checks? Would such dampening be the denial of a natural right or the denial of a special privilege?

A squabble naturally arises between pragmatic operations and presumed natural rights. Some of the tardy users of potato claims will maintain that they have earned the claims honorably in good faith, and that they should be permitted to use them in any way and at any time that they wish. Even though they want to use their claims in demanding the potatoes of the next season, they want the community to honor their claims fully without limitation, despite the fact that their deferred action may disrupt the whole farming routine of the community. They want the community to regard their wish to postpone their monetary demand as an inalienable right.

But if the community accedes to their wishes, while it presumably provides equitable protection to all the factor groups who cooperate in production—the workers, the renters, the risk takers, etc.—it would be extending to the tardy users of claim checks a special monopoly privilege to embalm their purchasing power, to disrupt demand and—with a lag—to lower prices and income.

Many people believe that saving their claim checks (or current money income) is synonymous with economic saving by society. That may or may not be so. Genuine economic saving occurs only when recipients of income do not spend all of it for consumption items, but spend a portion for capital goods or durable consumers goods. If they disburse the second portion as rapidly as the first, personal saving and economic saving are synonymous.

If employee A, for example, does not spend all of his current money income for goods and services, but "saves" some of it by depositing it in a bank, and the bank then disburses it for capital goods as rapidly as employee A spends his portion for consumption items, he has genuinely saved in both meanings of the term. The employee has saved money out of his income and has added to his property and reserves. The money not disbursed for consumption items has gone to purchase capital goods.

But if the employee merely saves his money or claim checks in a cookie jar, he is saving only in a personal sense while contributing to a disruption of the overall market. Individual behavior is of questionable merit if — when it is engaged in by everyone — it ends in disaster.

Inasmuch as the dollar claim checks which we use today not only do not depreciate if slowed down in use, but actually increase in value (in terms of goods as prices fall), it is well to examine what we have done to our institutional arrangements to generate such results.

In general, my thesis is (1) that a certain property privilege, namely, the opportunity to lengthen the interval between transactions below the rate at which goods are produced and the money claims against the goods are created — an opportunity which came about accidentally as the U.S. money medium evolved from its "commodity money" form to its "checkbook money" form — is a particularly disruptive one, and (2) that in a society of specialized workers, the mechanism of the free market simply cannot function well if in the aggregate our monetary income is disbursed for appreciable lengths of time more slowly than we receive it.

Unfortunately, few people view money and banking in terms of the property rights which envelop money. I shall present an analysis of money that will reveal graphically (1) how modern money consists primarily of claims against those evidences of private indebtedness which have been transmuted by our banking machinery into evidences of bankers' indebtedness and (2) how in the process of transmutation the money is given a fortified value which affords the holders of it opportunities of which they could not in earlier times avail themselves.

Custom and the state, by specifying permissible operating conditions can modify the distribution of income and in general can, within wide limits, mold the grooves to which economic behavior will conform. Certain laws relating to the contracts that are allowable before the haggling begins in the marketplace accidentally evolved to give a tremendous bargaining advantage to our recipients of money claims, an advantage which had entirely escaped the notice of our theorists. The whole world of economic theory was distorted and full of error because of the oversight referred to. "Equilibrium economists," "mathematical economists" and "institutional economists," in building their pyramids of logic, have all seemed to have ignored or overlooked the bargaining advantage referred to. None of the leading economists of the past—John Stuart Mills, Pigou, Böhm-Baverk, Marshall, Keynes—nor any of the outstanding or well-known ones of today have written anything about it.

*The tragedy of our age is that the economic theories of both the "old" and the "new" economics are built upon a shocking oversight and error based on a subtle monetary development that escaped detection.*

I shall describe the overlooked privilege, how it accidentally and subtly evolved, and in the light which its exposure gives, go on to re-examine the problems of our day. How to release fully the productive capacities of our men and machines, how to insure rapid economic growth in undeveloped as well as developed countries, how to stabilize prosperity, how to improve the distribution of income to the benefit of employees without price inflation, how to do all this under the economists' ideal of effective regulation with a minimum of governmental interference—this is the theme of this book. It is an effort to deal in an integrated yet non-Marshallian manner with the interrelationships of production, exchange and distribution within the framework of a freer market than we have ever had. It makes an effort to present a whole new orbit of functional relationships which, if sound, could cause a vast amount of accepted orthodoxy to wither away.

I will also show how the rules that have historically enveloped the free market system have been prejudicial to the worker and how more and more governmentalism has been invoked in efforts to improve the balance. In my opinion, the distribution of income as allocated by the initial bargaining in the market (not as reallocated by progressive income taxes, collective bargaining and transfer payments) between the factors of production (wages, interest, rent and profit) have favored the money saver. (See Figure 1, below.) The net result has been that the portion of income going to wages and entrepreneurial effort has usually been subnormal in relation to the portion of income going to interest and to that profit which goes to the occasional inert investor. In recent decades, the portion going to the savers of the U.S. has periodically—as we shall see—been more than enough to provide for that level of investment in plant and equipment that end market demand could profitably sustain.

Savings we must have in ever larger volume. Increases in manhour output and the standard of living cannot occur

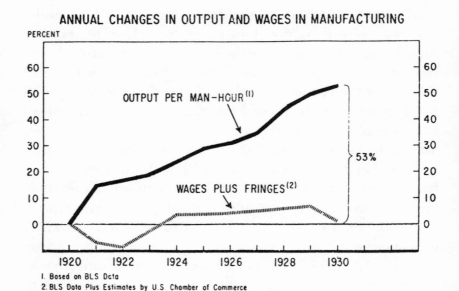

Figure 1

without a steady expansion of savings and the capital facilities for which the savings are spent. But the growth in the money available and used for consumption must be synchronized with the growth of the money savings used for investment.

In order to function well, the free market system requires that the income generated be so divided by the bargaining in the market that the fraction flowing to the workers for consumption be large enough to provide a steady market for the portion flowing to money savers for investment.

A particular condition, one which enveloped the market for many decades prior to the big depression of the 1930's, seriously impaired the bargaining power of the workers vis-à-vis the employers. Bureau of Labor Statistics data show, for example, that over the decade of the 1920's the output per manhour in manufacturing increased by fifty-three percent, while the average hourly earnings in manufacturing increased not at all.

The above chart reveals how, prior to the big depression of the 1930's the mechanism of the market system was unintentionally but inequitably stacked against the worker.

Figure 2 (p. 14) shows that, in contrast, governmentalist action during 1958–1970, with its combination of labor legislation, special tax legislation and bureaucratic welfare programs — which channel income from the rich to the poor — have stacked the system in favor of the workers. While the output per manhour in manufacturing went up by only forty-five percent during the twelve year span, the average hourly earnings in manufacturing rose by seventy-six percent.

I will explain farther on how it is possible, by means of a slight change in our monetary instrument, to cause wages to obtain via bargaining in the free market — without union or bureaucratic assistance — all that the increases in productivity justify, but not more than that.

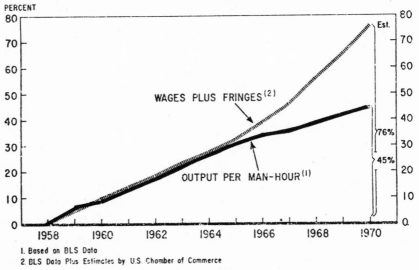

Figure 2

Sooner or later investors attune investment in capital facilities to the end market buying power of the consumers. By 1930 investment had so far outrun the balance that investors sat on their hands. The banking system was flooded with savings, but the savings would not move into investment at the rate of the 1920's. During the 1920's easy credit and rapid increases in the money supply had, of course, responded to the rapid rise in profit and investment and had contributed to the disbalance in the free market. But that development was also mainly a result of the preceding lopsided distribution of income which had developed between profits and wages. As profits zoomed, credit expanded, too. If profits had not increased out of line with consumer buying power — and the long term base for loan expansion — wild credit expansion probably would not have occurred.

When the flow of money savings into investment slowed to a trickle in 1930, the debacle of the 1930's began. Investment declined, unemployment rates rose into the fifteen to twenty percent range, and consumer prices fell by a fourth. (See Figure 3, below.) The decade-long collapse of the free market system incubated many of the employment plans that have come to be characterized as the "New Economics." These plans have succeeded in holding postwar unemployment to low levels. However, as Figure 3 also suggests, price inflation is one of the prices paid for low unemployment obtained in that way. (Later charts and diagrams will show that other evils — such as the breakdown of law and order and governmental encroachment on personal freedom — are, like price inflation, also necessary components of the governmentalism that the New Economics has already installed.)

As Figure 3 shows, both prices and employment remained relatively stable during the decade of the 1920's. Because

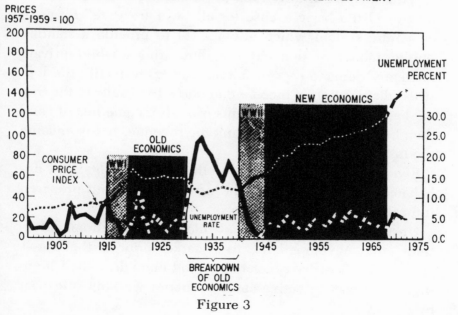

Figure 3

labor's bargaining power was weak, it had exercised no strong upward pressure on employment costs. So it was easy for producers to keep prices from rising during that decade, and even to make them decline gently.

Chapter 7 describes how it might be possible to introduce equity into the free market system—something the system has not had since the form of money now in general use began to consist dominantly of the collateralized debt obligations of bank borrowers. There I will describe two means which would cause checkbook money to have no more store of value than the commodity money it superseded. Such a plan would place the money savers under a continuous mild pressure to exercise a steady private monetary demand for the services of workers—and would prevent them from outbargaining the workers in the free market. The long-time dream of political economy to arrange for a built-in stabilizer of aggregate private monetary demand would have been realized.

With such an arrangement provided for, one would have destroyed the basic excuse for all "welfare state" forms of economic system which attempt (1) to provide a standby public monetary demand for those times when private monetary demand sags or falters, and (2) to rectify the lopsided distribution of income that normally results in the free market by taxing the recipients of high income heavily and then bureaucratically doling out the revenues to low income groups.

Figure 1 illustrated that something fundamental did unbalance the U.S. economy during the 1920's and prepared it for the collapse of the 1930's.

On the record, the laws and rules—or institutional situations—that enveloped the free market prior to the 1930's (and ever since) have not been good enough. I shall highlight what was defective and how better working rules can be designed.

# Chapter 2

## The Nature of Money
## (You Too Can Understand Money)

Now COMES the question of just what it is that constitutes the money medium used so extensively in the exchange circuits of the nation. The diagram below lists the several physical forms of money now in use. But it tells nothing about the institutional nature of money.

You probably have in your pocket both coins and Federal Reserve Notes. Such money, together with your checkbook deposits, constitute most of the money in the U.S. today.

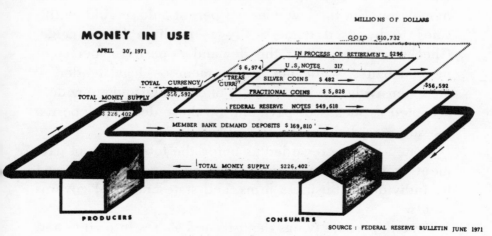

Figure 4

But what is the admixture of law and substance that these
many monies are made of? Where do these monies come
from? How rapidly does each circulate? What do they all
have in common?

Each money medium is a form of property that enables us
to shift easily from the ownership of one item to another.
Each serves as a store of value that enables us to keep our
buying power intact while we leisurely window-shop the
markets of the world. In addition, each is both an exchange
unit and a gauge of value against which people evaluate all
the things they regard as property – goods, services, wealth,
debt – every kind of asset, both tangible and intangible.

Our unit of account is the "dollar," which historically has
consisted from time to time of commodities like silver and
gold, but – as we shall see in Chapter 5 – has usually com-
prised merely the claims against the assets of the banking
system. Nowhere does economic literature functionally
portray the property ingredients that constitute the dollar.
In later diagrams we shall present both a written and a
graphic picture of the dollar's property content.

Narrowly defined, our money consists of coins and paper
currency. Some people regard our gold stocks as being
money too. But the law does not permit gold or gold certificates to be used domestically as medium of exchange.
Checks written against the demand deposits of our commercial banks, while not legally money – "legal tender" –
are extensively used as medium of exchange and are widely
accepted as means of payment. So these demand deposits,
too, are regarded as money.

Money may be regarded as being the total means of payment – coins, currency, and checking deposits – possessed
by individuals, business firms, and state and local governments.

Time deposits, savings deposits and shares in savings and
loan associations are highly liquid, but they are not a part of

the money supply. They are used for payment only after being converted into currency or checking accounts.

Our several kinds of money have different rates of use. Checkbook money, for example, turns over far more rapidly than does our currency. What is more significant, however, is that the turnover rate of the entire money supply may fluctuate greatly. Figure 5 below shows its variation from 1928 to 1954. Figure 7 shows its variation from 1919 to 1968. Figure 6 shows how when recessions occur, the rate has sagged. (See pp. 20–21.)

Note well, in the bottom panel of Figure 7, how the turn-over rate has risen steadily ever since 1945. But note also in Figure 6 how the turnover rate nonetheless periodically sagged prior to recessions. Figure 6 shows how it sagged during the last five recessions.

My aim is to show the faulty design of a monetary instrument which facilitates the sags to occur from whatever current turnover rate happens to prevail, and then to forestall

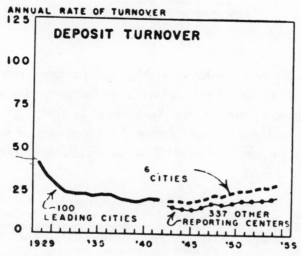

SOURCE: Board of Governors of the Federal Reserve System

Figure 5

## Velocity of Money Stock
## Plus Time Deposits*

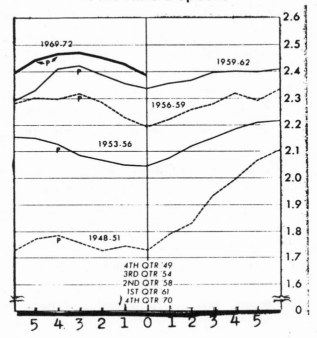

Quarters to and from trough of Recession.;
Source: U.S. Department of Commerce

Figure 6

or appreciably reduce the sags. My concern consequently is with the sags in spending, not with the turnover rate as such from which the sags occur, inasmuch as the sags reflect shrinkage in the monetary demand for goods and services and resulting unemployment. (The turnover rates have partly technical causes).*

---

* The rate is influenced by non-monetary factors. For example: The labor force grows by about 2% per year. And the productivity of each worker goes up by about 3% per year. This means that — other things being equal — the volume of goods being produced for exchange in the market increases by about 5% per year. This means too that we either need about 5% more chips in money form each year to exchange the added output, or require that each dollar do more work — that is, increase its rate of turnover to clear the market of goods.

In addition, if we have a situation where prices are lifted every year by 5% to

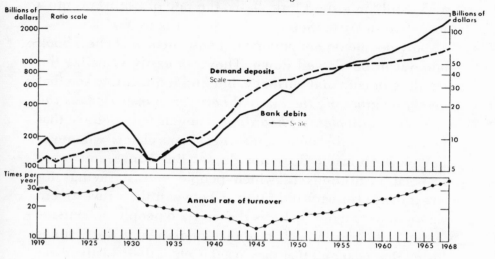

**BANK DEBITS, DEMAND DEPOSITS, AND RATE OF TURNOVER
IN "OUTSIDE" CENTERS, 1919-68**

Source: Board of Governors of the Federal Reserve System

Figure 7

Even during periods when inflation needles the turnover rate upward, severe sags in the rate occur and cause recession. And the sags usually continue until government deficit spending lifts the buying power of the end market. On

---

10% by governmental fiat or by labor union power, then either 5% to 10% more chips in money form will be needed to clear the market—or each dollar will have to have a 5% to 10% higher velocity.

Since 1968 we have had an increase annually in actual output of about 5%, and an additional inflationary price increase of about 5% per year. So we have needed annually either an enlarged money supply or a faster rate of money turnover to clear the market. We have had some of both. The money supply grew by about 5% per year during 1968–1972, and the turnover rate speeded up to make up for the rest. In fact, inflationary fears during those years speeded the rate by an additional amount.

But despite the steady upward trend in velocity during 1968–1972, the rate sagged sharply in 1969–1970 to cause recession. The turnover rate in itself is not the critical item; it is the prevention of the sag that is all important.

The three lifters mentioned above have, since 1968, raised Gross National expenditures (which are reported in current dollars) by about 10% per year. During 1968–1973, however, the supply of money rose by only about 5% per year. As a result, every existing dollar had to hurry and do more work. Which it did. Velocity rose continuously from 1968 to 1973. So, despite what many economists maintain, inflation since 1968 was probably not caused by excessive increases in the money supply, but by something else. We look into that in later chapters.

a trend basis the turnover rate rose rapidly from 1968 to 1972. Still, on a short term basis, the rate of use went into a nose dive in 1970. (See the top line of Figure 6.)

Many people do not understand how the use of checkbook money can be slowed down. They can easily visualize the hoarding of coin and currency, but find it difficult to see that *merely lengthening the interval between transactions is the economic equivalent of hoarding.* They usually believe that the bank uses the depositor's checkbook claims whenever the owner himself does not do so. But banks and other financial institutions to which people entrust savings for investment also vary the interval between their investment transactions. Figure 7 shows that in 1920 people in "outside center" cities used each of their dollars about thirty times during that year and that they used each of their vastly fewer dollars only about twenty times in 1933. So the average interval between each dollar transaction was twelve days in 1928 and eighteen days in 1933.

Figure 7 furthermore shows that after 1934 the money supply was expanded as large government "compensatory spending" programs were instituted to serve as recovery measures. It also shows that despite each annual expansion, the annual rate of turnover of the money (the velocity) did not improve. The hoardable type money that was injected merely turned over once or twice and lay down dead.

From the individual point of view, of course, "saving" can go up while investment goes down. In 1970–71, for example, personal savings did go up. But looked at from Mars, the amount of economic saving in capital facilities on Earth went down. During the inflationary — yet recession — year 1970, the volume of Personal Savings in Time Deposits, Savings Deposits, Saving and Loan shares increased from $444 billion to $523, by about $79 billion. But the sum total of all investment in 1970 for plant and equipment, residential and nonresidential construction, and state and local construction (financed by assumption through borrowed savings and not through taxation) increased by only $34 billion. Nominally, the savings institutions used some of the balance of the savers' deposits at a reduced rate (see the 1969–72 line in Figure 6) by buying federal government securities. But such "investing" in government securities is phony investing; it is not investing in capital facilities, as viewed from Mars. At best, it is spending for the current expenses of government—for war, transfer payments, subsidies, "education," etc.

### Personal Saving Rate*

*The ratio of personal saving to disposable personal income.
Latest data plotted: 3rd quarter

Figure 8

The high personal savings rate shown above highlights vividly how in 1970–1971 the rules enveloping our markets pampered our savers to obtain and hold enlarged nest eggs (which were about eight percent of personal savings), and then clobbered our dynamic risk taking entrepreneurs who cut back hard on plant and equipment orders.

If heat had been applied to the sleepy savings of 1970–1971 so as to generate lower interest costs for the dynamic entrepreneurs, and if Congress had been more understanding of risk takers' needs, the 1970–1971 recession would not have been so severe.

In a sense, all money is always idle between those electric moments when the ownership of the money is being legally transferred. At one instant I may own a twenty-dollar bill or one hundred dollars in my checking account; in the next, I may have transferred the ownership with electric speed to you. And the money is again idle until that moment when you transfer it legally to someone else.

If we are to understand money and the banking system, we must examine how our tangible monies, like gold and silver, are related to our intangible monies, like demand deposits and paper currency. We must also examine how we came to shift from barter to commodity money, to warehouse receipts, and then to modern currency and checkbook records of indebtedness.

As a point of departure, let us transplant ourselves into a simple, imaginative setting which will enable us to see vividly why any society that resorts to a division of labor must—if it is to keep functioning smoothly, regardless of what it uses for medium of exchange—display a continuous willingness to exchange its money for goods. For my purposes, Robinson Crusoe and his island will do.

## Robinson Crusoe Invents Refrigeration

If Robinson Crusoe works alone on his island, then the harder he works and the more ingenious he is, the higher will his standard of living be. Similarly if his companion, Friday, works alone in a detached manner, then Friday's standard of living, too, will vary with his diligence and efficiency. Should the two men, after a time, go in for a division of labor and begin to specialize, Robinson Crusoe making one half of the products and Friday the other half, the total output of the two men would undoubtedly increase above what it was before. If both men specialize and barter (that is, "spend") their products rapidly enough to maintain full-blast activity for each other, the standard of living of both will rise because of the specialization.

Note that at this stage the standard of living of the two men depends not only on their efficiency and willingness to produce, but also upon their willingness to exchange or "spend." Notice, too, that the moment they resort to a division of labor, they subject their existence to new dangers. Each of these specialists depends for his survival upon a so-called "effective demand" coming from someone other than himself. As soon as specialization begins in an economy, continuous exchange is necessary for economic stabilization and full-blast operation.

Let us imagine that at the beginning of the island's development the two men are more than willing to exchange those surpluses at which they specialize for the products of each other. Under such circumstances, all is well. Suppose that 1,000 more people migrate to the island, that each of these specializes, and that each barters his products for those of others so rapidly that full-blast operation for every worker is maintained.

Even if the newcomers had no spontaneous inclinations to exchange goods, they would have to keep on exchanging just in order to survive. In their economy of perishable goods, each specializing producer would be under pressure to exchange quickly (or "spend") his surplus specialty for the products of others, for tomatoes rot, fruit spoils, meat decays, lettuce wilts, butter turns rancid. So those who barter too slowly tend to have shriveled potatoes, sour milk, and rotten eggs on hand.

Just as various peoples over the world have selected some one commodity to serve both as a yardstick of value and as a medium of exchange—pounds of tobacco, sheep, cattle, furs, bushels of wheat, ounces of copper, etc.—so the Islanders

selected butter to serve as their medium of exchange. To
facilitate its use as money, they put the butter into quarter-
pound, half-pound, one-pound, five-pound, and ten-pound
packages. Because it was a common denominator of value,
each pound and package of butter did not simply traverse
a single direct path from producer to consumer, but shuttled
around many times over a vast number of paths between
producers.

Under a system of "perishable money," even an unbalanced distribution of income could not cause much of a
decline in aggregate monetary demand among the Islanders.
A lack of balance could bring forth luxuries for some and
relative poverty for others, but it could not generate unemployment. It was wholly incapable of generating depressions
in which one man or group of men could drastically decrease their rate of disbursement for long periods of time.
Even Crusoe, who was a shrewder trader and more efficient
worker than the others, was forced — when he became richer
than the others — to exchange his money accumulations for
products and services which added to his own well-being
or to capital equipment for the community. When Crusoe
acquired substantial "butter purchasing power," its depreciating nature, its limitation as a store of value, actually
forced him to use it in raising his own standard of living or
the island's capital goods activity. The perishability of his
butter money guaranteed that no men had to go unemployed
longer than crude storage facilities could delay deterioration
of the money. The use of demurrage money induced the
well-to-do to buy new boats, new nets, more furniture, etc.,
as the sensible thing to do. Mother Nature herself prevented
them from doing harm to the specialized workers.

Crusoe's butter money impelled him, for example, as he
got richer and richer, to hire Friday and the neighbors to
perform additional services for him. Sometimes it was to
produce "consumer goods" and sometimes "producers'

goods." Once Crusoe acquired claims to the community's output he was under pressure to exercise them. In this predicament he was naturally always bidding for workers. Men did not go unemployed longer than the island's crude storage facilities could prevent spoilage. Workers bargained so well with employers that an unbalanced income distribution did not occur. Under these circumstances, holders of money were just as desirous of getting rid of their money as the holders of commodities were of getting rid of their goods. Selling became as easy as buying. Money disbursed as a cost promptly boomeranged back as a demand and as a sale. The money of the island—not possessing an excessive store of value—became a dynamo of business and continually stimulated the economic growth of the land.

Now let us premise that this happy situation did not long endure; that a devastating change occurred; that the Islanders invented refrigeration. Naturally the new deferral power tremendously increased the money owners' bargaining power against job-seeking employees and capital-seeking entrepreneurs. They could almost insist on their own terms.

In order to forestall depreciation of their accumulated butter money, the big income recipients built brine-cooling coils into their warehouses. They were thereupon able to put their money receipts into cold storage and to hold idle indefinitely the butter money they received.

Fortunately, for years at a time, they spent their income for capital facilities even though their refrigerated butter money would have permitted them to lengthen the interval between their transactions. Occasionally, however, they chose not to invest their savings, but elected instead to "run from a goods to a cash position." Of course, by doing so, they cut off some of the income that had provided a big part of their market. Activity naturally declined. The savers discovered that lopsided income distribution in combination with their refusal to buy ever more capital equipment—a distribution

and refusal which installation of refrigeration had made
possible — reduced their own output and income and in the
end generated a "depression."

Eventually times became severe on the island. Unemployment grew, output declined, people starved and bitterness
spread. At first the Islanders were merely confused. Then
with growing bitterness and desperation, they supported
one crude governmental "recovery" proposal after another:
sales taxes and doles, progressive income taxes and handout
programs, fiscal and monetary programs of many kinds.

After endless grief and turmoil, experiments and plans, the
Islanders required, as a standby arrangement, that the Island
refrigerators have their cooling coils connected to a common
circuit. Then they could vote if necessary to set the refrigerators at temperatures that would make it costly for
owners to use their butter money tardily.

Suppose at that point in time, when the island's overall
activity had slowed down, that the government, in efforts
to correct the situation, had passed a Full Employment Act
and a Wagner Act, had gone in for compensatory spending
by borrowing the sluggishly used current income, or had
minted and disbursed a new quantity of money. Suppose also
that it had then given the new funds to the unemployed and
other low income groups along with more power to strike
and disrupt. Such actions would indeed have been clumsy
recourses for countering a breakdown of spending that could
have been prevented by merely lowering slightly the value
of the money loitering in the refrigerators.

Every society should design a monetary instrument — a
medium of exchange — that boomerangs back into the market
to demand goods once the money is paid out. For every
society, if it is to have business stability, must make use of
a boomerang money. If it does not, but uses a sanctuary
money instead, it dooms itself to improvise forever with the

hapless recourses of the New Economics, as this book will show. (We shall see that the demand deposit — the checkbook money that we use as medium of exchange today — possesses the same evil characteristic as does refrigerated butter money.)

By making it impractical for recipients of butter money to use it as an undue store of value, the Islanders kept demand stable, income distribution more balanced, exchange continuous and employment complete.

Thus life went on serenely. The very nature of the Island's money insured a full demand for each man's product despite the fact that each man specialized. Then one day an Islander discovered gold. Strangely enough this event was instrumental in unbalancing the idyllic Island world. People substituted gold for butter as medium of exchange and found that the deferral of spending was much easier inasmuch as temperature changes could not affect the value of the gold.

Then they compounded their troubles. For efficiency reasons they introduced a new kind of asset, the "certificate of indebtedness," as a secondary medium of exchange. They made it just as imperishable as was gold. Inadvertently, they made its deferability of use even more difficult to discern. By using both "certificates of indebtedness" and "gold" as media of exchange, the Islanders increased their vulnerability to sags in aggregate monetary demand. The Islanders did this when they carelessly decided to enforce with their police powers all kinds of contracts and debt obligations without adequate restrictions on the kinds of contract agreements that they would enforce. The next chapter traces the disruptive impact of such oversights in detail.

By examining in turn the characteristics of barter, commodity money, warehouse receipts, and the debt obligations of commercial banks, we shall see how cost pressures against using money tardily were accidentally and subtly removed from the money instrument as people moved to an ever more efficient instrument of exchange.

## Barter

Although barter provides some of the gains that derive from specialized production, it is an inefficient way to exchange surpluses. For it requires that each barterer must both want what another man has to offer and at the same time have what the other man wants in exchange. It is not easy to arrange for a simultaneous matching of wants.

Bartered commodities, however, have the big virtue that they do not possess an excessive store of value. Tangible commodities are all made from nature's materials and as a result deteriorate with time. Because all products depreciate, they can serve as stores of value to only a limited degree. They put continuous pressure on people to offer their surpluses in exchange — to accept the best price they can get for their specialties while staying in full production. They tend to induce a continuous exchange of goods — and consequent business stability. Farmers, for example, always stay in full production and offer their products in the market at the best prices they can get.

Barter may look like a simple transaction. Still it can occur only under governments which do not take away certain rights and privileges from the people. Under barter, participants are backed up by the enforcement of agreements and by the protection of their property. Only under such umbrella conditions can specialized producers obtain the efficiency and liberty that accompanies specialized production.

## Commodity Money

Still, barter is an inefficient way for producers to exchange their bulky surpluses. Consequently, people gradually shifted to exchanging their products for some widely accepted commodity such as furs and tobacco—as halfway steps toward exchanging their goods for those items which they really wanted finally to consume. Recourse to commodity money gave every producer a gauge of value against which to compare the market worth of all products offered for sale in the community.

The use of some widely accepted commodity as medium of exchange provided several advantages over barter. It was no longer necessary to get together a seller of goods and a buyer with commodity money. Recourse to relatively compact and portable commodity money made it feasible to set up trading posts and central markets. Men who were rich in commodity money could buy the miscellaneous surpluses of specialized producers, store them on shelves, and sell them later when other people were ready to buy.

Commodity monies like furs and tobacco gave every producer a gauge of value against which to array the relative market worth of all the products being offered for sale in the community. Such relative ratios of exchange against furs or tobacco became quickly known and provided all producers with a common denominator.

### Warehouse Receipts

Later, when people acquired confidence in law enforcement, they were willing to shift from commodity money to the use of Warehouse Receipts as money.

Warehouse receipts are claim checks that are exchanged for stored property. Such receipts early superseded Alaska's furs and Virginia's tobacco as media of exchange. Producers of these commodities deposited them for convenience and safekeeping in warehouses in return for receipts, and then used the claim checks as money instead of the commodities themselves.

Providing a convenient form of money involves costs. A

trapper would, of course, sooner go marketing with handy warehouse receipts in his pockets than with a bulky pelt on his back. But giving warehouse receipts for furs or gold, for example, put a cost load on the owner of the warehouse because he had to appraise the value of the depositor's commodity, incur the risk of making mistakes in doing so, and also spend time at keeping records. Consequently, he had to charge the trapper a fee for exchanging unstandardized bulky assets for a more convenient form of purchasing power. And a second real cost was involved because goods· cannot be preserved in a warehouse without care and attention. All of nature's products depreciate with time and need protection against the elements as well as against thieves. So a second charge had to be made for the average deterioration and loss. These two costs constitute a large part of what is called "interest." (See my book, *Money In Motion*, pages 87–88.)

Commodity money has to a mild degree the quality of being a hot potato. Because there is a dissuader involved in possessing it, it carries within itself an inducement to get rid of it steadily. Credit money should possess this same inducement. We shall see how that can be arranged.

Warehouse receipts became usable as money only because the government insisted that there be real tangible value behind each warehouse receipt, and that those who accepted the receipts in payment be privileged to turn them in for the tangible commodities in the warehouse. Our silver certificates of yesterday — warehouse receipts — circulated as money only because the courts enforced contracts and agreements. Contractual receipts can circulate as money only because the law enforces agreements.

Figure 9, which follows, illustrates the institutional arrangement that makes it feasible to substitute paper claim checks for hard commodity money. A Trapper (1), for example, who wants to buy goods and services (2) from the

Business Community (3) with his bulky furs (4) may much prefer to first exchange them at a Trading Post Depository (5) for convenient paper warehouse receipts (6) which he can then use—in making purchases. Warehouse receipts are usable as money only because the government insures that there is real commodity value behind each warehouse receipt and that those who accepted the receipts are privileged to turn them in (via the dotted line) for the tangible commodities in the depository warehouse.

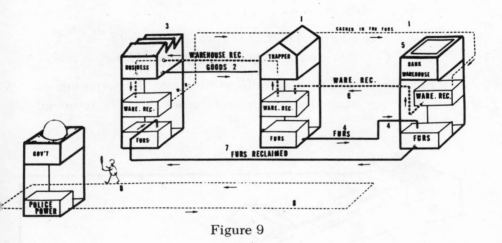

Figure 9

Our recent silver certificates—warehouse receipts—and our checkbook claims are in essence contracts that circulate as money only because the courts enforce our contracts and agreements.

Back of all the monetary systems that use paper of any kind as medium of exchange is the implication that the government will back up the line with enforcement of the promises on the paper. Only because the policeman stands ready on demand to escort (8) the furs—or other goods from the depository to the holder of the receipt, do the claims have value.

Once people acquired confidence in law enforcement, and warehouse receipts had come into active use as money, the gold certificate—a particular kind of warehouse receipt— came into very common use. For gold's compactness, uniformity, portability, and divisibility, had caused it largely to supersede goods like tobacco and furs as the preferred form of commodity money.

Then because of gold's low perishability, and the low cost of storing and warehousing it, the gold certificate soon superseded as money all other kinds of warehouse receipts and commodity money.

### Gold and Warehouse Receipts to Gold Came to Be the Dominant Form of Money

Figures 10 and 11 also help to illustrate the sequence of evolutionary steps by which society accidentally removed

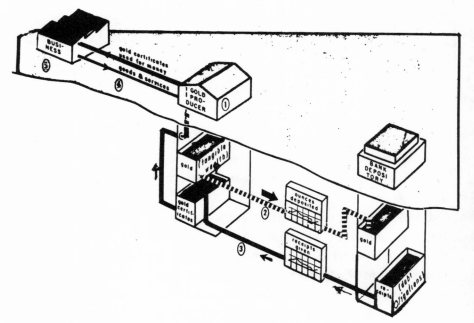

Figure 10

the ownership and loitering costs from that property which constitutes our money.

Even a gold producer (1) preferred to exchange his bulky gold (2) for lighter and handier gold certificates (3) and to use these in buying the goods and services he wanted (4) from the business community (5).

## Gold and Fractional Reserve Credit Banking

The gold certificate was usually worth as much as the gold itself and was a much more convenient form of money to use. Consequently, only small amounts of gold were ever redeemed or asked for from the Depository. The movements of the gold to the bank turned out to be mainly a one-way flow. In the main, the gold certificates stayed in circulation while the gold stayed in the bank.

And because the withdrawals were smaller than the deposits, it was feasible for bankers to nominally "lend" (against collateral of course) more warehouse receipts to gold than they had gold on hand. The circulating medium consequently came to consist of only, say, one part gold to several parts of nominal warehouse receipts.

Despite the popularity of both gold and gold certificates as money, they had their shortcomings. While they served as splendid gauges of value, they served too well as stores of value and reduced the amount of pressure on recipients of money income to disburse it promptly at stable rates.

All commodities have varying costs of care and storage. In the case of eggs and bread, the cost is high; in the case of gold, very low. Whereas the costs of care and storage spurred most producers, such as farmers and craftsmen, to offer their output for the best prices they could get, there was a negligible loitering charge on the gold certificate to put pressure on its owners to exchange it for current production quickly enough to assure full employment and a steady demand for goods.

### Debt Obligations of Banks

Until very lately, we in the U.S. used billions of dollars worth of Warehouse Receipts — our Silver Certificates — as money. We have, however, made a complete shift to another form of money. It came accidentally when we began to use commercial banks' obligations, our checkbook money, as our main medium of exchange.

We thus have a form of property without any carrying or ownership charges. How did we do it? It was not something we had with barter; nor when we used either commodity money, like furs and tobacco, or warehouse receipts for money. It came accidentally when we began to use collateral-backed contracts for money.

Checks are, in effect, contracts — the IOUs of banks — which circulate as money only because the courts enforce the claims against the banks. Behind all the monetary systems that use paper or checkbook money of any kind as medium of exchange is the implication that the government will back up the line with enforcement of the promises on the paper. However, how wise is it to enforce these promises as unconditionally as we do?

People rely heavily on the use of checkbook money because they find it a more convenient way to transfer to someone else a bank's indebtedness to them than it is even to use paper currency as medium of exchange. As a result, bankers also find today (as did the medieval bankers with respect to gold withdrawals) that *currency* withdrawals do not equal *checkbook deposits*. Consequently, bankers find it practical to "lend" — and promise to pay out on demand — more currency to borrowers than they as bankers collectively possess. Claims against bank deposits are also contracts and, in the form of checkbook money, are now used predominantly as our medium of exchange. It is these bankers' obligations created against such borrowers' debt obligations as mortgages, notes and bonds, that constitute the main portion of our bank money today. The average depositor reasons that his coin and currency might be lost or stolen, whereas his demand deposits cannot be. Then, too, his cancelled checks can serve as receipts.

As Figure 11 below illustrates, when tangible property like gold (1) was deposited in the banker's depository (2) the

## HOW BANKS CREATE DEMAND DEPOSITS IN EXCHANGE FOR GOLD & BORROWERS DEBT OBLIGATIONS

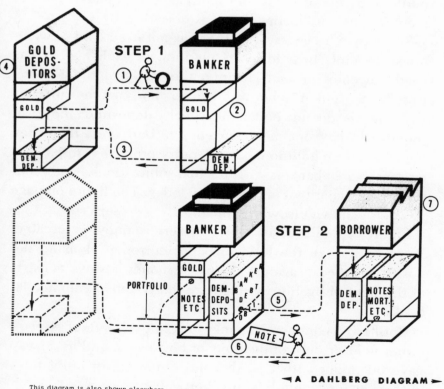

This diagram is also shown elsewhere more vividly in color.

◄ A DAHLBERG DIAGRAM ►

Copyright 1974 by Artur O. Dahlberg.

Figure 11

banker gave a demand claim (warehouse receipt) (3) to the
gold producer (4) in return. But if the banker knew that
only one tenth of the demand claims against him would be
exercised, he felt that it was feasible to "lend" out additional demand claims (5), providing he obtained a worthwhile asset (6) from the borrower (7) in return. He found it
feasible, for example, to give a borrowing farmer a demand
claim against the bank for $1,000 "in gold" if he could
obtain in return, say, a $1,000 mortgage against a $10,000
farm. Under such conditions, the banker felt confident that
if borrowers exercised their demand claims against him for
more gold than he had figured on, he could sell some of his
portfolio assets of notes and mortgages for enough gold to
meet the demand claims being exercised.

Since 1933, of course, the U.S. has not used gold or warehouse receipts to gold as its medium of exchange. It has
used currency instead—mainly, the IOUs of the Federal
Reserve System. And because bankers find that the currency
withdrawals do not equal the checks deposited, they can
promise to pay out more currency to borrowers than they
possess. These additional "book-entry promises" to pay out
currency are bankers' contractual obligations, and constitute the major part of our money today. The figure on page
37 is also shown elsewhere in color.

Figure 11 illustrates how modern money is created.
Whether it is in the form of paper currency, demand deposits, or checks against deposits, money always consists
of the debt obligations (which are the IOUs) of commercial
banks.

Until 1933, commercial banks took in two kinds of assets—
either gold or debt obligations of borrowers, and as a swap
gave out money (that is, demand deposits), or obligations
of their own of roughly equivalent value.

Gold, of course, is not now in domestic use. But the diagram illustrates how (prior to 1933), when an owner of
gold (4) deposited it (1) in the bank (2), the banker put it

in his asset portfolio and gave the depositor the bank's equivalent liability (3) as a swap.

The diagram also illustrates how, in a parallel way, a businessman with property (7) who wants money offers the bank (2) a debt obligation of his own expressed in some form such as a note, bond or mortgage (6), and how the bank puts it in the same portfolio with the gold, giving the borrower (7) as a swap the bank's own liability (5) in the form of a bank deposit.

Today, of course, commercial banks do not monetize gold. The two things they do monetize (or swap their own liabilities for) are private debt and federal government debt. If, in your imagination, you replace the gold owner's building (4) on the left of the diagram, with an imaginary federal government building, then it is easy to see how the federal government can also make money out of government debt obligations, and how it inflates the money medium. Since 1933, the federal government has had the power, to an unlimited degree, to exchange its debt obligations for commercial bank debt obligations. The banker cannot refuse to make the exchange. (Federal debt obligations today comprise about 17% of the total value of our commercial banks' portfolios.)

The difference in the value of federal debt obligations and obligations of private business borrowers is this: When a businessman tries to swap obligations with a bank, the banker looks him over carefully and appraises him as a producer. Does he earn enough income by producing goods or services for the community so that its purchases from him will enable him to retire his bank obligation at its due date? There is production behind the businessman's obligation. Behind the federal government's obligation, however, there is only the government's expropriation power. The banking system's assets are simply diluted and the buying power of demand deposits in terms of goods and services is made to decline steadily.

# Chapter 3

## How We Give Money an Excessive Store of Value

DOLLARS are brought into being by commercial banks when they convert into bank deposits the obligations of borrowers, who by giving collateral, fortify their debt obligations to the banks with reserves of wealth. Businessmen and farmers could conceivably use their own personal obligations locally as media of exchange without first converting them into bank deposit equivalents. But in order to make their own assets — their wheat or personal notes — into a widely usable exchange instrument, they exchange at the bank an obligation against themselves (like a mortgage or a note) expressed in dollars, for the immediate dollar obligation of the bank. It is by making such exchanges with collaborating bankers that businessmen, farmers and other borrowers create new money today. By simply leaving their dated notes with the bankers and receiving demand deposits of roughly equal value in return, borrowers convert claims against their properties into money.

Observe well in the following Figure 12 that all note, mortgage and bond obligations which borrowers convert into money always have collateral value $(a + b)$ behind them, and that therefore the deposit dollars which banks create against the borrowers' obligations are as fully protected against depreciation as are the borrowers' obligations. Note, too, that when borrowers purchase goods and materials with their new deposit dollars, they do so in the belief that the new money, which they themselves quickly disburse, will continue to circulate at the rate at which they send it out. The borrowers expect the respending of the money by the many recipients to provide them with some of the revenue with which to meet their notes at maturity.

Figure 12 illustrates the evolutionary step by which society accidentally and unintentionally removed the carrying and loitering cost from that property which is now used as medium of exchange and why, as a consequence, money has an excessive store of value. Because of that development, full employment and a steady demand for goods

## HOW BANKS CREATE DEPOSITS IN EXCHANGE FOR OBLIGATIONS.

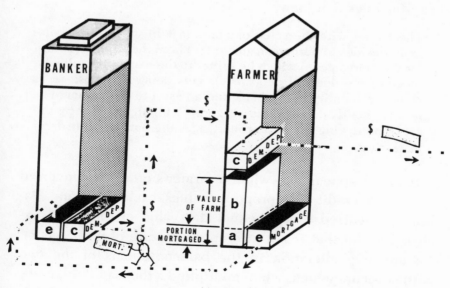

Figure 12

is no longer assured unless government compensatory demand is periodically thrown into the breach.

Figures 12 and 13 bring out how a farmer, owning, say, a $10,000 farm (a + b), and who borrows and encumbers $1,000 against it at (e), ends up owning $1,000 of demand deposits (c) which has its value insured with the additional $9,000 worth of farm.

Today the practice of exchanging borrowers' debts for bankers' debts seems simple enough (and is usually portrayed in textbooks in simple T-tables). But such tables fail to show the subtle way in which the practice of exchanging borrowers' obligations for bankers' obligations—both of which have their values expressed in fixed terms—alters drastically a basic property relationship between lenders and borrowers far more than T-table portrayals suggest.

In T-table presentations it superficially seems that when a farmer borrows $1,000 at a commercial bank and helps thereby to create money, only an exchange of $1,000 debts occurs between the two and that the case is closed. Figure 12 illustrates that view.

> The farmer with the value of a farm (a + b) shown in the diagram decides to borrow an amount (c) from the bank. In return for the mortgage (e) which he brings to the bank's portfolio, he receives the demand deposit (c). This demand deposit is, as shown, a liability to the bank and an asset to the farmer. The farmer spends these dollars. Figure 12 highlights that by the act of borrowing the farmer mortgages the portion of his farm market (a).

It might appear that when a farmer's credit is converted into bank credit, the property values exchanged and liabilities incurred exactly equal the value of the debts exchanged. But that is not a complete picture of what occurs. An auxiliary alteration in the balance sheets of the two parties occurs which, when multiplied a thousandfold, gives the possessors of money in our economy a new bargaining power advantage over all producers and possessors of tangible goods. Moreover, it operates to expose our otherwise superb free market system to its dreaded instability of demand and employment. It is an alteration which up to now has gone completely undiscussed in economic literature. What, then, is the nature of this alteration?

In borrowing money, the farmer (as shown in the following Figure 13) does more than merely exchange $1,000 debt obligations with the banker. He transfers to the banker a mortgage liability (e) not only worth that much at the time of the loan, but also a *contingent liability* (f) against his entire collateral (his farm, a plus b) — which will probably be worth at least $1,000 at the maturity date, even if the nation's overall dollar demand for goods collapses, and property values in the economy — including that of the farm itself — tumble drastically.

### ;ORROWERS' OBLIGATIONS HAVE COLLATERAL BEHIND THEM.

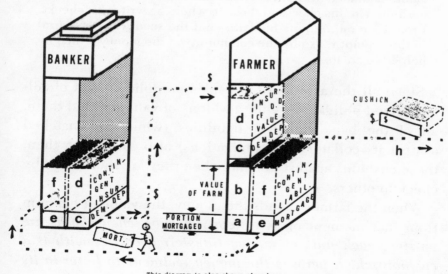

This diagram is also shown elsewhere
more vividly in color

Figure 13

In pledging that he will repay $1,000 at a future date, the farmer implicitly puts up the whole value of his farm as collateral to insure that he will repay the money on that future date. He says that, even if during the loan period the nation's income recipients re-use their money so slowly that prices fall and property values tumble, he will sacrifice his farm if need be to obtain the needed $1,000 for repayment.

When the farmer borrows at the bank, he subtly puts a cushion or reserve of value (f) behind the mortgage liability (e) that he gives to the bank. He transfers this cushion (f) to the bank's portfolio. Then he receives this cushion (d) back with the dollars (c) which the bank credits to his account. This occurs, because, for the mortgage (e) and contingent liability (f) that the banker receives, the banker creates and gives to the farmer a matching bank liability—made up of the demand deposit (c) and the contingent value insurance (d)—which necessarily matches the bank's own contingent claim (f) against the farmer. (In this way the bank's liability given to the farmer always equals arithmetically the liability that the borrowing farmer gives to the bank.) After receiving back the contingency value insurance (d) from the bank, the farmer transfers (h) this cushion with his checks to those to whom he writes his checks. From then on, he puts his faith (and the security of his farm) in the prompt reuse by the community of the money which he helped to create.

Since all the assets in the bank's portfolio consist of collateralized obligations with cushions of value behind them, all of the bank's deposit liabilities (which are matched against its collateralized obligations) also carry with them these cushions against decline when they are transferred by check to others.

When the farmer spends the money, the value of his farm from that moment on is in jeopardy. *For when checks are written, each unit of money transferred carries with it a cushion which permits the money recipient to loiter in its use without suffering a loss*—even though the loitering may help to shrink business and tumble prices. The recipient can do this with impunity because the value of the dollar itself does not shrink immediately when the value of the collateral bleeds away. Not until the value of the collateral becomes worth less than the face value of the mortgage, is the cushion of value used up. Only then are the dollars that are slowed down by the laggard spenders worth less than when the laggard spenders accepted them. Not until all the collateral behind the assets in the bank's portfolio has melted away — as happened to the farm mortgages in Midwest banks during the depression of the 1930's — is the bank insolvent and unable to pay off one hundred cents on the dollar. * In the material that follows, we shall look more closely at the points I have just raised.

---

* The fact that all the checkbook money of today has its value fortified with collateral, and can thereby give its possessors the opportunity to slow down its rate of use with relative impunity, is so important that I wish to insure here that I have driven home this point. Thus I shall picture the factual relationship with additional graphic evidence.

Apparently the public and professional understanding of both the nature of money and the institutional substance that lies behind the process of money creation is so distorted that even our banking terminology reflects it.

According to popular and accepted concepts and terms, those responsible citizens who possess property values, which the community recognizes and is willing to protect with its police power, and who wish to obtain a bank's present obligation to pay our Federal Reserve currency on demand in exchange for their own obligation to obtain and repay at a later date, are called "borrowers." That term is inaccurate and misleading.

The participating farmers, businessmen, and consumers who exchange their obligations really *borrow nothing from the bank. They merely swap assets with the bank.* They are swappers, not borrowers. They are equals who exchange intangible property obligations of equal value. That is the essence of money creation. *Commercial banks do not make "loans" when they increase the money supply.* They do not "lend" money except the time deposits which are entrusted to them. Not one dollar of the bank's cash or reserves is "lent out," in the process of money creation. The bank's cash is untouched in the exchange transaction. The volume of cash merely acts as a restraint, or as a guide, to the bank's judgment as to how many obligations it is advisable to swap with members of the community.

Yet bank literature, discussion, and statistics create in the public mind a very different functional picture of the reality of money creation by using such terms as "borrowers" and "loans": As a result, public policy is often harmfully affected by the prevailing mental confusion.

Savings banks usually lend out existing money in return for an interest fee, but commercial banks merely transform borrowers' debt obligations into their own debt obligations for a fee.

COMMERCIAL BANKS DO NOT MAKE LOANS.
A commercial Bank (2) does not lend out its beginning
cash (3) to "borrowers", but creates and gives new
deposit obligations (8) to them in exchange for their
collateralized obligations (9).

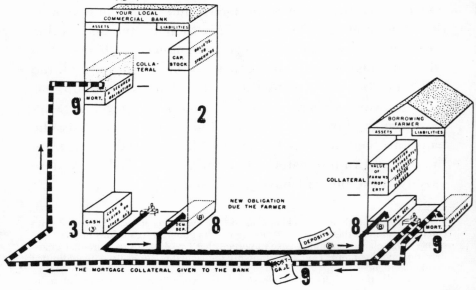

Figure 14

The diagrams shown make it easier to understand why,
when we provide our money with insurance against declines in face value, we must first: continually bait our
possessors of money with subsidies, guarantees, premiums,
and extra increments of interest payments in order to keep
them disposed to disburse their money without delay; why,
secondly, we must assure savers of money that they can—
without penalty—respend it tardily and cause people to
clamor for more and more compensatory spending, either
as "planning" or as relief; and how, thirdly, the government's power over the people expands steadily as it allocates
and directs the flow of ever larger buffering sums among
them.

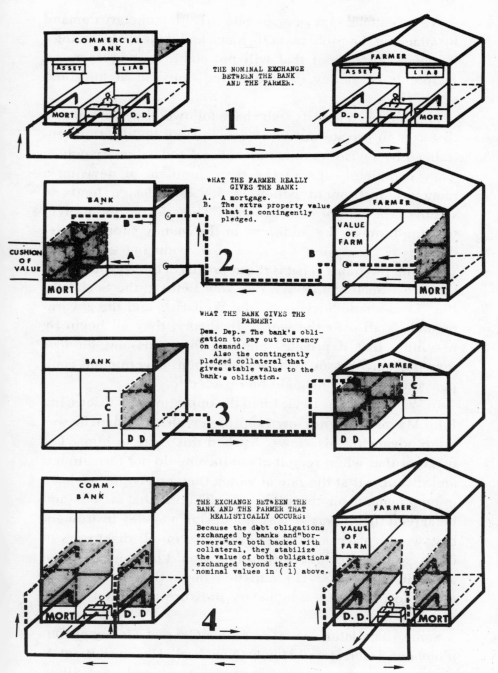

Figure 15

We can attack sags in aggregate private monetary demand by attacking the problem at its roots, and do it by designing a monetary instrument that will put continuous pressure on recipients of money income to redisburse it at high and stable rates.

The "new economists" who have followed Keynes contend that sags in private monetary demand can be offset or neutralized by a wise combination of fiscal and monetary policy. They completely ignore the basic problem of devising a monetary instrument which by its very design tends to stabilize the rate of use of money. They devote themselves to "fine-tuning" the additions to the money supply, to reducing or increasing taxes, or to introducing ever more spending programs. That is the approach of the New Dealers, the Great Society analysts, the New Leftists, the Socialists, the "Democratic Socialists," the Welfarists and the governmentalists all over the world. In theory, they all begin by reasoning that if private spending for goods and services sags for any reason whatsoever, then government compensatory spending should be resorted to.

In Washington in 1934, I had the opportunity of discussing John Maynard Keynes' own approach with him, when he was there advancing his views. I posed this issue to him: "Let us grant that when recipients of income do not turn around and disburse it at the rate at which they receive it, we have unemployment for the difference. Then if that is so" — and he agreed that it was — "why not design a money instrument that would place a monetary pressure on all disbursers of funds so that the rate of spending would be stepped up to adequate velocity?" He said that theoretically this was a good idea, but such a monetary pressure could not be devised.

Some years later, however, in his *General Theory of Employment, Interest and Money* (New York: Harcourt, Brace & Company, 1936, p. 355) Keynes wrote favorably of Silvio

Gesell's proposal to increase the rate of money disbursal by placing a tax on currency:

> It is convenient to mention at this point the strange, unduly neglected prophet Silvio Gesell, whose work contains flashes of deep insight and who only just failed to reach down to the essence of the matter. . . . I believe that the future will learn more from the spirit of Gesell than from that of Marx. . . . But there is a great defect in Gesell's theory. Having given the reason why the money-rate of interest cannot be negative, he altogether overlooks the need of an explanation why the money-rate of interest is positive. . . . Gesell argues that the growth of real capital is held back by the money-rate of interest. . . . Thus the prime necessity is to reduce the money-rate of interest, and this can be effected by giving the money a cost just like other stocks of barren goods. This led him to the famous prescription of "stamped" money. . . . The idea behind "stamped" money is sound.

As will be brought out, the idea behind—and the need for—"stamped script" is not sound and is not necessary.

Unfortunately, although Gesell understood well the functional need in the aggregate for a stable rate of use of money, he did not understand the institutional nature of modern money. (As brought out on page 54, neither did Keynes understand it.)

Gesell maintained that all money was fiat money—that it had acceptance only because the government's enforcement machinery stood behind it. He did not see that modern demand deposits and currency consist basically merely of the monetized debt obligations of bank borrowers (and—indirectly—of their property). Gesell's proposals for stabilizing aggregate monetary demand and for buttressing the mechanics of his proposals were therefore defective and historically have not been able to enlist the support of the monetary theorists of the world.

Of course, as I bring out later, the money rate of interest

is always positive because, in the process of converting borrower's obligations into money, a cushion of value is placed behind each dollar created. In my opinion, it is not the saver's "liquidity preference," as Keynes maintained, but money's undue store of value that explains why the money rate of interest is always positive and never goes to zero. *Interest is not solely a reward for saving, it is also partly a bribe for not hoarding.*

There seem to be two relatively simple ways in which to give money an ownership cost which does not involve the use of the taxing power or the discretionary power of the state. Such approaches are very basic to making the free market system viable and acceptable. All other recourses lead to governmentalism with all its attendant evils.

It is my opinion that the causal relationship between the accidental institutional removal of carrying charges from the medium of exchange and the resulting inadequate demand for goods—a relationship which Keynes also overlooked and gave untenable explanations for—is the missing link of economic theory.

# Chapter 4

## One Form of Money Disrupts the Stability of our Free Market System

PREVIOUS chapters illustrated the evolutionary steps by which society accidentally and unintentionally removed the carrying and loitering charge from that property which is now used as medium of exchange, and why, as a consequence, full employment and a steady demand for goods is no longer assured unless government compensatory demand is periodically thrown into the breach.

Borrowers do not arrange that the dollars they disburse shall pay a penalty if tardily used. No carrying costs or pressures to spend are placed on the money sent out, with the result that the recipients of the money have the opportunity to slow down indefinitely the money they receive. The prevailing pressures to prevent the recipients from spending tardily are inadequate. (The loss of interest revenue that results from not investing their "money-savings" promptly exercises some pressure, but that pressure is usually more than offset by their gain in holding cash from the dip in security and property values that occurs when tardy spending on a large scale begins.)

Economic law decrees that, for business stability, money must in the aggregate be respent at the same rate at which it is received; yet our monetary arrangements enable re-

cipients to spend it or slow it down without cost as they see
fit. And no one criticizes the logic of that arrangement.
Running tacitly through the historic writings of almost all
economists is the premise that money recipients should be
permitted to withdraw from the markets at will without
penalty and that they should only be coaxed back. It is this
premise that should be challenged. Economists today do
not seek the explanation for the lengthening of the interval
between transactions — the slumps in velocity — that occasionally occur.

For example, in his textbook, *Economics* Professor Paul
Samuelson even asks the question "What good does it do
us to raise the concept of velocity of money? The older
economists," he writes, "thought it did lots of good. Today
the new generation of economists tends to believe that the
concept of velocity is of limited usefulness. It puts off
answering a question by asking another question. Thus, one
of the reasons given for the Great Depression of the 1930's
was the reduced velocity of circulation of money. But why
was velocity reduced? To know that is already to know the
answer to the riddle of the slump. [It is that riddle to which I
address myself.] Similarly those who thought recovery could
be ensured by increasing the quantity of money were disap-
pointed by the unexpected decline in the velocity of the new
money."

Samuelson points to "One bitter lesson we have learned
since 1929: There is no inherent tendency for money to be
spent for goods at a constant velocity. If my current income
is low, and if my expectations are pessimistic concerning real
investment projects, then I may hold large sums of cash from
1930 to 1940 without at all increasing my spending. Call this
hoarding if you like; but if interest rates are low, and if I am
pessimistic concerning the future values of securities and
real estate, then to hold cash is the most sensible speculation

that I can make." * Obviously such writing is merely commentary, and is not functional analysis.

This book concerns itself particularly with the riddle of the slumps in the rates of use of money. It seeks to call national attention to the tragically overlooked fact that as we gradually shifted from commodity money (on which nature and society impose a carrying cost or demurrage cost) to bank deposit money (which is fortified in value with cushions of collateral) the holders of money were unintentionally and inadvertently given a costless opportunity to slow down their disbursements.

Economists do not seem to have noticed that declines in aggregate monetary demand result largely from the accidental removal of carrying costs from the medium of exchange. In fact, many of them specifically have argued that money as an exchange instrument is a neutral tool which of itself would cause no serious derangement of the level of production. As a group they have accepted Say's and Ricardo's view that, even though monetary demand is left uncontrolled, it will never be seriously lacking. As John Maynard Keynes says:

> The idea that we can safely neglect the aggregate demand function is fundamental to the Ricardian economics, which underlie what we have been taught for more than a century. Malthus, indeed, had vehemently opposed Ricardo's doctrine that it was impossible for effective demand to be deficient; but vainly. For, since Malthus was unable to explain clearly how and why effective demand could be deficient or excessive, he failed to furnish an alternative construction; and Ricardo conquered England as completely as the Holy Inquisition conquered Spain. Not only was his theory accepted by the city, by statesmen, and by the academic world, but controversy ceased; the other point of view completely dis-

---

* Paul Samuelson, *Economics* (New York: McGraw-Hill, 1951).

appeared, it ceased to be discussed. The great puzzle of effective demand with which Malthus had wrestled vanished from
economic literature. You will not find it mentioned once even
in the whole works of Marshall, Edgeworth, and Professor
Pigou, from whose hands the classical theory has received its
most mature embodiment.

But Keynes, too, failed to notice how the evolutionary removal of carrying charges from the medium of exchange,
via the adoption of collateralized bank money, explained the
almost chronic deficiency of effective demand. In his writings, at least, he did not recognize the impact of that removal.
Instead, he found the cause of inadequate demand in
"liquidity preference." In so doing, he gave a semantic name
to the trouble, but he did not explain it. He did not spot
either the collateral reserve of value behind the face value of
modern money, or the opportunity to defer demand with
impunity, which that reserve gives to the possessors of
money. Failing to see how the practice of using collateralized
bank obligations as money automatically operates to give a
hoarding privilege to the holders of that money, he fell into
the trap of recommending—as suitable correctives to inadequate private demand and serious unemployment—
compensatory government spending. And unfortunately he,
in his turn, with his faulty analyses and recommendations
for government economic intervention, conquered not only
England but the whole Western world as completely as the
Holy Inquisition conquered Spain.

Keynes and his followers have completely overlooked the
curative possibilities of those monetary approaches which
could insure directly that the private holders of money on
balance reuse their money in the markets as rapidly as they
receive it.

Economists generally agree that booms occur whenever
people try to run from money into goods, and that growth
stops and recessions occur whenever they try to run the other

way—from goods into a "cash position." People occasionally prefer money to goods because they realize that money somehow differs from goods in that it is much less vulnerable to sudden losses in value. Stockbrokers, for example, when they try to shift their customers into "cash" in periods of uncertainty, recognize that money is an island of safety to which their customers can run. But historically no one has investigated how it came about that we possess a form of asset which, unlike other forms, has no ownership or carrying costs like depreciation, obsolescence, taxation or warehouse charges.

Because money has no ownership or demurrage costs, economists have always implicitly assumed that modern money must be lured back into the markets by means of rewards whenever people slow down its use for any reason whatsoever. But why must money always be lured into use? After all, modern checkbook money is a man-made instrument, and its exemption from ownership costs is a man-made arrangement. The exemption is not a gift of nature.

The use of sanctuary money as our medium of exchange leads to occasional sags in aggregate private monetary demand and contributes to many subsidiary disruptions such as sagging employment, government pump priming, deficit financing, and price inflation. It would therefore be a mistake for us to concern ourselves initially with subsidiary disruptions such as, for example, federal deficits, price inflation, deficits in the balance of payments, etc. That would not be to start at the beginning.

In a monetary economy, specialized producers who have surpluses which they wish to trade for other things, must exchange them indirectly. Usually their products are first exchanged for some one thing of economic worth, such as gold or silver, or checkbook dollars, which is easily evaluated, highly imperishable, readily acceptable, easily subdivided, and highly compact. That unique thing, money, is then in its turn exchanged for the goods and services which are most desired. By the roundabout process of comparing products with a standard of value, services, commodities, and privileges can all be equated with one another and exchanged.

By this means, too, each contributor to the productive process can be given a quantity of money presumably equal to his share of the money sale value of the commodity or service produced, instead of his share of the particular product which he helps to create. This quantity of money is put into circulation as wages, salaries, taxes, commissions, royalties, rents, interest, dividends, and profits, and becomes the money income of the country. By resort to the instrument of money we convert each contributor's share of a particular product into the vastly broader opportunity of claiming in the markets diversified products of approximately equivalent value.

Modern money, however, does more than this. It gives the holder complete freedom in respect not only as to *what* he will take in payment, but as to *when* he will take it. By making use of the device of money, producers of all kinds are given the privilege either of taking their reward in the period during which they produce the goods and services, or of suspending as long as they please the exercise of their right to choose products—either consumer goods or capital investments—in settlement of their claims. Continuity of exchange, full-blast exchange, should probably be the goal of all plans for rapid economic growth. For without it, full use of specialized facilities is impossible.

Demand deposit money is a component part of the U.S. system of agreements that circumscribe our financial transactions. Such money is a highly efficient tool for carrying on exchange. Its social contribution could have been unimpaired, but the laws that define it and circumscribe it are too loosely drawn. The result is that today demand deposit money also performs a disruptive role. This chapter will show how its excessive store of value resulted from an inadequate limitation on the content of the debt obligations that were entered into between the commercial banker and the bank borrowers when the bank loans were made. This chapter will also show how that inadequate limitation inadvertently granted a new special privilege to society's money savers—and placed society's workers at a severe disadvantage in bargaining with employers in the wages market. (When union monopolies did not exist.)

If a person wishes to participate in the benefits that accrue to a community that resorts to a division of labor, he should use in the markets without undue delay the claims to the community's output that he receives for his own output; he should use them at the rate at which the goods themselves are produced in the community. That requirement is a price which he should logically pay for the privilege of belonging to a community that goes in for a division of labor and for exchanging the surpluses of its many producers.

In a free society, market disruption is not caused when the community's savers exercise their right of holding or retaining physical items — real wealth — as long as they please. But when society's money consists of the IOUs of bank borrowers which have been transmuted into the IOUs of banks, and those IOUs are so designed that they can be used sluggishly or held out of the transaction stream without cost, a needless disrupting privilege is being extended to the money creators.

Borrower-producers have deadlines to meet at the bank. They stand ready to produce to meet monetary demand. Is it reasonable under such conditions for the savers of the IOU money, which the borrowers innocently cooperated with the bankers to produce, to have the privilege of keeping the producers at arm's length?

Normally, the money savers of the community do disburse

their income for goods, services or capital investments as rapidly as they receive it. But the design of the money they hold inadvertently gives them the opportunity of disbursing their income at a rate that is not synchronized with the rate of production. And sometimes they drastically reduce the aggregate monetary demand of the community. At such times they impair the bargaining power of the workers in the wages market and cause the industrial activity of the whole community to dip.

In a free society of persuasion and not coercion, a key desideratum is that the courts and police enforce agreements and contracts that people enter into freely. Today our bankers and borrowers, in creating checkbook money, freely but innocently enter into agreements which facilitate sags and lags in aggregate monetary demand. In respecting and enforcing such contracts, society lays itself open to recession. All over the world voters and legislators try to neutralize recessions caused by such agreements with ever more federal spending and governmentalism.

Just as a free society will not enforce contracts between people who sell themselves into slavery — even if they do so willingly — so a free society sets limits to the contracts that it is willing to enforce. If borrowers and bankers were to fully understand the subtle disruptive impact of the kind of agreements that they enter into today in creating checkbook money, they would choose freely in their own self-interest to modify those agreements slightly. They would choose to align the value of those agreements to the average receding values of all the depreciating products which all borrowers produce. A very slight modification could insure the maintenance of aggregate monetary demand for goods and services and at the same time take the pressure off the community to resort to governmentalism whenever sags in private monetary demand occur. Collectively they would choose to have their community enforce only those agreements involving money creation which gives them the advantages of the checkbook exchange instrument which we now have, without the disruptive potential that it carries. How this could easily be done is brought out by the following illustration, which carries the Robinson Crusoe illustration ending on page 29, one step further:

### *Borrowers and Banker Could Protect Themselves against Recessions and Bankruptcies*

Normally, if a borrower at the bank can not meet his $1,000 loan at maturity, he may be driven into bankruptcy. If his assets are liquidated and he is foreclosed for, let us say, $500, then the banker suffers too. For whenever banker's borrowing clients are not patronized, their obligations, which constitute his portfolio of assets, necessarily decline in value. When too many obligations fall too far in value, bankers and borrowers are forced to walk into bankruptcy together.

Bankers and borrowers could have forestalled their occasional common bankruptcy (as in 1933) if, when they initially agreed on a loan the banker had said: "Listen, Mr. Borrower, let us play safe on this transaction. You know as well as I do that we are making our exchange of obligations on two assumptions: (1) That you can collect from the stream of buying in your field of business about the same percentage of patronage as in the past; (2) that during the coming loan period the public's inclination to spend money will remain as great as before; that is, that "the conditions of demand" will remain stable. As a banker, I do not worry about a change occurring in your ability to get your share of business any more than you do, but neither you nor I have any assurance that the present level of demand for goods will remain stable. Yet our solvency hinges largely on it. We have no control over this "demand"—and it could decline violently.

So let us protect ourselves by insuring that there will be a stable market for products when your note matures. Some arrangement such as this might do:

"Let us stipulate that each of our obligations — your annual interest obligation to me, and my demand deposit obligation to you — shall decline in size by, say, two percent per year. Then let us try to induce all other bankers and borrowers to do the same. In that way we can insure that recipients of money will not spend it tardily, and that there will be a demand waiting for your products when you get them produced. In that way we will not have exposed ourselves unduly to forces beyond our control. As it is, tardy spending occasionally bankrupts people like you and me. Then people make investigations. We bankers are often damned for our reckless evaluations and loans. We have sinned some in that regard, it is true, but the usual cause of occasional business failures is neither reckless evaluation nor dishonesty, but our past ignorance of the system of organized indebtedness over which we have had control."

Thus we see that massive bankruptcies grow out of the concession to bankers and borrowers: (1) to work together to create monetary obligations, (2) to stipulate by indirection that these are appreciably insured against declines in buying power, and (3) to make the obligations into assets more desirable at times than wealth itself. People fail to perceive that they give the bankers' debt obligations an undue store of value while they make them into media of exchange. The explanation for occasional recessions lies in the contractual machinery which comprises our money. We do not wish to have our use of "obligation-money" hamstring the exchange of physical wealth itself. But the rules and property rights which we accidentally attach to our catalytic money are not properly designed to prevent it.

It would be unreasonable to deny a possessor of *physical*

*products* or facilities the right to keep them out of use indefinitely if he so wishes. But it is quite another matter to grant him the man-made privilege of deferring the use of the IOUs of men who, when they incurred them, did so in the expectation that they could redeem them with new production before a due date at the bank.

A system of cooperative production can function only by synchronizing the rate of use of claim checks with the rate of production. This synchronization is thwarted by today's money system.

Money should properly be enough of a reservoir of value to permit specialized producers to get from the possession of one kind of specialized product to another—say, from wheat to butter, or from wheat to gold to butter—without suffering greater losses in the process than they would incur if they stayed idly by with their own surpluses. But money should not be so good a store of value that producers can retire into it and stay away so long that they force other producers to lower their activity and prices in efforts to lure them back into the markets again.

We have inadvertently created through our banking machinery a form of economic asset which has no carrying costs. And that asset we use as our medium of exchange. It is therefore possible today for a producer of cotton, steel, shoes, or any other specialized product or service to exchange the surplus of his specialty for present day money, and then slow down the disbursement of it without incurring any carrying charge on the asset that he holds. He can slow down society's exchange tool, money, and force other specialized producers to lower their prices in efforts to bait him back into the markets again. Sometimes the government too tries to neutralize his contraction in monetary demand—caused by the use of a "sanctuary money"—with a wide variety of compensatory spending programs, all of which bring on expansion of governmentalism and bureaucratic power. If it did not do so, the price level would fall as it did in 1930 and make money as an asset ever more valuable to those who had decreased its rate of use.

If my conclusions are tenable regarding both the nature and disruptiveness of modern money, and the curative power of a carrying cost on money, then a revolutionary opportunity opens up for all mankind. For if we remove money's accidental defect, we can proceed to correct the other smaller disruptive and inequitable characteristics of our free market system.

During recent decades, people have been looking in a floundering way for a new system of society, a "third way," somewhere between capitalism and communism which would provide on the one hand for job security and rapid growth, and on the other for freedom from bureaucratic control.

Capitalism is one version of a free market system wherein the pattern of production and consumption is dependent mainly on the preferences of consumers, but which nonetheless utilizes as its medium of exchange an instrument which impairs the continuity of private monetary demand. For that reason it has unwittingly prejudiced the bargaining in the supposedly free market in favor of the holders of money capital and against the workers, so that the workers were chronically forced to bargain at a disadvantage. This was so until they enlisted the power of the state to help them bludgeon their employers. The use of a money that is hoardable with impunity has periodically led to such serious unemployment, fear, and distress that millions of people have entrusted their hopes for a better life to socialists and trade unionists, who strive to invoke the power of the state to fix the wages in the market, in place of relying on the free decisions of the bargainers themselves.

I differ from most advocates of the free market system in that I do not view the system as ever having been tried out to best advantage. The capitalist version of it has not been a well-balanced free market system because the collateralized demand obligations of the banks have been used as its medium of exchange. As brought out before, historic capitalism has in consequence been continuously loaded against the worker, and has increasingly required government compensatory spending to neutralize the propensity of money-savers not to disburse their money as rapidly as they received it from those who were instrumental in creating it through bank borrowing.

If we were to provide for a genuinely free market system — free from both favoritism in the rules to the money-savers and from the power of the unions to coerce the market's wage decisions — our economy would operate full blast and provide job opportunity to its workers. Then, operating under a chronic scarcity of workers, instead of under a chronic scarcity of jobs, the worker-consumer could bargain for himself automatically in the market place during the initial slicing of the pie and gain a large portion of the national income. In that way he could prevent more income going into money-savings for potential investment than can be supported by the prevailing dollar demand of the end markets. The dream balance between consumption and investment would tend to result automatically. The bureaucratic practice of recent decades of trying to achieve the proper balance — after first letting unbalance arise in the free bargaining arena — by bureaucratically taxing the rich heavily and then redistributing the income directly or through government supported jobs to the poor, would cease to have economic justification. So would the union practice of coercively lifting wage rates. The union approach and the government approach toward improved income distribution and growth — whether rooted merely in a desire to improve income or to install socialism — would be patently obsolete.

# Chapter 5

## The Nature of Your Dollar

To UNDERSTAND the merits of the two proposals presented in Chapter 7—both of which, it will be shown, would stabilize aggregate private monetary demand—one must first understand two things: (1) how checkbook money consists of the transmuted debt obligations of bank borrowers which have cushions of value behind them, and (2) how gold is quantitatively and functionally related to the value of the demand deposit obligations which banks give to borrowers in return for their notes, bonds, mortgages or other obligations.

All money has been of two basic types: tangible property or intangible IOUs; tangible wealth or intangible debt. In tangible property form, money usually possesses an intrinsic value. Gold, silver, copper, tobacco, sheep and furs all have considerable use-value in the world of production and consumption. In contrast, legal evidences of indebtedness have no intrinsic value. They are sheets of paper or records of indebtedness which rely for their value on the widespread belief that government will enforce the agreements that people make to transfer values between themselves.

How are the values of specific units of *tangible* property like gold arithmetically related to the value of specific units of *intangible* bankers' obligations? Both kinds of units make up our money today. How is one kind of money functionally related to another? How are the metal coins in our pockets related to our paper currency and demand deposits?

Let us assume that the first American bank began business (under the abandoned old gold standard) with $1,000 (or 23,200 grains of gold) as capital. Since the law stipulated that the monetary unit, the dollar, must contain 23.2 grains of pure gold, let us assume that the banker lent out his gold in chunks with 23.2 grains or multiples of 23.2 grains in each. Under such circumstances, how could it develop that the banker managed and dared to "lend" out more gold than he had? It developed out of his habit of demanding contractual "security" for his loans.

Borrowers who initiated loans at the bank were usually businessmen with property who by means of a note converted a part of the value of their property into bankers' promises to pay out "gold on demand." Since everyone was willing to accept the banker's promises on sight, the loan was a convenient means of converting the value of the businessmen's property into acceptable and usable money.

The process of converting pledges into money permitted bankers to "lend" more gold than existed only because they "lend" no gold at all! Bank borrowers always use as purchasing power only the part of the current value of their own assets that is converted into a new form and guaranteed to the public by the banker.

In creating deposit money, bankers and borrowers promise one another an unequal quantity of "dollars" to be delivered at different dates. In making a $1,000 loan a borrowing farmer, for example, has the banker assign a $1,000 value to such a fraction of his assets as he pledges will be worth, say, $1,015 (at six percent) ninety days later. The borrower plans to harvest and sell goods before that date, and it is this product which he plans to exchange for at least $1,015 of the public's dollars before the ninety days are up. The banker plans on such performance too.

However, since both realize that something may go wrong with the borrower's plans, the borrower gives the banker a note which the courts regard as being a contingent claim against his property. The borrower in substance says that if he fails to pay the banker $1,015 within ninety days, the banker may commandeer the pledged property and sell it to reimburse himself. The banker (before 1933) was willing to promise 1,000 gold dollars "on demand" (even though he realized that there might be no new additions to the country's gold supply to make his promise a realistic one) because the borrower put up, as collateral, assets which the banker believed at the time of the loan could be exchanged for much more than $1,000 in gold and which he felt convinced would be worth in gold at the loan's maturity — even in a forced sale — at least as much as the face value of the loan. Thus the banker in effect said that for a fee of $15 (six percent for ninety days) he would guarantee that the borrower's security, which might be worth many thousands of dollars at the time of the loan, would be worth at least $1,000 at the termination of the loan, and that he as banker would convert for the duration of the loan period a prior claim against the borrower's assets into a claim of $1,000 against himself. In a nominal sense the banker underwrote the borrower's pledge by taking the responsibility for its value at maturity. In a realistic sense, however, the borrower himself underwrote the banker's evaluation and took the larger risk because he insured his note with a contingent claim against his other possessions.

The fact that bankers usually go bankrupt (as in 1930– 1933) only after large numbers of their failing clients first go bankrupt indicates that borrowers and not bankers are the primary underwriters of the debt exchange. Functionally speaking, the banker simply puts a part of the present value of the borrower's assets into a new dress which has a more acceptable form and credits it back to him. After the money is created, the borrower has part of the value of his assets expressed in their dollar equivalent and can more readily disburse his purchasing power for labor, supplies and materials.

Note that in the asset-conversion process the banker has lent no gold or titles to gold; he has remained the custodian of his own gold the whole time. He has merely kept it as a reserve. He has merely incurred an obligation to pay dollars. And while he has incurred an obligation to the borrower, he has received in its place the borrower's equivalent (though numerically larger) obligation to repay dollars to him.

Before 1933, we took for granted that the banker always balanced his new deposit debts with contingent claims against borrower's assets which had values far in excess of the amount of his loans — and that he got no poorer as the bank's loans increased. We found no reason therefore to investigate whether the banker really possessed that mysterious asset, gold, which he claimed that he had in his vault when he first began his role as banker. Normally our banker's $1,000 gold supply was never looked at or asked for.

Yet in a nominal sense, whenever the banker had "lent" exactly $1,000 no more and no less — against a borrower's assets a "dollar" could be regarded as a realistic claim to 23.2 grains of gold. (See Step 1 of diagram on next page.)

For the banker actually had 23,200 grains of it in his vault available for meeting a $1,000 claim. Thus at the beginning of the banking process, when the bank's gold reserve of 23,200 grains exactly matched the value of the deposit created against it, the "dollar" could be regarded as being 1/1000th part of the gold in the bank, that is, as a claim to 23.2 grains of gold.

When, however, the banker "lent," say, $2,000 against the secured obligations of borrowers and there was only $1,000

WHAT IS A DOLLAR ?

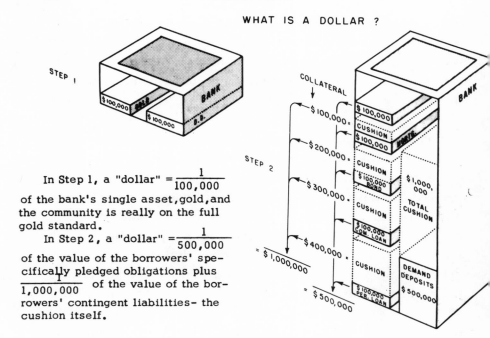

In Step 1, a "dollar" $=\dfrac{1}{100,000}$
of the bank's single asset, gold, and the community is really on the full gold standard.

In Step 2, a "dollar" $=\dfrac{1}{500,000}$
of the value of the borrowers' specifically pledged obligations plus $\dfrac{1}{1,000,000}$ of the value of the borrowers' contingent liabilities— the cushion itself.

Figure 16

worth of gold in the banking system, each "dollar" in circulation could not be, despite any legal definition of it, a realistic claim to 23.2 grains of gold. It was then at most a claim to 1/2000th part of the bank's assets which consisted of a mixture made up of 23,200 grains of gold plus borrowers' obligations which were in the nature of contingent claims against their property. As soon as bankers began to issue obligations to pay out gold on demand against borrowers assets, the gold dollars became merely yardsticks of value, gauges against which bankers could evaluate the assets of borrowers. The gold in effect was locked up like a gauge at the Bureau of Standards, while the assets evaluated or measured against the gauge circulated in their transformed state as the medium of exchange.

As soon as a bank promised to pay on demand more gold

than there was in the banking system, a dollar ceased to be a realistic claim to a certain number of grains of gold, and the deposit "dollar" became only a fractional claim to the assets of the bank—assets consisting of gold plus a stew of pledged values which were backed by contingent claims against farms, goods in process, real estate, railroads, factories, etc.

Our analysis of the nature of the dollar has thus revealed that when banking was in its initial stages and loans were exactly equal to the gold holdings of the bank, the "dollar" as a fractional claim against the assets of the bank was arithmetically actually redeemable in gold. A system of 100% gold reserves then prevailed. Moreover, the claims in use were, in effect, warehouse receipts. The analysis showed too, however, that when the loans outstanding exceeded the gold holdings of the bank and the assets of the bank came to consist mainly of borrowers' notes and collateral as well as of gold, a dollar was realistically redeemable only in a hodge-podge of assets only some of which were gold. A review of that analysis should make it easy to understand how, when the assets of a banking system come to consist, say, of approximately one tenth gold and nine tenths of contractual assets (such as notes secured by contingency claims against borrowers' farms, land, business, etc.), the modern dollar too became but a fractional claim to bank assets which consisted of one tenth gold and nine tenths of other things.

Thus the value of the dollar is not determined by nor tied to the value of gold. It is tied to the value of the assets in the bank's portfolio. And the value of gold is tied by decree to the value of that dollar.

Banking policy has not, however, been laid out with that conception of gold's relation to the dollar. Nor has economic theory recognized the above relationship. Our own government has unrealistically assured foreign central banks and, indirectly for a time, the foreign owners of money, that they could exchange any or all of their dollars, not for one tenth gold and nine tenths miscellaneous assets, but for ten tenths gold, so many ounces for each dollar. Clearly, remaining on that kind of a gold standard was impossible whenever the owners of more than one tenth of the money dollar wanted to have their money redeemed in gold. Normally, a checkbook dollar was more worth owning than a gold dollar because it was a better medium of exchange. Only when people were preferring to go continually from a money to a goods position could banking systems avoid stampedes for gold.

We may now summarize the money-creation process: men with variable but clumsy assets, like goods in process, farms, factories, "accounts receivable" and even speculative prospects — assets which cannot be conveniently broken up and handed out as money to workers and manufacturers in exchange for labor and materials — come to the banker when they want to engage in exchange to get him to help to certify that they too have assets which, if offered in exchange, have a dollar worth at least equal to the $1,000, $2,000 or whatever sums they wish to borrow. The borrowers want the banker to underwrite their judgment that their assets have a definite worth. For this assistance they are willing to pay him an interest fee and to extend to him for the duration of the transaction a contingent claim against their assets.

Until the U.S. went off the full gold standard, bankers pretended to be lending gold. Actually they were evaluators of the assets of borrowers, who converted clumsy assets into negotiable "dollars," which were intended to be so unquestionable in worth that they would be accepted on sight at face value. Then, after making an exchange of debt with each of the borrowing clients, the bankers balanced the indebtedness accounts of all of them. They did the bookkeeping. They were the treasurers for a community that dealt in pledges. In effect they balanced one man's promise to produce butter against another man's promise to produce potatoes, and by so doing assisted all producers to exchange goods with one another.

### The Dollar As a Gauge of Value

As a bank proceeds to convert borrower's debt into bank debt, its portfolio grows to include more and more assets besides gold, with the result that the gauge of value — the unit which is used to appraise all the new borrowers' debts that are being converted into dollars — becomes not gold alone but that fraction of the portfolio's value which each outstanding deposit dollar makes up. For example:

In our premise for Step Two, the bank has a portfolio of $500,000 and has $500,000 in deposit liabilities outstanding. We show that the portfolio contains $100,000 of gold, $100,000 mortgages, $100,000 railroad bonds, $100,000 of commercial loans, and $100,000 of personal loans. The value of a deposit dollar is then 1/500,000ths of the value of that stew of assets. If at such a time, the bank considers making a new $1,000 loan against a new obligation such as a mortgage or a note, the banker would naturally ponder whether the new obligation that he is thinking of monetizing is really worth 1000/500,000ths of the whole existing bank portfolio. Clearly the gauge of value used is a dollar which represents 1/500,000ths of the value of the bank's total assets, of which gold constitutes only a minor fraction.

But even if all the gold in our banking system's portfolio were suddenly disposed of, the bank's gauge of value for appraising the new obligations of borrowers would not change. For a unit slice of all the composite assets in the portfolio would continue to serve as the yardstick of value for all loans to be made in the future. A unit slice of the total value of the assets in the portfolio (and not the value of gold alone) would determine and define the value of the dollar.

Let us look again at the contents of the asset and liability bins of a commercial bank. (See Figure 16). Let us assume that it has four items in its portfolio, namely: a consumer loan, a commercial loan, a government security and a bin full of "gold or reserve deposits and currency."

Suppose each item in the portfolio is an obligation nominally worth $100,000. If against this $400,000 nominal worth of assets the bank has issued $400,000 of demand deposit credits, then "a dollar" would seem to consist of a 1/400,-000th claim against only the nominal value of the four assets in the bank. But things are not always as they seem.

If say, all of the bank's asset items totalling $400,000 were collateralized so that in the aggregate the mortgages, notes and securities accepted by the bank and put into its portfolio had collateral values behind them worth a total of say $1,000,-000, then obviously a dollar would realistically have strength greater than merely 1/400,000th of the nominal value at which the bank carries the items in its portfolio. For in addition the dollar would also be a *contingent* claim to the protective worth of the collateral behind the portfolio items. Today every single dollar used as medium of exchange has a collateral backing which fortifies its value in relation to other forms of goods and property. Consequently, the value of checkbook dollars does not decline whenever business recedes and all other property values go down. This fortification of money against decline enables the owners of dollars – if they so choose – to spend their money laggardly in the markets without penalty. The manner in which modern money, because it is collateralized, can facilitate and contribute to disruptions of the stability of aggregate monetary demand is a subject which goes completely undiscussed in economic literature. Nor have I been able to find in economic literature a functional portrayal of how the property ingredients that constitute the dollar are arithmetically related to one another.

The diagram on page 68 highlights vividly that American checkbook money is not fiat money, but consists of claims against the assets contained in the portfolio of the American banking system. It also highlights that this portfolio contains debt obligations which are worth far more than the face values attributed to them in the portfolio. All the debt obligations carry a cushion of value that backstops the value of the borrower's nominal obligation. Such property is not fiat money at all. U.S. money consists of conservative claims against the property and performance of the outstanding members of the business community. The highly prevalent view that our money has value only because the public is willing to accept it is analytically faulty and misleading.

That American money consists of the monetized and cushioned debt obligations of top-notch performers in business — as shown in the diagram on page 68 — is a very different view of money than almost all economists have maintained. Professor Paul Samuelson, for example, author of *Economics,* the most widely used textbook in the subject in the U.S. states that . . . "all American money is essentially fiat money," and that "it is money because the government decrees that it is money. . . ." If the diagram and analysis above are valid, then his view is completely untenable, and reflects no realization that money is the transmuted property of borrowers.

Because the "T" table (which is so commonly used in textbooks to portray the balance sheets of commercial banks) fails to make any entry, for example, in the asset column for the collateral values that lie behind those nominal values of the assets in the bank's portfolio, it completely misrepresents — through omission — the property content of modern checkbook money. (See the two "T" tables below.) The net result is that "T" tables merely present those nominal balance sheet relationships which facilitate trade; they do not call attention to the sanctuary from spending which collateral gives to checkbook money. To this sanctuary business cycle theorists should properly concern themselves.

TABLE I

An Illustration Of A Conventional Balance Sheet For A Commercial Bank
For Operating Purposes

| Assets | | Liabilities | |
|---|---|---|---|
| 1. Cash and Reserves | $300,000 | 1. Capital Stock | $300,000 |
| 2. Premises ,etc. | 200,000 | 2. Demand Deposits | 200,000 |
| 3. Mortgage Loans | 400,000 | 3. Demand Deposits | 400,000 |
| 4. Security Loans | 100,000 | 4. Demand Deposits | 100,000 |
| 5. Commercial Loans | 500,000 | 5. Demand Deposits | 500,000 |
| | $1,500,000 | | $1,500,000 |

TABLE II

An Illustration Of A More Realistic Balance Sheet For Business Cycle
Analysts

| Assets | | Liabilities | |
|---|---|---|---|
| 1. Cash and Reserves | $300,000 | 1. Capital Stock | $300,000 |
| 2. Premises , etc. | 200,000 . | 2. Demand Deposits | 200,000 |
| 3. Mortgage Loans | 400,000 | 3. Demand Deposits | 400,000 |
| 4. Security Loans | 100,000 | 4. Demand Deposits | 100,000 |
| 5. Commercial Loans | 500,000 | 5. Demand Deposits | 500,000 |
| 6. A Buffer of Collateral Worth say ,an estimated: | 1,000,000 | 6. A Buffer of Worth (provided by the borrowers) which insures the value of the bank's obligations valued at | 1,000,000 |
| | $2,500,000 | | $2,500,000 |

Figure 17

Today all textbooks on economics fail to alert students to
the disruptive role which the collateral behind bank assets
plays. A vast amount of today's banking and business cycle
theory consequently is built on "T" table relationships which
patently do not represent the true situation. Tables I and II
below highlight how deceptive and inadequate the "T"
table methodology is for portraying the real balance of
property values that is set up between commercial banks
and their borrowing customers.

Although it is pointless for purposes of mere banking operations to take into account in a "T" table the full value of the property contingently pledged by the bank borrowers, it is nonetheless necessary for economists to do so in making business cycle analyses. (This theme was developed more fully and dealt with more completely in the author's book, *Money In Motion*, John de Graff, Inc. Tuckahoe, New York, 1962.)

Money is a tool of freedom. In evolving from its early commodity form, such as furs and tobacco, into the highly efficient form of checkbook money, it made possible the operations of free markets on a large scale along with the free choice of both goods and jobs and the existence of many of the civil liberties that accompany free markets. But in evolving, it also accidentally acquired such a large collateral value that the guarantee of its prompt reuse was reduced. So even though modern money is a splendid tool of freedom for diffusing economic power, it is still designed to facilitate recessions and to induce job instability.

# Chapter 6

## Why We Need a Stabilized Monetary Demand

A PARAPHRASE of the story which the English economist, Edgeworth, told in the *Economic Journal* many years ago brings out vividly the vital role which the rate of spending plays in the economic process:

Two cronies, Pat and Mike, owned a keg of beer which they decided to take to the County Fair with the intention of selling its contents at ten cents a glass. Pat, it happened, had a nickel in his pocket while Mike had nothing. Enroute, Pat stopped and bought a glass of beer from the reservoir owned in common. Since Pat owned half of the beer supply, he paid Mike only five cents for the drink. A little later Mike got thirsty, bought a drink from Pat and passed the same nickel back to him. As they toddled toward the Fair, the drinks went down while the nickel shuttled back and forth until the keg went dry. Pat and Mike's behavior makes vivid for us the catalytic role which is played by money.

The above story throws no light on why we have fluctuating rates of spending today, but it does reveal that the money in existence at any moment can, like the nickel, have a highly variable rate of use.

Of course, only that particular spending of money which brings goods and services into consumption is directly conducive to production. A circulation of money which serves merely to carry on transactions that bring goods no nearer to the jaws of consumption has little economic significance. For example, dollars which circulate merely to exchange existing railroad bonds for industrial bonds, or one kind of stock for another have no "income velocity"; they have merely "transaction velocity." Only increases in "income velocity" are directly conducive to increased production.

If we divide the total volume of bank debits in a year (exclusive of those debits that merely reflect the buying and selling of securities) by the average volume of currency and demand deposit dollars in existence during the year, we get the average number of times a dollar is used during that year. Figure 5 on page 19 shows how that number has varied over a period of many years.

Output can be stimulated only when "income velocity" is stimulated. Only when claims to goods are offered in exchange for goods will goods be made and sold. American industry is like a great big slot machine within which is mounted the most productive machinery that the world has ever seen, and which, to the limit of its productive capacity, ejects more goods the faster nickels are spent or dropped into the slot.

Even though the economists of the world understand well how the free market system tends to produce what consumers want in a milieu that permits vast liberty of action in buying, hiring, producing, pricing and selling, they seem discouraged and heavy hearted. They probably intuitively sense that the free market system contains a serious fault in design that has not yet been isolated. They know that our system requires — for internal functional operativeness — that recipients of income collectively spend or invest it as rapidly as they receive it. Otherwise growth and full-blast activity will not be maintained. They also know that people with money are nonetheless in a position to slow down the tempo of their spending and investment decisions at any time and to stall business activity.

Because they have not isolated the weakness in the world's monetary system that permits this holdback of spending, they make no effort to correct that basic weakness. Instead, they fall in with governmental attempts to offset the weakness with programs which require the public to surrender ever more discretion over disbursement to agents of the state. These programs often do propel activity upward, but it is at the price of ever more bureaucratic interference with our lives.

Economists know that ideally the market system should be so designed that when excessive production of plant and equipment and inventories occurs, the excesses can be corrected and adapted to without a downward spiral occurring in overall aggregate monetary demand and confidence.

Chapter 7 will describe how a gradual and systematic reduction of the store of value of modern money—whether gold or dollar debt obligations—can so alter the operations of the free market system that the aggregate private monetary demand for goods, services and workers can be permanently stabilized and intensified; how the distribution of income can be permanently altered to benefit the workers and entrepreneurs, and how it can be made to reduce the loitering opportunities given to the savers of money.

It will further show that "the working rules" of today's free market system (called Capitalism) are accidentally designed to favor the savers of money capital. A modified free market system (one that neutralizes the opportunity to spend tardily—and could well be called "Marketism" or "Unshackled Capitalism") would not contain that favoritism. Such a modified system, would—in the array of systems —fall somewhere between Anarchism and Capitalism.

## Different Systems of Society

If our thinking—with respect to subjects as electric as a concern over systems of society is apt to be—is to be even partially divorced from the disruptive play of our emotions, it is necessary to outline to some extent the content of the terms.

The simple diagram below highlights the kinship of the different systems. It shows their juxtaposition with respect to: 1) Systems of Exchange; 2) Promptness of Exchange;

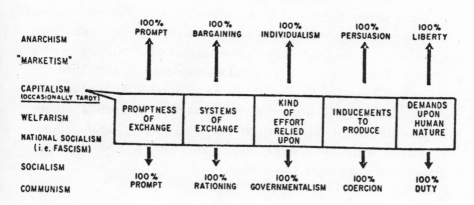

Note that—because it uses a sanctuary money as its medium of exchange—Capitalism is unique in that it is the only system that provides its savers of money with a disruptive arrangement that permits them to use their money tardily.

HOW TO READ CHART: The diagram above shows how the major systems of society differ in those aspects of group living that they emphasize. Anarchism, for example, emphasizes Bargaining, Individualism, and Persuasion, whereas, Communism—at the other extreme—emphasizes Rationing, Governmentalism, and Coercion. Note that as emphasis declines, for example, from 100% Persuasion to 0% Persuasion, and then climbs in the opposite direction from 0% Coercion to 100% Coercion, the very structure of society changes.

Figure 18

3) Kind of Effort Relied Upon; 4) Inducements to Produce, and, 5) Demands upon Human Nature (as these aspects are reflected in the rights and duties, powers and privileges, liberties and exposures that citizens possess under the different economic systems).

In 1939, I was employed by the Temporary National Economic Committee to analyze the many recovery plans then being reviewed in yearlong hearings before that Congressional Committee.

Among the many proposals submitted to the TNEC, very few advocated recourse to Welfarism. Relief for humanitarian reasons was, of course, advanced. But not Welfarism as a system of political economy. Today it is here as an integral part of the "New Economics." Personal income taxes, for example, have been escalated sharply since 1942. Concurrently, more and more government revenue has been transferred directly to selected community groups through so-called Transfer Payments. In 1939, total federal revenues were about $5 billion per year and total federal Transfer Payments about $2.5 billion. In fiscal 1971, total federal revenues were over $200 billion, and total federal Transfer Payments were over $80 billion.

## Different Systems of Society

With very few exceptions, the theoretical systems of society have never existed except on paper. They have been mainly hypothetical. It is therefore difficult to describe them exactly. However, Capitalism, Fascism, Communism and State Welfarism we can, as it were, view in the flesh. Other movements have been sporadic and hypothetical.

Let us contrast the theoretical systems at the two extremes and try to show how Marketism and Capitalism fit between them. Anarchism and Communism are obviously the antithesis of one another. Capitalism and Marketism are in the nature of halfway houses between the two. The others are scattered to the right and left.

The shades of anarchistic doctrine have been various. Political anarchists like Godwin wished to abolish the State and all forms of coercion as a matter of "Justice." Aesthetic and philosophical anarchists like Shelley, Thoreau, and Emerson advocated all noninterference with personal ideas.

Anarchism, on the whole, wants no group or governmental interference whatever with private affairs. All of its social control is to rely upon persuasion, love, and example. It is Anarchism, not Communism, that requires that "all men be like angels." Anarchism is probably inherently inoperative, for without some form of group control or government the strong would manhandle and exploit the weak.

The Anarchists want no enforced cooperation. Under anarchism, if the individual does not care to join with and cooperate with others in, say, a collective farming venture, he is free to do as he pleases. Under Communism, he has no such latitude.

Communism insists upon enforcing all measures coercively until some future date when it shall have created a "classless society" and educated all of its people to a compliant point of view. For a beginning period, however, which may turn out to be a long time, it is willing to use extreme coercion and to sacrifice the individual for what it regards as the good of the State.

As a system of society, National Socialism (sometimes called Fascism) provides—as Hitler and Mussolini conceived it—not for direct confiscation of private property, but for governmental determination of business' wages, prices, output, investments, and other operating matters. It is an indirect approach for replacing Capitalism with coercive Governmentalism.

Because our monetary authorities have never given thought to placing pressures on money ownership to insure its adequate rate of re-use, they are often driven instead to advocate (as remedies for our occasional unemployment) several types of remedial governmental effort.

One is that the government should neutralize the tardiness of disbursement by borrowing the laggard money savings and then substitute itself as the spender. Keynes was an early advocate of this recourse.

A second is to have the government create (by selling its obligations to the commercial banks for new bank deposits) a new batch of money to balance that which went to sleep and then buy goods and services with the new money.

A third is to have government lure the laggard money back into the markets by granting to hesitant private spenders tax concessions, subsidies and favors of one kind or another.

A fourth is to impose heavy progressive taxes on corporations and persons in the upper income groups and then bureaucratically divert these sums to powerful pressure groups in the lower income brackets. Federal transfer payments were $2.4 billion per year in 1940. Today they total over $80 billion.

A fifth is to circumvent the whole free market system and attune buying power to production by vast central planning controls over production, employment, resources, wages, prices and income — so that in theory, at least, the volume of monetary demand will always be able, as in Russia, to move into consumption whatever modest output comes forth.

There is a sixth nongovernmental recourse that is continually proposed by economists of the classical school; namely, to remove the many stultifying controls and regulations with which naive voters and bumbling politicians have overlayed the free market system for generations. The advocates of this recourse are usually learned men who understand the irrationality (when adequate monetary demand prevails) of such arrangements as tariffs, wage and price controls, subsidies, double taxation, central planning, etc.

But these men have not recognized the manner in which the free market's otherwise fine operation is disrupted by the removal of carrying costs from money. These economists understand well the mechanics of the free market system and the built-in inefficiencies and tyrannies of the Administered State. Most of their analyses of economic operation are sound. Tragically, however, these men have ignored money's imperfect design and have all too often attributed our chronic breakdowns to political interference alone.

Economists who have generally leaned toward the use of the first five remedies for growth and stability mentioned above are largest in number. Because their favored remedies call for further participation in economic operations by the state, these can and do put up only halfhearted and confused defenses against Communist theory, Russian aggrandizement and governmentalism in general. Governmentalism will never be defeated under their leadership.

The current vogue in economic theory premises that central government must continually expand its taxes, borrowings, and expenditures in order to obtain a satisfactory rate of growth. This book, in contrast, reverts toward the classical view, in that it again puts savings and investment in the center of its analysis. It does this with the single difference that it proposes to so modify the monetary instrument that the instrument itself will maintain a rigorous alignment between savings and investment. Classical economics, by regarding and accepting the monetary instrument as a neutral factor, exposed the free market system to periodic failure, and also unintentionally and inadvertently induced public recourse to the many amateurish improvisations of the New Economics.

Regrettably, all advocates of change overlook the cancerous defect in the free market system discussed above. None seem to realize that the free market system on which the United States still in the main relies, simply will not operate without more disruption and governmentalism than people will tolerate when it attempts to use as a medium of exchange a money that has an excessive store of value.

A healthy free market system requires that the exchange of money claims be at such a high tempo that the factor that limits output is the labor supply or the productive capacity of the nation and not the willingness of the people to exchange their claim-check money for goods. Such a requirement would be almost automatically met if personal income were well distributed among many people, because the spontaneous wants of most people chronically outrun their purchasing power.

But when relatively few in the upper income groups get too much of the income — as a result of the bargaining advantage in the market that the safe deferability of spending that "sanctuary money" gives them — then slow economic growth or even recession frequently occurs. For the big savers of money in effect often say: "We will spend for investment or we won't spend at all. And since it happens that we believe that we have overinvested for the time being and that it is not now profitable to spend for investment, we shall wait awhile."

At such times, our system should answer them: "The yield on your investment is a secondary matter. Since our economy is disrupted if you do not spend or invest your money income at about the same rate at which you receive it, we wish to insure that you spend for consumers' goods if you cannot gainfully spend for investment. Buy yachts, if you will not buy factories; we don't care what you buy, consumers' goods or producers' goods, but get busy and buy something, for we cannot stand idle while you hesitate about whether to use your currently generated claims to output at the rate at which you receive them."

Sometimes economists recognize that anarchy in the "conditions of demand" chronically exists, but they always tacitly imply that our working rules should permit it to be thus. Unthinkingly, they premise that the privilege to spend tardily should be continued. This assumption runs tacitly through all the thinking of our classical theorists and through all the writings of the economists of today. Where in the analyses of the eminent men of the past, or of the outstanding ones of today, do you find any recognition of the fact that our occasional shortcomings in demand result largely from the excessive store of value possessed by modern collateralized money?

In the main, the theorists of capitalism support a body of theory which premises that the lure of investment gain is by itself an adequate inducement to motivate owners of money savings to exchange it for goods, even when owners acquire a money that can be disbursed tardily with impunity. The theorists reason that the lure of gain should be adequate. Realistically, however, our occasional recessions do not square with their logic. Say's law premised that the individual's decision to save is identical to and concurrent with his decision to invest. Say consequently excluded the possibility that money could have an influence of its own on the stability and activity of the nation. Keynes, in contrast, noticed that the free market system did not automatically maintain full monetary demand and full employment. In my opinion, however, Keynes failed to explain why the system did not do so.

Nonetheless, Keynes did seemingly succeed in inducing governments to take responsibility for maintaining full employment. In stressing liquidity preference, he dwelt on money both as an asset and as a medium of exchange. But he did not spot the cushion of value behind the face value of the money asset. And consequently he did not understand why the "liquidity preference" that he did observe was at times so pronounced and widespread. Unlike D. H. Robertson, however, Keynes did notice and stress that a monetary economy differs greatly from a barter economy and that variations in the quantity and rate of use of money has an influence of its own on business stability. Still, he did fail to notice the tremendously different role played by a commodity money and a "debt-obligation" money. Consequently, he did not deal with the disruptive role of sanctuary money, nor with the promising potential that lay in the use of a hot potato money.

Most economists have dealt with savings and investments almost as identities. Few of them focused on the overextended "time-interval-between-transactions" which is made possible in our system by the use of collateralized demand-deposit money — the variable this book focuses on.

Historically, the free market mechanism operated in a chronic state of underemployment. The entrenched dogma of the classicists — that there was an automatic tendency toward full employment in the mechanism — broke down badly in the face of the reality of the 1930's. Even before that decade, "underemployment-equilibrium" chronically characterized the free market system in a mild way until it broke down completely during the 1930's. Even at its peak of cyclical employment, as in the late 1920's, the free market system did not reach full employment, and jobs were scarce.

If nondeferrable hot potato money had been used during that whole historic period, economic resources would have been used continuously for something. In lieu of periodic idleness, the money-savers would have been under constant pressure to use their claims for big ticket personal consumer items or for additional capital facilities.

Originally, people exchanged their specialized products for a wealth item: the gold, the butter, the furs, or whatever they happened to be using for money. Then with the development of law, and enforcement of agreements, people shifted from circulating commodity money to circulating claims and obligations. This shift has befuddled mankind more than any other monetary change.

In a barter society, when an unequal distribution of income results, the poor people possess almost nothing at all, while the big savers hold physical assets like granaries full of grain. But when in a credit economy a very unequal distribution of income results, the poorer workers possess nothing but labor services which they cannot sell while the money-savers hold potential claims to goods and services compactly stored away in currency and checkbook entries. Of course, it is neither feasible nor desirable to circulate bulky wealth today; the circulation of certificates and records of indebtedness is in itself a splendid economic invention. But the new manner in which "money-savings" are stored has had extremely important and disastrous effects.

If finished goods alone were bartered or exchanged slowly (instead of those puzzlingly deferrable commands-over-goods which are kept in the banking system), it would be obvious that those who owned the claims to output would simply not exchange them for labor's services rapidly enough to keep industry running or the poor from suffering. Unemployed people themselves would see the wealth accumulations and realize what it meant when the lumber, the wheat, the clothing, etc., were kept in warehouses and not offered promptly in exchange for the efforts of their hands. But unemployed people who are confronted with a maze of banking machinery, which operates to conceal the fluctuations in the expenditures of bank money, do not know where to attack the problem.

The money-saver's behavior is much less exposed to criticism when he can unobtrusively store his potential command over goods and services and can let the farmers, the manufacturers and the workers, whose products he will someday request, themselves store the goods and services as best they can. The oats, butter, fruit and grain, which the owners of the money claims will someday command, are warehoused by the farmers themselves until the people with the laggard money see fit to tap the bins. Likewise, the carpenters, some of whose muscle energy the money-savers will someday direct to build new plants, are warehoused on the relief roles at the expense of the state.

Although today most people realize that money must not be respent tardily if the economic system is to run properly, they propose to do little more than to coax our money-savers to use it promptly. In the main they have accepted the Keynesian view that the government should borrow the money-savers' loitering sums, pay the money-savers an interest fee for the privilege and substitute itself as the spender. Such primitive adjustment will not do. What is needed is a recast of the property content of money so that the willingness-to-purchase is continuously pushed out, not coaxed out. Not only now, but in the past as well, we have given money too large a store of value. It is time that we stop reassuring ourselves 'that the money-savers' desire to invest in facilities under all circumstances will keep the money moving steadily. It is time to insure prompt spending with a money of improved design.

Even though the defect built into our money is devastating in its impact, it is very easy to remove it—as the two proposals presented in Chapter 7 will make clear. And if a free market, free of tardiness of demand were to eliminate unemployment automatically and the practice of extending statism during recessions; if it were to assure everyone a lifetime of job security and alternative job opportunity; if it were to assure us a labor and investment market wherein employers are always looking for workers instead of workers always looking for jobs, the virtues of the system would be so obviously compelling that it would undoubtedly rekindle and refire the proselytizing fervor among Americans that once drove them to sing to the whole world the virtues of their system. There would be no need for and little demand for more bureaucracy or statism in its many forms.

If the proposed market system actually has the potential which I am attempting to depict, and if it has the alternatives which I shall point out, it will be unnecessary to take recourse to any form of governmentalism. People could have all and more than Statism and Welfarism supposedly have to offer by merely modifying slightly the rules enveloping their free market system in the manner which this book will point out.

The challenge is there. In the next chapter, I shall outline a plan proposed to meet that challenge—a plan that not only avoids the economic evils of governmentalism, but one which in addition will permit us to possess—to a degree never hitherto possessed—that flower of all economy, the nonregimentation of thought and the luxury of liberty of expression. The plan advanced calls for the creation of no new economic machinery, but merely a more intelligent operation of the machinery that we already have. For that reason the plan has the great merit of being immediately applicable. As stated, Capitalism has always been made to operate under an uncertain and unreliable aggregate private monetary demand. The following pages point out the possibilities of a market economy which is designed to operate full blast under chronic scarcity of labor. It points out how these possibilities are so different—so desirable and tremendous—that it all may seem too good to be true.

# PART 2

## Two Suggested Solutions

see also page

# Chapter 7

## Two Proposals for Stabilizing Private Monetary Demand

*The Conditional Enforcement of Contracts
between Banks and Borrowers*

In earlier publications the writer explored at length several seemingly obvious means by which the government could neutralize the excessive store of value of money and proceed to align properly the relative value of money and goods. Many years ago—in *When Capital Goes On Strike* (Harpers, 1938) and in TNEC monograph, *Analysis Of Recovery Plans* (U.S. Government Printing Office, 1940)—I proposed a federal tax of about two percent per year on bank deposits and currency to assure that money income be disbursed at a more stable rate. I outlined the mechanics of that proposal in great detail. After going over the feasibility of the proposal with several leading monetary experts, I was confident that the plan was workable. But the plan had two undesirable features: (1) it called for one more tax on the citizen—one more revenue for the government—and (2) for one new administrative chore for the government.

Nonetheless, the tax on demand deposits which I proposed in *When Capital Goes On Strike* would have activated the economy by pushing savers of money to disburse it more promptly. Even though the proposal was far more cumbersome than the two described below, it was functional.

A monthly tax on the ownership of money would of course be one possible institutionalized means of speeding up the disbursements of income for goods or facilities. My proposal of 1938 elaborated on that idea. It was a workable plan but was probably politically unacceptable because I accompanied my proposal with a complex plan for taxing currency as well as demand deposits. *The proposal in this chapter avoids that complexity completely.* In retrospect, my 1938 proposal was merely an early, clumsy model of a good device.

In his book, *Program For Progress,* John Strachey, the very left-wing but able British economist, and who became Minister of War in Clement Attlee's cabinet, made this appraisal of my 1938 proposal for a tax on demand deposits: *

> . . . there is one method by means of which an expansionist programme could be implemented without the creation of new money. . . . Mr. Arthur Dahlberg, in his recent book entitled *When Capital Goes On Strike,* puts forward the proposal that the government should impose a tax on demand deposits. . . . Mr. Dahlberg believes that the volume of more or less stagnant money would drop rapidly if it were taxed. The first effect would no doubt be to drive the demand deposits into time deposits. But as this happened the bankers would find it necessary first to lower and then to abolish the interest which they paid on such deposits. . . . So the general effect of the tax would be greatly to decrease the advantages of holding money in the bank, relative to investing it. By this device, Mr. Dahlberg believes, wealthy individuals and corporations would be driven to invest their money as quickly as they received it. It would be too expensive for them to attempt to hold it idle. . . . The expectation of even the most modest rate of profit would be more attractive than having to pay for keeping their money idle. Thus investment would be driven up to a volume sufficient to keep the economy in full employment. Nor would there be any need for government intervention.

---

* John Strachey, *Program For Progress* (New York: Random House, 1940).

This plan is, substantially a modernized and much improved version of the proposals of the German currency reformer Silvio Gesell, whose suggestion took the form of stamped money. . . . A tax on bank deposits would be seriously considered as a part of a policy for securing, and even more perhaps for maintaining, full employment. . . . There is nothing either fantastic or unsound about the proposal itself.

Its main advantage is that it provides a method by which the recipients and holders of liquid money can be prodded instead of tempted into activity. And this is an extremely important advantage. For the only thing which will tempt the holders of money to invest is to raise, in one way or another, their expectation of profit. And to do this involves . . . taking measures which tend to decrease the share in the total product going to the wage earner; which tend, that is to say, to increase the maldistribution of wealth, and so to produce slump by an insufficiency of purchasing power in the hands of the people to clear the market of consumers' goods and services.

Another feature of the Dahlberg proposal which many people would no doubt feel was an advantage is that it avoids any increase in government initiative or participation within the economy. As against government spending and lending, and as against government banking, a tax on deposits is undoubtedly an individualistic measure, since it seeks to activate the economy by pushing private initiative into action again, instead of by substituting public initiative, in any degree for it. (Mr. Dahlberg is himself antisocialistic in bent). A tax on demand deposits even avoids the bugbear of a progressively increasing national debt. Indeed it could be plausibly argued that in contemporary American conditions it was just about the one tax which might really result in balancing the budget!

All the same, and in spite of these genuinely conservative features, a tax on bank deposits would almost certainly be strongly resented by the wealth-owning class. The idea of pushing holders of money to invest, instead of tempting them deferentially, is so novel that it might well be thought much more radical than it really is.

Author's note: Readers are urged to examine the analytical justification for these proposals in the previous chapters. Without such an orientation the proposals cannot properly be understood and as a result will not seem reasonable.

Today the writer no longer recommends the mechanics of
his 1938 proposal. He has now devised two superior and
simpler ways of imposing a carrying cost on the ownership
of property held in the form of money—a cost which is
aligned with and synchronized with—and approximately
equal to—the carrying cost that bears on all other kinds of
property.

*And neither of these ways involves the imposition of any
tax whatsoever. Nor does either of them call for any governmental bookkeeping or administrative effort whatsoever.
Neither, moreover, confronts the government with additional
problems of enforcement, surveillance or compliance.*

The pressure placed on money to stay in steady use need
not be severe nor imposed in the form of a tax, as the writer
once believed. There is no need to have the state obtain
one more increment of the nation's income through the use
of such means as stamped scrip or taxes on deposits. Fortunately there are simpler and more equitable ways of
reducing the excessive store of value of checkbook money,
and of increasing the stability of private monetary demand—
ways which would divert the demurrage cost directly (as
factor payments) to the dynamic entrepreneurs and workers.
That is, there are two ways by which it is possible to modify
the arrangements enveloping the free market mechanism
so that—without "collective bargaining" and bludgeoning
of society by labor unions—a portion of the income that now
goes to interest would go directly to wages.

### Proposal #1

The preferred and simpler way would be—as was mentioned earlier on page 60—to enforce only certain kinds of
monetary contracts which commercial banks and their
borrowing customers make with one another.

Theoretically, the most desirable way of obtaining the
desired continuity of spending would be to legislate that the

courts will not enforce the new dollar demand obligations that commercial banks incur to borrowers and depositors unless the banks and the depositors jointly agree—before the borrowing and depositing is done—that the bank's obligations to the depositors shall be lowered monthly (on the average bank balance) by, say, the rate of two percent per year.

In practice this means that when commercial banks accept checks for deposit, or create and lend new demand deposits to borrowing customers, they and the customers and depositors must work out terms on interest and repayment that relate to a new kind of demand obligation—one that is set to be lowered in value by, say, two percent per year. Under such an arrangement, money without a carrying cost would simply never come into being to cause trouble. (However, this Proposal #1 would not carry the emotional appeal that Proposal #2 would probably do.)

## Nonenforcement of a Certain Kind of Contract

The following illustration will show how Proposal #1 would work. Suppose that you are a merchant or a farmer who borrows $1,000 at your local bank. You borrow this money only, of course, if you have the need to spend it for important purchases. The dollars that you in effect mint at the bank by converting your note or mortgage into demand deposits and then disburse becomes income for people in the community. Normally, these recipients turn around and disburse the money as rapidly as you send it out, and the economy stays in equilibrium. But sometimes they lengthen the interval between their transactions.

Next let us premise that legislation is in force that stipulates that the contract between you and the bank will not be enforced unless your asset, the newly minted demand deposit—the bank's debt obligation to you—declines in value monthly by, say, the rate of two percent per year. Of course, since the bank's obligation won't be worth as much to you as before—and it won't have to pay out to you in the future as withdrawals as much as before—you will not have to pay him as much as before to keep your mortgage monetized— perhaps only two or three percent interest per year instead of four or five (under conditions where price inflation has been halted by the means described in Chapter 13).

Knowing that the law so provides, the banker will, when making his agreement with you, stipulate that the value of his liability to you—the demand deposit made out to your credit—will carry a demurrage deduction of two percent per year. This means that the money you receive for your note or mortgage steadily declines in value and will continue to decline in value even after you shift its ownership to other persons in the community.

Someone may ask what happens to the two percent demurrage deduction? Who gets the two percent? Under the arrangement described, no one would get it—neither the government, the bank, nor anyone else. You, your banker and your community would simply be doing business with an item of property, a monetary unit, that declines slowly in value just as though you were using depreciating furs, tobacco or butter as your medium of exchange. And just as the U.S. Treasury does not obtain as revenue the incremental loss of value of a house or a car that is depreciating, so it would not receive as revenue the loss of value of the monetary instrument. A demurrage deduction would not have the characteristics of either a tax on property or of a tax on money.

It would seem offhand that the banker would profit by an arrangement like the above. But he would not. Even if a customer borrows $1,000 and transfers the money from bank to bank, the money stays in the banking system as a demand deposit until he pays off the debt. While in the circuit, the $1,000 declines in value to $980 after one year. The banker's liability also declines to $980, and the bank (or the banking system) would seem to be $20 ahead. But the bank can now afford to lend money out at lower interest rates. And competition between the banks (which is very severe) would force him to do so. The banker consequently would be no better or worse off than before. The real gainer would be the bank borrowers who would be able to borrow money for about two percent less than before.

A state often specifically limits the kind of contracts that it will enforce. At the time of the Civil War, the U.S. decided that it would no longer enforce contracts in which a man sells himself into slavery. Nor will it today enforce agreements made illegally between gamblers.

The courts of today protect the ownership of all kinds of wealth (except such items as gold and narcotics)—i.e., all kinds of Certificates of Ownership. And with a few exceptions, it protects the ownership of all kinds of Certificates of Indebtedness. This book advances, as one of its alternative proposals, that the state reduce slightly its unlimited protection of one kind of contract; namely, the Certificates (and Records) of Indebtedness of commercial banks. This book proposes that the state not lend unlimited protection to the ownership of those demand deposit debt obligations which are made between commercial banks and their business borrowers and depositors unless the principle of the debt obligation is set up to decline gradually at a demurrage rate that parallels the average depreciation rate bearing on all other kinds of goods and property.

Note To The Reader:

Because understanding Proposal #2, following in the next section, requires some familiarity with the usual transactions between depositors, member banks, Federal Reserve Banks and the U.S. Treasury, it is recommended that readers, not particularly interested in returning to a modified gold bullion standard, omit reading Proposal #2 and resume their reading on page 108.

Proposal #1 is very basic because it explains how to design a demurrage money which does not possess an excessive store of value. Proposal #2, in contrast, presents a means for so handling gold that it could cause a demurrage cost to bear on the kind of money that we already have.

*Proposal #2*

### Return to a Modified Gold Bullion Standard

Somewhat parenthetically here, I shall outline a second way of imposing a demurrage cost on the ownership of checkbook money which would have an emotional appeal to many people. This second plan is recommended for only a short introductory period of, say, five to ten years during which the basic idea of a demurrage cost on money demonstrates its merits. Proposal #2 is an expedient only, however, and not an essential part of this book's central thesis, (as is Proposal #1).

It happens, nevertheless, that Western society—because of its confused monetary thinking—has tried to devise and live with a monetary system that is based partly on the use of the tangible money, gold, and partly on the use of the intangible debt obligation of commercial banks. And it is consequently possible to take advantage of this confused thinking, with its clumsy designs, and devise an attractive change in its hybrid system which would probably make the acceptance of a demurrage money plan much easier for those people who have a staunch faith in the inherent value of gold as money. To those many people who advocate a return to the use of gold as a currency at a higher Treasury price per ounce, the second proposal will probably have a strong emotional appeal. This second proposal will please them because it would call (1) for the return to the full gold bullion standard, (2) for the Federal Reserve System to use gold again as a central bank reserve, and (3) for the free personal use of gold as currency. If we returned to the gold standard and all depositors could again obtain gold for their deposits and jingle it in their pockets — even under the proposed conditions where the Treasury value of their gold was scheduled to decline in value by two percent per year — they would feel themselves living in a safer milieu than is the case now, where built-in price inflation reduces the value of their deposit money by from four to eight percent per year.

Although both plans #1 and #2 would work well, the first plan is the more basic of the two and has the best internal consistency. It would, however, be the more difficult plan to sell to a public that has little understanding of money.

Under both proposals — as we shall see — owners of demand deposits would be under pressure to disburse their money for goods, services, and facilities at stable rates. Under both proposals it would be costly for them to lengthen the interval between transactions, and under both it would be made unfeasible for them to avoid the loitering cost.

## Structure of the Proposal for a Modified Full Gold Bullion Standard

Legislate: (1) a return to the full gold bullion standard, under which gold coins could again be freely held and used as currency; (2) that the U.S. Treasury reinstate a worldwide offering or support price for gold based initially on, say, a price $5 per ounce higher than the average highest price of gold during the last six months in the London gold market; (3) that the Treasury thereafter steadily lower its support or purchase price for gold by two percent per year from the high initial price; (4) that all depositors may demand gold for their deposits — should they want it (which is improbable) — and (5) that all commercial banks must, when checks are presented to them for payment, offer to pay off in gold.

*How to Design Plan #2 to Fit a Very High Free Market
Price for Gold*

The question naturally arises: Would the above plan be a
good idea if, when resorted to, the free market price per
ounce for gold has risen to very high levels?

After the U.S. devalued the dollar twice within fourteen
months in 1970–1972, the free market price for gold rose into
the range of $80 to $90 per ounce. The possibility exists that
Congress will raise the Treasury's nominal offering price
drastically before the proposals made above are acted upon.
The Treasury purchase price may at such a time be at the
$50, $70, or $100 per ounce level. Still the public response
to the #2 proposal would be the same regardless of the
offering price for gold prevailing when the plan for a demurrage cost on gold is first imposed.

In order to appraise the probable future calmed-down
price for gold, one must look at the size of the likely future
demand forces in relation to the likely future supply situation. In retrospect, how large were these forces during the
decade before March 1968, when the major monetary nations decided not to buy gold from anyone except from one
another?

During that decade, the annual production of gold was
valued at about $1.4 billion. The annual demand at the time
came from three sources: (1) about $500 million per year
from industry; (2) about $500 million per year from central
banks for use as reserves, and (3) about $400 million per
year from hoarders and speculators.

In March 1968, in Stockholm, the central banks withdrew
completely from the markets for gold, and by so doing reduced their purchases from about $500 million per year to
zero. Concurrently, worldwide fears over the prevailing
monetary turmoil caused the hoarders and speculators to
increase their demands for gold by more than the central

banks decreased theirs. The result was that the free market price for gold rose sharply.

The Western world's annual production of gold has stayed steady around $1.4 billion worth (at $35 per ounce), or 40 million ounces, since 1968. But the demand since that time has changed drastically. Since then it has come almost exclusively from only two sources — from industry for about $700 million to $800 million per year, and from frightened hoarders and speculators for the balance.

After the U.S. devalued the dollar twice within fourteen months after the Smithsonian Agreement in 1970, turmoil and fears increased. The annual production of gold stayed around the $1.4 billion level * and the industrial demand for gold increased only very little. But the hoarder demand for gold exploded and prices rose. The basic situation is that only if hoarder-speculators keep up an intense demand for gold of about $600 million to $700 million per year or more will the free market price stay near the high levels of 1973. It is scarcely likely that demand will do so indefinitely unless the U.S. Treasury also lifts its offering price to the same very high levels. Proposal #2 does propose that Congress shall lift the Treasury's offering price to the high speculation levels to begin with, and then reduce the price systematically thereafter by two percent per year.

Let us premise that the free market price for gold is hovering in the $50 to $100 per ounce range when Proposal #2 is adopted. If the U.S. then establishes an offering price for gold, even higher than the prevailing free market price, regardless of whether it is $50, or $70 or $100 per ounce, but also simultaneously stipulates that its offering price will

---

* South Africa alone produces about $1.1 billion of gold per year of the $1.4 billion total. Being in almost a monopoly position, she can hold back or release her current output and affect the market price of gold considerably, as she has done in recent years. When she holds back her output, and when the hoarder-speculators continue their fears amid hopes and buying urges, the price of gold jumps into very high ranges.

be lowered by two percent per year, a downward pressure on the speculators price of gold would probably begin.

This would be so because the high speculative price would have weak demand underpinning and would be held up mainly by faith in the inherent value of a precious metal. The free market price for gold would probably crumble. But the Treasury's offering price would decline only very slowly, from, say, $100 per ounce to $98 after one year, to $96.04 per ounce after two years, etc.

By beginning at a high figure, the Treasury's offering price would probably hover for a long time above the "supply and demand" price for gold. That free market price would probably tend to decline by more than two percent per year as soon as the speculators realize that their demand for gold is rooted much more in fear than in use. Consequently, it would be the Treasury's declining support price that would fix the world's real going price for gold—just as its historic $35 support price was far above the free market price for gold for 20 to 30 years, and was the world's real going price for gold for that length of time. The best backstop market price for gold for Frenchmen, Swiss, or Arabs could again be the offering price of the U.S. Treasury.

Because the Treasury's thirty-five dollar offering price for gold after 1933 was for many years far above gold's free market "use-value," the world unloaded much of its gold upon us. As a result, the U.S. gave the world about twenty billion dollars worth of useful goods over a twenty year period in exchange for some five hundred and fifty million ounces of gold—which it then proceeded to bury in the ground. Such was the penalty for not understanding how the value of gold is related to the value of product, on the one hand, and to the value of demand deposit money on the other. Under Proposal #2, foreigners would again unload gold on us if the U.S. Treasury's gold price remains at high levels after the free market price begins to decline. But a governmental accumulation of an inventory of even twenty to thirty billion dollars worth of the commodity, gold, would in political economy be a small price to pay for acquiring a means for stabilizing the nation's monetary demand for goods—and for enlisting the support of the gold enthusiasts in a needed monetary change.

When the gold support price has gradually come down to its "supply and demand" market price, and the owners of gold cease offering their gold to the U.S. Treasury, it would be advisable to shift to Proposal #1, under which the demand deposit obligations of commercial banks to borrowers and depositors (which constitute our checkbook money) would begin to be reduced in value by two percent per year.

Only the U.S. has enough resources to resort to Plan #2 for an introductory period of years. Other countries—should they decide to take the initiative in adopting a demurrage money—would have to do it by limiting their enforcement of loan contracts between bankers and borrowers which are written to recede in value over time, as was suggested under Proposal #1. The U.S. can resort to Proposal #2 only because it has the resources to pay excessive prices for the metal gold for those interim years while the panic prices for gold is declining toward the free market level. (Historically— after 1933—the U.S. paid an excessive price for gold when it lifted its offering price from about $20 per ounce to $35 per ounce.)

## Introducing the New Program

Suppose that Congress were to pass the suggested legislation and were to require that the Federal Reserve maintain, say, a five percent reserve against member bank deposits (now at over the $250 billion level), and, further, were to stipulate that the Treasury must maintain a high but gradually receding offering price for gold, then the value of all demand deposits at all commercial banks—which constitute our checkbook money—would decline by two percent per year.

It would work like this: When the Treasury begins to buy gold from the Federal Reserve—which acts as the Treasury's agent in buying gold from all sellers—the Treasury would pay the Federal Reserve for its purchased gold with gold certificates. (It did just this in 1933 when it commandeered the Federal Reserve's gold and put it in the ground at Fort Knox.) These certificates are warehouse receipts (that is, debt instruments) and would decline in value by two percent per year as the matching gold itself also declined in value by two percent per year.

But these certificates of declining value are also the Fed's reserves against member bank deposits. They are the assets which match and backstop the value of the deposits which the member banks carry with the Federal Reserve. Thus if the gold certificates lose value by two percent per year, so will the deposits of the member banks at the Federal Reserve. (See the diagram opposite.)

And if the member bank's deposits (or reserves) at the Federal Reserve declines by two percent per year, so will the value of all the demand deposits of the depositors and customers of the whole commercial banking system because the commercial banks insist on it by spending only loans of demurrage money.

If all member banks were also required to place a sign over each bank teller's window saying "All checks presented here will be paid off in gold unless the customers specifically ask for currency or demurrage checkbook money in its place," and if the Treasury made a policy of giving gold upon request to the Federal Reserve banks for gold certificates whenever some member bank wants depreciating gold to give to one of its depositors or customers in return for his checkbook money, then the value of all the demand deposit money in the banking system would slowly recede in value. The plan would be in operation.

If Congress were to stipulate that the Federal
Reserve's gold certificates were again to constitute part of the Fed's required reserves ( R),
and that the Treasury must begin to lower by
2% per year its purchase price for gold(beginning at some arbitrary price above the prevailing free market price), then the value of all demand deposits would also decline by 2% per year.


NOTICE TO DEPOSITORS.
"We cash all checks presented here either in
depreciating gold- when gold is asked for- or in
depreciating dollar claims against ourselves. We
do this because the value of our own reserves at
the Federal Reserve,M, lose value gradually as
the U.S.Treasury gradually lowers the value of
the Federal Reserves's gold certificates,R,by
2% per year."

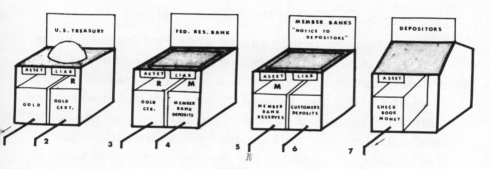

IF THE ASSET AT 1 LOSES VALUE SLOWLY, SO WILL THE ASSET AT 7

Figure 19


If the U.S. Treasury buys gold for a few years at a receding
price of two percent per year while the free market price
declines, so would the value of its current gold inventory
(which constitutes part of its international monetary reserve) go down. This inventory is now nominally worth
about $11 billion (at $42 per ounce). It would, of course,
be worth much more at some higher initial per ounce evaluation if Proposal #2 is adopted.

In today's world, very few people would be likely to ask
for gold in exchange for their deposit money because checkbook money is a far more feasible medium of exchange than

is gold. (The next chapter explains why, under the proposal outline, ordinary people would not be tempted to try to avoid the demurrage cost on checkbook money by fleeing into currency on which no demurrage deduction would be imposed.)

The plan described above (Proposal #2) for using depreciating gold to make demand deposit dollars into hot potato money is advanced—as was stated earlier—as a transitional means only in order to take advantage of the Western world's hybrid monetary system of relying on the use of both gold and credit instruments in its international exchange.

### The Role of the Volume of Money

The volume of money in use, if properly related to the need and growth of the economy, should be and can be a neutral factor in influencing a change in a country's price level. In the U.S., the Federal Reserve system is designed to attune the volume of money to the operating needs of the nation. It does this in the main by modifying the reserves that it makes available to the member banks as a base for the volume of loans and investments that they make. Obviously, if the total activity and output of the nation suddenly doubles, twice as much currency and demand deposits for carrying on the exchanges would tend to be needed.

With modern advances that continually occur in transportation, communication, data processing, etc., there is, of course, a gradual increase in the amount of work that each dollar can do. So over a period of time the need for more money declines somewhat in relation to the volume of business being done. This volume of business being done grows with the number of workers in the labor force and with the growth in output per man-hour. On the basis of those two growth factors—other things being equal—the upward trend in total output would call for a steady annual increase of about four and one half percent in the money supply. But, as noted, continuous growth in the amount of work that a dollar can do suggests that only a net increase in the money supply of about three percent per year would be called for.

Most monetary authorities maintain that the annual growth in the money supply should be somewhere between two percent and four percent. However, the Federal Reserve authorities, while they always as a minimum have in mind permitting the money supply to rise enough to take care of the growth needs of the nation, are also disposed to use their vast control powers over the money supply to dampen booms and to counter recessions. In 1966, for example, by means of a tight credit policy the Federal Reserve authorities held the growth of the U.S. money supply at zero for nine months. In 1968, in contrast—believing that the recently imposed surtax would cause a recession—they eased credit to such an extent that the money supply grew at about an eight percent annual rate.

In making the proposals advanced in this book for insuring that those money recipients—who are normally the "money savers"—reuse their income at the rate at which they get it, and for insuring that their money not be used as an excessive store of value, it is premised that the central bank authorities will merely attempt to attune the growth of the U.S. money supply to the secular growth of U.S. activity, and that they will not restrict the money supply to a zero rate during one year and then inflate it to a ten percent rate during another year. It premises that they will hold it to a secular uptrend of about three percent per year.

Let us suppose that if two percent of the money supply bleeds away each year, and a three percent net increase is needed each year, money creation through bank borrowing, etc., should proceed at a growth rate of about five percent per year. This means that the monetization of loans and investments should proceed at that tempo if changes in the money supply are to have only a neutral effect on the price level. During the past decade, this monitization increased at an average rate of six percent. If the loitering in spending were really nullified by an annual two percent demurrage cost, real growth in overall business activity could easily hit six percent per year, while the net increase in the money supply was only three percent. A secular downtrend in prices would set in as a result.

Even though a gradual demurrage cost of two percent per year were eroding the value of all the demand deposits during the year ahead, the total volume of the nation's money supply would not concurrently decline. The $250 billion of demand deposits at the beginning of some year, for example, would bleed away to $245 billion by the end of the year if a two percent demurrage cost were prevailing. But new loans and new money would be being made during that year. And this new volume of loans and money creation would be geared to the volume of business being done. With business activity being intensified by the demurrage cost, the volume of business would expand, and money creation with it. From 1950 to 1972, as an indication, the average annual expansion of the money supply was six percent. Price inflation during that period accounted for less than three percent of the rise. Business expansion accounted for the remainder. The point is that as a demurrage cost gradually erodes the existing supply of money, new money comes into being as a normal accompaniment of business activity and growth, and would more than offset the erosion.

Under such conditions, *the changes in the rate of use of money, and not fluctuations in the rate of increase in the money supply, will thereafter be the cause of the ups and downs in the level of U.S. activity.*

Oddly enough, those monetary theorists who in recent years have maintained that the rate of growth in the money supply should be held to a steady rate of advance — say, to a rate between two percent and four percent per year — demonstrate no parallel concern over a needed steady rate in the use of this money supply. While they wish to stabilize the rate of monetary growth, they implicitly premise that there should be permissible anarchy in the rate of use of the money itself.

In the United States, monetary policy is chaotic because the rate of use of money is anarchic, and because the quantity of money is subject to discretionary and almost anarchic variation by the Federal Reserve authorities. Our monetary authorities concern themselves only with varying the money supply according to their notions of the need and growth of the economy. They also seem to believe that by controlling the money supply alone they can indirectly adequately control the rate of use.

But, as mentioned above, they use their great powers to modify the reserves available to the member banks for other reasons, too. For example, they vacillate between tight credit and easy credit to repress business booms as they see them and to counter recessions. They also occasionally modify member bank reserves in order to prevent interest rates from going to high levels.

Just as they try to prevent interest rates from going too high, they also occasionally try to prevent them from going too low. They know that if rates are too low in the United States relative to yields obtainable abroad, hot U.S. investment money may flow abroad in enough volume to impair the U.S. balance of payments.

A central theme of this book is that it is highly desirable to reimpose an ownership or carrying cost on property held in the form of money — a cost which was in operation when money was in its earlier forms of commodity money and warehouse receipts. Such a reimposition would be a tremendous stabilizer of the rate of use of money and a logical accompaniment to stabilization of the rate of increase of the money supply itself.

Picture, if you can, a situation where the United States' money supply is controlled to increase at a steady three percent per year rate, and where the rate of use of that very money supply is indirectly stabilized at a high rate of use by a two percent per year demurrage cost. With such stability built into the monetary system itself, there would be little need for the frenetic and often blundering actions of the Federal Reserve authorities to control the intensity of the private monetary demand for goods and services.

For a variety of reasons, the whole Western world gradually went from the use of commodity monies — including gold — to the use of debt obligations as its money. For better or for worse, the world went specifically to the use of those bank obligations which had been routinely swapped for the matching obligations of private and government bank borrowers.

Great danger lies in the use of such a monetary instrument. After all, who should be given the power to decide which obligations shall be transmuted into money, and to decide when the transmutations should cyclically occur? Some of the historic wrestling with such issues is dealt with in Chapter 21, on page 291. Other aspects of the problem I shall discuss in the following section. First a word about gold.

### Bearing on the Advisability of Returning to a Gold Bullion Standard Without a Government "Support-Price" for Gold

The manhandling of credit systems has historically been so severe, arbitrary, and frequent that many thoughtful people — in order to avoid bureaucratic interference — want to go back to the use of a commodity money, in particular, to go back to the use of the commodity, gold. They want the gold to have a floating "supply and demand price," and not to have its price supported by a standing government offer.

But gold, like the debt obligations of banks, is also an exchange instrument with such a high nondepreciating store of value that recipients of it can withdraw from using it in the markets without a direct cost penalty.

Suppose that gold were again to be the money in use, and that the owners of ten percent of it were suddenly to lose confidence in, say, a particular government policy, in the outlook for peace, or business stability, or in the wisdom of wage and price control, and that they were to withdraw from the markets for a time—and merely stand on the sidelines with their gold.

The remaining nine tenths of the gold would then, of course, be worth more to the public in terms of baskets full of goods. Producers would offer more baskets for each unit of the nine tenths of the gold still in use. This, of course, means that consumer prices would fall, that wages, too, would fall in the free market, and that unemployment would increase. The gold on the sidelines would not come in to take advantage of the lower prices. Aggregate monetary demand would become inadequate. The price level would be falling; every day that the owners held off using their gold, it would gain in buying power. (Before 1931 the writer—suspecting that business would decline further— had put his holdings into gold, and he held the gold all through 1931 while the price level fell by twelve percent during the year. But by sitting on the sidelines, the writer made a paper gain while he helped to choke the economy.)

The premise that the hoardable gold money on the sidelines will come back into the markets as promptly as wages and prices fall—and thus maintain overall demand and activity—is fallacious. Stable confidence—that is, the stable willingness to spend for either consumer or capital goods—is also a necessary factor for business stability. And it is not a stable factor in total aggregate demand. When business confidence is frightened and impaired by falling prices or political fears, it always declines. Historically, at least, it has always done so.

So gold, with its high store of value, is as disruptive as the cushioned debt obligations of bankers as a destabilizing medium of exchange — unless the government were steadily lowering its support price for gold.

### The Demurrage Cost as an Aid to Business and Consumer Confidence

A demurrage cost on money would be an institutional incentive to disburse one's income promptly and at a stable rate. It would be the equivalent of an addition to public confidence. A free market system cannot work well unless people retain confidence in it. This book has tried to point out that there is and has been an institutional flaw in the free market mechanism which makes it needlessly difficult to 'maintain the needed confidence during all conditions of activity — particularly during periods when adjustments to business miscalculations are being made. Consequently, the pressure on people to utilize their income at a high and stable rate for either investment or consumption is an empirical contributor to confidence.

Just as Federal insurance of bank deposits is an institutional device for underpinning the confidence of people, and just as unemployment insurance, the amortization of mortgages and social security payments are all providers of added underpinning for consumer confidence and the disposition to disburse one's income continually at adequate rates, so would a loitering cost on money, insuring to all of us a continuous demand for our services, be one more powerful bit of underpinning for the maintenance of confidence.

The advantage of a money designed to lose some of its store of value slowly over time is that every fresh credit dollar minted at the commercial banks — jointly by the business borrowers and the bankers — and then sent on its way to buy the market's goods, is under continuous pressure to return without disruptive delay to purchase domestic goods and services from some producers who are also bank borrowers, and in the process to be liquidated through loan repayment.

We could even today go back to the full gold bullion standard in the U.S. and elsewhere without adding more gold to the $40 billion of central bank reserves that the world already collectively possesses. We could do it immediately if we lowered the Treasury's offering purchase price of gold by two percent per year.

Even though everyone were again privileged to ask for and to obtain gold coins, not many people would want them if they knew their value would decline continuously by two percent per year.

The academic and lay worlds have been so mesmerized by the supposed inherent value of gold as a medium of exchange that nowhere in economic literature is there even a rigorous portrayal of the relative value of gold and the banking system's checkbook "dollar" — no portrayal of how they are functionally tied together and quantitatively related to one another (as was done on page 100). That is a major gap in economic literature.

Under Proposal #2, the U.S. could begin to mint $25, $50 and $100 "gold pieces." If, with the price of gold receding, you were to receive someone's check for, say, $500, and wished to turn the check in at the bank for gold, you would be entitled to receive, say, ten $50 gold pieces for your $500 check.

The coins could be stamped with the year of issue, perhaps by half years. So, if you turned in your $500 check in, say, July, 1975, you would be given ten $50 gold pieces stamped "1975 — 2nd half."

Inasmuch as the U.S. Treasury's offering price for gold would be receding by two percent per year while you were holding your coins, you would find that if you gave one of your $50 gold pieces to someone after you had owned the coin for, say, two years the recipient would say that since your particular $50 gold piece was worth $50 in 1975 it is worth only $48.02 now in 1977. So he would be willing to give you only $48.02 for it. No one owning depreciating demand deposits would want to exchange them for gold coins if the coins were depreciating at the same rate. What is more, it is not practical to use gold coins to pay telephone bills or light bills, or to buy automobiles or to shop in supermarkets with them. Gold coins are for safety deposit boxes, not for medium of exchange.

There would only be an inducement to own gold coins if one could run with them to foreign countries which had not as yet adopted a demurrage money. Meanwhile, the U.S. Treasury's offering price for gold—while it would be declining—would nonetheless be far above the world's free market price for gold. So the U.S. Treasury would be offering more for the coins than would the free market elsewhere.

If the annual gold production remained near the 40 to 50 million ounces level for a few years after the plan's adoption, and the industrial demand for gold were to expand to, say, only the $900 to $1,000 million per year level (while the demand from the central banks remained near zero), the hoarding demand for gold would probably begin to fall off.

If owners of gold saw a high windfall offering price for gold established by the U.S. Treasury, but also saw that that price was scheduled to recede steadily, they would probably be disinclined to accumulate more gold. They would probably conclude that their gold coins would have no place to go to advantage except into the purchase of U.S. goods and services.

Even though people everywhere would be happy to return to a full gold bullion standard, it would be unwise to return to it if it were not for the fact that gold still constitutes a major reserve asset for many of the credit currencies of the world.

But even though, on a permanent basis, it would be silly to return to the full gold bullion standard, it would be very desirable to do so for an introductory period. As mentioned above, if the U.S. Treasury's offering price for gold were lowered very gradually, the return to the full gold standard would enable the U.S. and the whole Western world to use the return as a means for intensifying continuously the aggregate monetary demand by checkbook money for goods and services—which is one of the dream goals of all free market economists.

This proposal is so novel that many people may be disturbed by it. But, even if frightened, they would be able—if the proposal were adopted—to exchange their deposit money for gold on demand, and be able at little cost to sit on the sidelines with gold for, say, six months, at a cost of only one percent, while they watched developments. So no feelings of panic would develop. Meanwhile the owners of deposit money could do nothing but disburse their money more steadily for goods and facilities and thus stimulate business activity and security values.

Although a proposal for neutralizing money's excessive store of value is unorthodox, many people might like the idea. In recent years many leaders have ruefully concluded that central state planning—and the value-fixing that usually accompanies it—are questionable roads to social betterment. Many may view with disfavor any remedial measure that retains the free market mechanism, but many are also weary of merely talking the language of free choice and then naively championing the machinery of governmentalism. Some people might come to regard this new approach as the greatest central planning effort of all—for it would insure that end markets are always adequate to absorb the efforts of the nation's willing workers.

The liberal ideal of greater welfare for toiling mankind is one that is held by most decent people. The end desired is one to which mankind on the whole subscribes. But many people are beginning to doubt that the end can only be reached, or reached at all, by government management of industrial details. Still, some people deeply so believe it can be reached in no other way that they are willing to sacrifice some liberty "temporarily" while they bureaucratically do their "central planning" and build their value-fixing worlds. Many of them realize that the maintenance of a centrally planned and price-fixed economy requires (for compliance and enforcement) the abandonment of free speech and rules of law, and of both humanity and tolerance; also, that it requires the adoption of propaganda as an enforcement means. Yet they are so convinced that federal planning will eliminate the evils of society that they are willing to sacrifice some of the finest fruits of whatever civilization already prevails. In their opinion, the end often justifies their coercive means. One may blindly believe that one can throw liberty away temporarily in the gamble for more bread, but it is a hazardous thing to do. Liberty is elusive; once gone, she is difficult to lure back. For the sacrifice of means to ends ever destroys the very institutions and cultural verities that make for reason in the obtaining of one's ends. When legal means are sacrificed to ends, idealism has become fanatical.

Sadly, it is the cancerous monetary defect now imbedded in the free market system that helps to drive people into the all-consuming statist fire. Only the removal of that defect and the successful establishment of the stability of total private monetary demand can provide us with a realistic hope of dislodging those many "non-economists" and sentimentalists who, in education, politics and opinion formation, have in recent decades acquired vast power over our lives — people who can advance no other recommendations for social betterment than more and more governmentalism.

We hold in our hands the possibility of releasing through simple monetary action both industrial and emotional potentials that would quickly smother the weak appeal of a totalitarianism that rests its industrial case on the elusive promise of more goods through centralized planning, while placing its emotional case on an ability to incite—through organized dishonesty—ignorant and bewildered people against those who are more orderly and advanced. With chronic disruptions of demand removed, with dynamic performance everywhere about him, and with an improved understanding of his system to fortify him, the innate decency of the American would probably induce him to fight actively and courageously against the diabolical extension of the communist state.

# Chapter 8

## How the "Age of the Gothic" Maintained Private Monetary Demand

THERE WAS a period in history when for three centuries money was not exempt from ownership costs. That was the "Age of the Gothic."

It is always difficult to isolate the exact cause of a specific historical development. We know, for example, that Rome fell and that for centuries moralists, militarists, biologists, agronomists, anthropologists, political economists and others have all advanced in a myopic manner their own selected reasons for its fall. In a similar way, we know that for three hundred years medieval Europe experienced a tremendous and continuous building boom. The cathedrals, castles, and town halls are still there in large numbers for all of us to see. But "the cause" of that historic boom is still conjectural.

Most historians have merely reported the occurrence of the enormous building boom and have not sought to explain it. It happened, however, according to the researches of Dr. Hugo Fack, that during the three centuries of that boom the main money of the time was being impelled into use, not merely lured. And one can reasonably surmise that the novel historic monetary arrangement was a major causal factor behind the boom.

For six hundred years after the fall of Rome, Europe was a

land of wretched existence. Then, for reasons which most historians have ignored, an advance began that continued for three hundred years, an epoch of dynamic activity, cultural advance and general good feeling. In France, Germany, Italy, Switzerland and Spain, impressive castles and marvelous cathedrals arose to testify to the prosperity of the time. The *Encyclopedia Americana* says that "The great period of cathedral building in Western Europe was the 12th and 13th century. . .. Between 1170 and 1270 approximately 80 cathedrals were constructed in France alone."

For a few centuries, the people clearly had an economic surplus — a continuing surplus. Influenced by a religious orientation intensified by the crusades, the people cheerfully diverted that surplus into the building of religious structures. The American tourist, as he wanders over Europe and views the physical accomplishments that still remain, must wonder what brought on that epoch of prosperity. There is strong evidence to suggest that it was brought on accidentally by a monetary practice of the time which operated to push money into prompt and stable use and to deny the recipients of money both the opportunity of lengthening the interval between transactions and of using their money excessively as a store of value.

In his booklet, *The Gothic*, Dr. Hugo R. Fack examined at length the impact of the unhoardable money of the time on the continuing prosperity. He wrote:

> . . . from 1150 to 1450 were built the sublime Gothic domes, the splendid city halls, the spacious and beautiful guild houses, vast public market halls, luxurious private mansions and fantastic castles which the modern observer admires at thousands of places in Europe. . . . The splendid cathedrals of Cologne, Wuerzburg and Strassburg in Germany, of Salisbury, Canterbury and Wells in England, of Burgos in Spain, of Rheims, Paris (Notre Dame) and Chartres in France, to cite but a few, are incomparable masterworks for all time . . .

Writers of that period agree that the era was an age of plenty—
that general prosperity had spread to all who worked—that
wages were unbelievably high—that the satisfaction of material wants gradually led to working a smaller number of
hours—that homes were richly equipped—that peasants were
wearing silver buttons on vest and coat, in double line mostly
and using big silver buckles and ornaments on their shoes.

According to Johann Butsbach, one of the chroniclers of
that period, "the common people seldom had fewer than
four courses at dinner and supper." As Butsbach recounts:

> Monday was a free day, the so-called "Blue Monday." That
> day was set apart so the people could attend to their private
> affairs. . . . Since the number of official holidays, moreover,
> was at least ninety the journeyman actually did not work
> more than four days a week and on these four days the hours of
> work were strictly regulated. When the dukes of Saxony tried
> to increase the working time from six to eight hours a day, the
> workers revolted. The life of the people became so voluptuous
> that the dukes, Ernest and Albert of Saxony, found it neces-
> sary to issue special regulations—gastronomic and otherwise.
>
> The soul of the people began to express itself in folklore
> and folksong. The great epics of the Nibelungen, of Tristan
> and Isolde, Gudrun and Waltharius and others were written.
> Minnesang and chivalry flourished.
>
> The question naturally arises: How did it happen that this
> period became filled with material abundance—even without
> having available the productive power of modern machines?
> How was it that the joy of life rang through the land from high
> and low?

Apparently, it was not the result of some governmental
five or ten year plan. No bureaucratic government of alpha-
betical agencies arranged it.

To quote Hugo R. Fack again:

> It had been an old custom for rulers to issue money stamped
> with their insignia, name or portrait and these coins would

remain valid even after the death of the ruler because the coins had a definite metal value which permitted them to be preserved and stored or hoarded.

At the start of the Gothic, however, traditional practice underwent an amazing transformation. Rulers began to recall the money issue of their predecessors in exchange for new coins with the insignia of the new regime. And in order to fill their treasuries, this change-over, termed 'renovatio-mone-tarum'—renewal of money—became subject to a special re-minting charge or seigniorage fee of ten to twenty percent. Since this reminting fee proved to be a very profitable means of taxation, all the many secular and clerical princes, who had acquired the minting right from the government, gradually de-veloped the habit of recalling their own money issue each year. [The open practice of lowering the value of coins on an annual schedule provided a continuous goad to the use of the existing money, whereas the clandestine practice of clipping coins did not. The open practice was a crude improvisation, but it did operate to insure stability of demands.]

As a matter of expediency the coins of that day were made of very thin metal plate and stamped only on one side. They were called thin-pennies, deniers, and in order to facilitate their use for smaller change, the coins were provided with dividing grooves to permit the breaking of them into halves and quar-ters. From this the coins received their name: Bracteats, i.e., coins that can be broken. These thin-pennies, or bracteats, were the main money coins in Europe from the 12th to the 14th century, report the historians.

The *Encyclopedia Britannica* says that "In Germany and France . . . the consequence of the extended right of coinage was a depreciation in weight and in the middle of the 12th century the one-sided deniers called bracteats appeared. . . . In France, the denier, which at first weighed $\frac{1}{28}$ gramme ($19\frac{3}{4}$ grains) was for centuries the chief of European silver coins."

"The regular periodic withdrawal of coins for reissue against a seigniourage charge . . ." writes Fack, "was not conducive to the withholding of money for any length of time. Money withheld was always threatened with loss of value. . . . Thus, hoarding became impractical, and holders of money were just as desirous of getting rid of their money as were the holders of commodities of getting rid of their goods . . . selling became as easy as buying. Money became the dynamo of business. . . ." No longer could money, by being used tardily, impoverish the producers who needed it for exchanging their products. Money became what it has not been in recent times: a medium of exchange without an excessive store of value.

Even so, the people did not understand the cause of their continuous prosperity. During the whole three hundred years, they strongly opposed the periodic reissue of the money and put up a continuous fight for the re-establishment of so-called "perpetual money," which was so designed that it could be saved and slowed down in use without loss. The people naturally resented the tricky tax system which diverted ten to twenty percent of their buying power to the princes year after year. But they did not realize the big contribution to continuous activity and growth that the prompt reuse of money provided.

"The chronicles of that time," writes Fack, "show the unpopularity of the periodical reminting of the money. Instead of demanding that the fee be reduced . . . and that the period between the remintings be lengthened, they simply demanded the removal of reminted money and the adoption of 'eternal money' instead. The first to yield to the pressure was Duke Rudolf IV of Austria. In 1359 he renounced his right of annual monetary renewal. Of the free cities, Augsburg was the first to yield in 1350 and Brunswick in 1412 completed the list."

One of history's greatest blunders may have occurred when the people, in their ignorance, abolished a money having a demurrage cost and shifted back from the use of a boomerang money to a sanctuary money. With the removal of the ownership charge on money, there was an inadequate incentive for money to circulate with adequate promptness. And the economically depressed Middle Ages returned.

People of the world are still shackled to a sanctuary money that has no demurrage or carrying costs. Hoardable gold and silver coins with intrinsic value are disappearing as media of exchange, but in their place we have adopted the credit money of today which—with its face value fortified as we saw with reserves of collateral—is an even more deferrable money than metal coins. *Hoardable money still rules the world.*

Even so, this book has attempted to show that the U.S. monetary system is fortunately so designed that there are two practical recourses to which the U.S. can resort which would automatically operate to impose an ownership cost on all forms of credit money and to impel them all to move with stable promptness into the markets as a demand for goods.

# Chapter 9

## Likely Reactions to
## My Two Proposals

SUPPOSE that you are a business borrower and wish to borrow $1,000 from the bank in your usual manner. In return for your note, the bank would be required to offer you gold with a slowly declining value. But you do not want gold. Instead you want a credit balance against which to write checks because you borrow only in order to spend promptly for payroll and supplies. You would probably tell the banker that you would prefer to accept slowly depreciating deposits in place of inconvenient and slowly depreciating gold. The monthly deduction on your deposit would affect your bank balance very little because as a borrower you would pay out most of your money quickly. But it would put additional pressure on the recipients of your money to use it at a stable rate.

Congress could even stipulate at the beginning that all commercial banks be required to offer to meet all cash withdrawals by paying out depreciating gold. Because customers and depositors do not want to use clumsy gold as their medium of exchange, but want instead a convenient credit balance against which to write checks, only a few people would try to arrange with the banker to leave the proffered gold at the bank in exchange for a new and slightly lower deposit credit. While the banker would be willing, he would probably say: "I shall be happy to substitute for the gold—which legally I must offer you for the checks you present—a new deposit entry here at the bank. But I shall have to lower the value of this new deposit balance a little every month at the rate of two percent per year in line with the falling value of the proffered gold." He might even put a sign over his teller's window saying "All those who present checks here must accept gold or currency or, in lieu thereof, a deposit credit here that will be debited at the rate of two percent per year."

Congress might also stipulate that all bank depositors who have not asked for gold or currency within one month, be sent a cashier's check on the bank at the end of that period. When redeposited, these checks would begin to be debited at the rate of two percent per year.

If commercial banks were permitted to pay off demand deposit claims with gold of declining value, no one—incongruously—would want gold. In the 1920's, for example, when U.S. gold reserves were only about four billion dollars, and all depositors were privileged to exchange their checkbook money for gold, no one wanted gold. So if the purchase price were also receding by two percent per year, it is highly likely that few people would want any of the U.S. Treasury's present holdings of about ten billion dollars in gold. Everyone would still prefer to use checks as his medium of exchange. And, in always preferring to own slowly depreciating deposit money instead of depreciating gold, everyone would end up living under an arrangement where all demand deposit balances would be debited a little every month—at an annual rate of about two percent per year. So even if legislation stipulated that depositors could demand gold for their deposits and that commercial banks could at their option pay off depositors with gold, no one would want gold. We would end up using as our medium of exchange the very kind of debt obligations that we use today. But these new debt obligations would be under continuous pressure to remain actively in use.

## The Shift from Demand Deposits into Currency
## Can Easily Be Forestalled

Everyone would, of course, speculate over ways in which to avoid the bank's monthly carrying debit. Because "coin and currency" and demand deposits are alternative forms of money, it would seem necessary at first thought to devise some special means for forestalling people from exchanging their deposits for coin and currency when the depreciation is begun.

However, I became increasingly convinced that there would be no need to set up obstacles or deterrents to the exchange of demand deposits for coin and currency. *The current disadvantages of owning coin and currency— beyond a certain minimum amount—as compared with owning demand deposits are already so large as to forestall any meaningful shift from demand deposits into owning more coin and paper currency.*

It already costs the American people more to keep their money in the form of demand deposits than it does in the form of coin and currency. Over 80 million people in the U.S. have checking accounts. If on the average they maintain checkbook balances of, say, $400 each and pay service charges to their banks of eight cents on every check that they write—and write about thirty checks per month—then they would be preferring to pay $2.50 per month or $30 per year to the banks for the convenience of making payments with checks rather than with currency. Depositors realize that checks have the big advantage of minimizing the danger of theft—because check writing restricts the cashing of the checks to the designated recipients. In contrast, currency is in itself negotiable and is valuable to any and every possessor. Checks, moreover, can be written for exact amounts. Payments need not be made in inconvenient coin and currency denominations.

Consequently, the depositor with the average balance of $400 would have to pay the bank an additional $8.00 per year, or about 66¢ per month for the convenience of using checkbook money rather than currency. It is highly unlikely that people who are already willing to pay $2.50 monthly for the convenience of using checkbook money would, because of an additional monthly charge of about 66¢, choose to operate with currency out of a cookie jar. Certainly, corporations and businessmen who own a large percentage of all demand deposits, would not choose to shift a single additional checkbook dollar into currency in efforts to escape the demurrage cost.

It is very unlikely that resort to some form of clumsy stamped script would be needed to forestall a flight from demand deposits into currency.

### It Would Not Be Feasible to Hoard Checks

If a carrying charge were imposed on demand deposits, some people might try to hoard checks instead of currency. If Jones, say, works for General Motors, he might try to save his paychecks in safety deposit boxes. Of course if he were to do so, General Motors' checking account would be debited monthly instead of Jones'. Under such behavior, the practice would quickly arise under which writers of checks would stipulate on the blanks themselves that the check is void or reduced in value if not cashed within a stated period. Check blanks might carry a notice like this: "After two months the face value of this check will decline by one percent per month until deposited." Such pressure would cause Jones to deposit his paycheck because, at a two percent per year demurrage cost, his personal deposit would decline in value at the rate of only one twelfth of two percent per month.

### Interest Paid on Time and Savings Deposits Would Fall

Let us suppose on the first day of a new year that Jones owns $50 in currency, $900 in a savings account and $500 in a checking account. As made clear above, if Jones' bank were to impose a two percent annual carrying charge on his demand deposits, it is highly unlikely that Jones would exchange his $500 demand deposit for still more currency.

Nor would Jones try to exchange his $500 demand deposit for time deposits. An inclination to do so would be forestalled because the bank—when it imposes its two percent annual deduction on demand deposits—would concurrently have to reduce by two percent the interest that it is willing and able to pay on time deposits. If it did not do so, depositors would line up at the bank's time deposit window and hurriedly reclassify their demand deposits as time deposits.

If and when demand deposits are gradually devalued at the rate of two percent per year, Jones would wonder whether his savings deposit would also incur a two percent annual deduction in the same way. It would not. Instead of incurring a charge on his time deposit, Jones would find that his savings bank would lower the rate of interest that it pays on his deposit.

Savings depositors entrust savings institutions to act as investing agents for them. These institutions presumably invest the funds in ways which employ labor. And all is well if they actually do disburse the deposits as rapidly as the deposits are delegated to them. But suppose that the savings institutions only partially fulfill their function of investing. Suppose that Jones deposits his $900 check in a savings bank at the beginning of the month and that during the month the bank invests only $300 of it in new ventures that use the money. Disruption is then going on. For the savings bank now owns a new $600 demand deposit in some commercial bank which it is laggardly using. But since the commercial banks would be placing a loitering cost on all demand deposits, a new pressure would be put on the new $600 of the savings institution's money holdings to speed them into investment.

The savings bank would naturally deduct the new charge, placed on its deposit balance by the commercial bank, from the aggregate interest payment that it pays to its savings depositors. For collectively, the depositors are disbursing their dollar savings tardily by way of the savings bank. Of course, it would not seem to the depositors that their deposits are incurring a monthly charge, but that they are receiving a lower interest return on their money savings.

The deduction by commercial banks of a loitering cost on all demand deposits of say two dollars per year on each $100 deposit does not mean that the commercial banker would make two dollars more per year in handling each $100. For, under the new regulation, all the projects in which he invests in order to earn income will be able to obtain funds for investment from the savers of old money—and competitively from him—for two percent less interest than before.

## No Gain Would Result from a Flight into Foreign Currencies

Nor would owners of demand deposits be able to shift them profitably into foreign currencies since the monthly deduction on demand deposits would apply to all balances regardless of who holds them. Germans, for example, would not exchange their marks for deteriorating U.S. deposit dollars unless they were paid a premium for doing so. Their purchased dollars would be subject to whatever deduction was being imposed on dollars generally. As a result, Jones would soon realize that he could not buy marks or other currencies with his penalized dollars without paying a premium for them that would cancel out his prospective gain.

If a monthly carrying charge on dollars were being imposed, then any and all foreigners who had purchased dollars, or received them as payments in trade, or received them as gifts from either relatives or the U.S. government, would be under pressure to re-use them promptly.

Implicit in such an induced rapid re-use of money income would be the automatic termination of one of the world's worst economic troubles: the periodic creation of unemployment in countries with unfavorable balances of trade and payment. If a monthly carrying charge on dollars prevailed and foreigners were to obtain a favorable balance of payment against us, they would be under much greater pressure to use their claims promptly in buying our goods and services. No longer could they feasibly resort to the occasional practice of merely saving their dollar claims and building surpluses instead of buying our goods. No longer could they feasibly shout across the ocean: "It is more of your money, not more of your goods that we want." They would have to use their dollars in our markets as promptly as we would have used them ourselves. We would not have to suffer domestic unemployment while they merely spend their acquired dollars for some of our gold—an action that employs no one here—or while we wait for them to buy our goods and services. Under a carrying charge on money, that part of the problem of unemployment that results periodically from lags in international demand would completely disappear.

### A Depreciating Charge on Money Would Spread Contagiously from Country to Country

Because that country which first imposes a carrying cost on its money will have a big advantage over the countries with which it trades—in that it will have insured the prompt

continuity of both its domestic and its international trade—
the practice of having banks impose a two percent per year
carrying cost on bank debt obligations used as money would
spread rapidly and contagiously from country to country.

In 1934, for example, when the U.S. *raised* its price for
gold to $35 per ounce, those foreign governments which
used gold as bank reserves had to follow suit. If they had not
done so, a Frenchman, say, would have purchased gold
from his government at its old $20 per ounce price, shipped
it to the United States, and made a profit on the transaction.
Similarly, if the United States were back on the full gold
bullion standard under Proposal #2 (see page 100), and
were then to *lower* its price for gold and offer it freely in
exchange for deposit money, people would buy gold here at
the new low price, ship it to France for a higher price and
make a gain there unless the French government forestalled
the action by also lowering its purchase price of gold. France
would do this because it would not want its central bank to
add to its reserves an asset that is being systematically
lowered in value. Consequently, a carrying charge on U.S.
money would not for long lower the value of the dollar in
relation to foreign currencies. There would quickly be no
foreign currencies or markets for gold to which American
dollars could advantageously flee.

### *Debt Instruments Would Carry Lower Yields,*
### *but Not a Depreciation Charge*

Someone might ask, "Why place an ownership charge on
bank money only?" Should not all forms of debt be debited
regularly—bonds, mortgages, commercial paper, etc.?"
Earlier pages have revealed, however, that it is only the
sluggish use of the catalytic agent, money, that stifles exchange and drives industry back to lower stages of operation.
Moreover, as we saw above under time deposits, an annual
two percent cost on owning money would automatically

lower by two percent per year the onerousness of being in debt; for interest rates in general would be that much lower than before.

Some people might think that if an ownership charge were placed on money, then paper in the form of titles, warehouse receipts, etc., would come to be used as money instead. But most titles and warehouse receipts depreciate as rapidly as the goods to which they constitute title. Moreover, they are not mechanically well-adapted to serve as media of exchange.

People might try to avoid the loitering charge by buying titles to autos, houses, yachts, and factories. But that is the very result desired: the steady and continuous exchange of money for goods.

As the debit on deposits operated to drive down bond yields, refunding operations would go on at a brisk pace. All callable bonds would probably be quickly retired. Business costs would fall as a result. Entrepreneurial profits, wages, and activity would rise as interest rates began to fluctuate around a level about two percent lower than that which had prevailed before the new support price of gold was lowered.

## The Gold Outflow Would Stop

If the Federal government—after adopting Proposal #2—were to reduce its new high offering price of gold, would the world want to buy the then available gold? Probably not.

Would not the demand decline if Congress reduced the offering price for gold continuously from an initial price higher than the then current free market price—and far higher than its then probable "use-value"—by two percent per year? What if under the new plan Congress gave notice to the world that the U.S. was gradually easing what had been one of its price support programs? Indirectly, it would be telling the world that ten years from now its Treasury price for gold would, for example, be down by more than twenty percent from the initial adoption price. Under such conditions, would wise managers of foreign central banks want to exchange any of their earning assets, like U.S. government obligations, for a steadily depreciating asset?

Faced with a receding U.S. Treasury purchase price for gold, the hoarders of the world might try to inundate our Treasury with offerings of their past accumulations. If you were a French peasant or an Indian prince with a cache of gold, what would you do if you learned that the world's price support program for gold was going to be steadily eased? Arithmetically, of course, you could gain nothing by fleeing into dollars and exchanging your gold for U.S. currency and deposit dollars under the new arrangement, because both the gold and the demand deposit dollars would be incurring an equal decline in value of two percent per year. The only remaining rational place to which to flee would be into the purchase of physical goods or facilities (via investment) which have a fair promise of enduring value.

## How Severe Should the Annual Carrying Charge on Money Be?

Just how large an annual decline in the value of demand deposits should be arranged for could probably be ascertained empirically. There is an objective way of finding out what is an advisable rate.

(Figure 6 on page 20 shows that the rate of use of money sagged the economy into recession four times between 1956 and 1969 — once every three or four years.) The demurrage cost could begin at a one percent annual rate the first year. Then, if and when a business sag occurs, the annual rate could be increased to two percent. If and when a later sag occurs, the rate could be raised to two and one-half percent. And so on.

The annual depreciation rate need not be too accurately

established; any rate would be better than the zero rate that prevails today. The main point is that the rate should be so high that people would continuously try to go "from a money to a goods position."

The two percent annual cost recommended under the two proposals presented in the previous chapter would do two things to the savers of money: It would cause them to search out entrepreneurs with more alacrity, and to accept about two percent less from the entrepreneurs to whom they delegate their funds. Faced with an enlarged demand for their services, the entrepreneurs would in turn be under greater pressure to seek out workers to help them with their tasks. In the double process, the sums diverted from the money savers would thus not go to the government, but would be split between the nation's workers and entrepreneurs.

Is there danger that the demurrage cost would bring on an unwarranted boom, that industry would hit a pace it could not hold? Probably not. Because jobs would always be plentiful under the proposal outlined above, every worker would have complete liberty to choose leisure in place of goods if and when his desire for goods was satisfied. Under such circumstances it would be difficult to drive people into an unwarranted boom. People using their own sense of values as to what is worthwhile could and would escape into leisure if they found that they were working too hard.

### Real Personal Savings Would Increase

At first glance, we are inclined to shudder at an arrangement which impels us to disburse our money savings more steadily than in the past. Our immediate reaction is that we would be forced to live forever without savings. But it is only the saving of IOUs and claim checks for disruptive periods of time that would become impractical under a carrying charge on money; and that kind of saving is not real economic saving anyway.

Oddly enough, continuous spending or disbursement is a necessary step in the genuine saving process. For only when money is spent for the ownership of long-lived assets, that is, for capital facilities, does real economic saving occur. If, after one puts one's money into titles to facilities or securities—that is, into the partial ownership of plant and equipment—or into savings banks which in turn disburse it for capital goods items, one can build up a portfolio of equities, or of claims against the savings institutions which acquire such equities. These portfolio holdings constitute real savings, real ownership of facilities, and can be reconverted into cash in later years for use in one's old age.

Peculiarly enough, the stabilized spending of money would not result in anyone having less to spend. On the whole, everyone would have more certain purchasing power than before. What you as an individual are induced to spend is income for the other fellow, and what others are induced to spend is likewise income for you. While you are under indirect pressure to employ others, others are indirectly under pressure to employ you. It is a theoretical impossibility to reduce the income of all the people by impelling them to disburse income—including money savings—more promptly. From the social point of view, all that can happen is that people are driven into continuously demanding goods, into producing goods, and into creating and obtaining new dollars which correspond to the new goods.

# Chapter 10

## Better Rules Are Needed to Envelop Our Free Market System

E CONOMICS, it is said, is the science of scarcity. The implication is that the prevailing capacity to produce goods is the factor that limits our standard of living. The implication is often even stretched to imply that if we merely increased our productive capacity and improved our science and human skills, life in general would improve. This is the accepted view in universities, business, and government. Law and public policy are based upon it. Congress even maintains a National Committee on Productivity. The government also provides scholarships to engineers, and maintains billion dollar programs to increase the productivity of the unskilled.

The above view has deep historic roots. Adam Smith, John Stuart Mills, Ricardo, Böhm-Baverk, Marshall, the Austrians — Jevons, Taussig and others — have all premised that scarcity was the problem, and that increased productivity was the crucial means for resolving our material woes. As of now — in the United States at least — that view is outdated.

The advent of checkbook money has so changed and impaired the "effective demand" for goods and services that it is "inadequate effective demand," not productive capacity, that is today the limiting factor in resolving our material problems.

There is little doubt that our economic system does possess some deeply rooted defect. It experiences recurrent recessions, unemployment, and distress. It also experiences an income distribution which would be very lopsided were it not that government now gives labor unions the power to bludgeon employers and, furthermore, taxes the rich heavily for revenue which it bureaucratically transfers to the poor. Economists have all failed to provide a satisfactory and theoretical base for the conservatives to use in defending the free market system.

During World War II (just as during World War I) monetary demand—the urge to buy, rooted mainly in large federal disbursements for war—unlocked the country's productive capacity, the dormant capacity which had been stagnant and inactivated during the whole dead decade of the 1930s. Figure 3, page 15, shows how unemployment during the war went down to one to two percent from an average level of fifteen percent during the 1930s.

After World War II, however, U.S. production facilities were again not fully utilized, and unemployment rose to hover around the five percent level. Clearly, the major problem in political economy during recent decades has not been to provide more capital facilities, or more money savings for such facilities. Rather, it has been to unlock adequately the sluggishness of the claims held by those who exclusively are entitled to command the facilities to perform.

Perversely, economic analysts and public policy makers continue to look at our relatively stagnant activity, poverty, and unemployment problems through the obsolete scarcity analysis of Adam Smith and his successors. They clamor for more savings, for more "investment tax credits," and for more training programs for unskilled workers — even when the rate of use of existing facilities hovers in the seventy to eighty percent range.

No, it is the rules of the game on the demand side that needs a looking into. Over the long pull it is, of course, basic that we have rules that generate appreciable savings out of income — savings that are willing to flow promptly into investment in order to build ever more and better facilities. (This is particularly true for the underdeveloped and developing countries in Asia, Africa, and Latin America.) Unless we do so provide — that is, accumulate savings and produce ever better facilities — we lose what is perhaps the most laudable feature of the free market system: The ability to deliver for almost everyone an ever more plentiful supply of goods and services in return for lessened effort.

But we have played our production game with loaded sanctuary money so awkwardly that the savers of money — who are determined to buy capital facilities with the money or nothing at all — have, on the record, received not only enough of the community's output to overbuild U.S. facilities periodically (in relation to U.S. end market buying power), but to invest over $80 billion U.S. dollars in capital facilities in Europe and elsewhere.

Figure 20 shows how money savings have flowed into investment annually since 1956. Over a period of time, the amount of savings invested in new facilities bear a rather sensible ratio to the amount of money spent annually to constitute the end market for goods and services. This is logical, for one must have plant if one is to turn out goods.

The U.S. Economics Corporation, the research and consulting firm founded by the writer, constructed the above chart. It shows what the investment/consumption ratio was in the U.S. from 1956 to 1971. It also shows how the amount invested in facilities has swung above and below the par ratio. Roughly, U.S. history (and the formula that is based

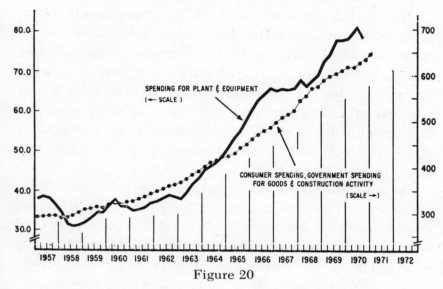

Figure 20

upon it) demonstrates that for every $1 billion increase that we spend for consumers *goods* we need to spend about $130 million for new investment, and that for every additional billion we spend for *services* — such as electric power and telephones — we need to spend about one third as much (one third of $130 million) more for new facilities.

The chart highlights the situation which usually prevails under the current rules that envelop the free market: namely, that the system provides money savings in abundance to our (occasionally) invested minded people — so much in fact that they even occasionally whip themselves into periods of excessive investment in relation to which consumer buying power can provide a market. This was the case during 1965–1970, for example. *Excessive* savings, when promptly invested in capital facilities, lay the basis for a later recession. Too much saving for a rainy day itself brings on the rain.

Despite the empirical record shown, analysts and public policy makers chronically maintain that the need is for more

savings and investments, and not for arrangements which
(1) operate to induce the savers — whenever they reduce
their rates of disbursement for investment — either to blow
their entire current income for yachts and other big ticket
items, or (2) for new rules of the game which cause less of
our currently generated income to flow to those who will
only spend it for facilities or for nothing at all, and more to
those who will happily spend it promptly for consumers'
goods and services.

These analysts and policy makers believed that periodic
crises were only "dislocations." Even the ten million unemployed of 1933 did not call forth more than the sophomoric
cures of compensatory spending and build-ups of union
power. The severe disruptions of 1938, 1949, 1954, 1958,
1961, 1966, and 1969, they merely labeled "recessions,"
and then prayed that the ship would right itself. But the
disruptions which they regarded as being only incidental
are today the very essence of the situation which I shall
now describe.

Historically, machinery increased product and more and
more of the supplies with which to make machinery. A
mammoth physical apparatus has grown up around us. This
apparatus is owned by economic men who do not permit its
use without compensation. Hence, most of the output is not
distributed to meet even intense human needs, but only to
meet human ability to pay.

The power of today's machines to turn out ordinary consumption goods like shoes, food, automobiles, and appliances could — if fully utilized — bury us in a pile of products
a mile high. But the ownership of the claims, which can
command the machines to run, belongs to economic men
who do not consume enough. These economic men call for
more and more machines instead — that is, for more investment.

Our U.S. industrial system runs excessively to the production of plant facilities. These do not adequately turn out all they can of consumption goods. Their rate of use sometimes slows down to recession tempos. Relative to our country's total activity, there is an inadequate demand for consumption goods. Those who need them do not have the money, and those who have the money do not want to buy an irrational amount of such goods for themselves, but want to put most of the money into ever more facilities. Hence, our massive advertising effort to get people, who have the money, to buy more and more — our ghastly effort called salesmanship.

Our power to produce goods has outstripped our power to align it with a balancing monetary demand. Machinery, plus standardization, plus lopsided income distribution, together have created a situation which frequently brings our productive machinery to a recession stop.

Because production has been too victorious in the U.S. in relation to effective demand ever since the early nineteen hundreds, it has precipitated several business crashes; and the public has been saved from several more crashes by the high demands of four wars and the growth of a few large sensible consumer demands such as those for automobiles, appliances, and aircraft.

Economists have ignored too much the economic lessons of war. For the time being, war harmonizes production and consumption. It speeds up the industrial machine to the limit. The data and history presented in Chapter 23 shows how the labor scarcity engendered during war changes the free market bargaining power of workers to their advantage so completely that they obtain more of the output and comforts of life than ever before.

In nonwar periods, in contrast, the workers would like to buy more but cannot; the investing class could buy more, but will not. It is possible to imagine a world wherein this

is changed—where the working man works under a new set
of rules in a different kind of free market system with liberty,
and a more equitable distribution of income.

The system that was expounded from Adam Smith to
Alfred Marshall could and did call forth vast quantities of
goods—and inventions for making more goods—but it did
not call forth social justice for the working man. The evolutionary shift from hot potato commodity money to postponable checkbook money accidentally loaded the bargaining in the market against the worker (as this book will show)
and in favor of the reluctant money-holding investor. The
subtlety of this shift escaped, and still escapes, the notice
of analysts and economists. Instead, they invoke collective
bargaining, compensatory spending, progressive income
taxes, transfer payments, and other patent medicines to
ameliorate the lot of the working class. All such recourses,
however, at best merely start the machine going all over
again in the same old way.

The distribution of buying power between wages, profits,
interest, etc., does not seem to be functionally balanced.

Wages, profits, interest, rent, and local taxes are merely
five names for the rewards that flow out to employees,
entrepreneurs, lenders, and owners of fixed property (and
to the community providers of necessary government
services), who cooperatively produce a product or service.
The relative breakdown of rewards between the cooperating
contributors can be diagrammed. (See page 206.)

Everyone in his heart is interested in establishing "fair
wages," "fair profits," "fair interest rates," etc., and wishes
that he knew how to do it. The "fairness of the relative
rewards in producing billions of products in millions of
establishments cannot be achieved by a bureaucratic fixing
of wages, profits, interest, etc. It can only be done by personal demand expressing itself in relation to the supply of
each factor in a free market *under the laws and rules that the*

*community sets up.* If that is so, then the question arises: how wise, or rather how functional, are the laws, and rules that have enveloped the free market in the past, and still envelop it today—the rules under which the participant producers bargain with one another for their share of the total reward?

The laws of property and the laws circumscribing the range of behavior of the employees, entrepreneurs, lenders, and owners of property (and the community providers of necessary government services) in cooperatively producing a product or service have always been unfair to some one or other of the contributors. As John Stuart Mill wrote in *Principles of Political Economy:*

> The principle of private property has never yet had a fair trial in any country. . . . The social arrangements of modern Europe commenced from a distribution of property which was the result, not of just partition, or acquisition by industry, but of conquest and violence; and notwithstanding what industry has been doing for many centuries to modify the work of force, the system still retains many and large traces of its origin. The laws of property have never yet conformed to the principles on which the justification of private property rests. They have not held the balance fairly between human beings, but have heaped impediments upon some, to give advantage to others.

Marginal utility analyses—while helpful within any particular institutional frame of reference—have not zeroed in on the enveloping laws and rules which provide the frame of reference within which the analyses proceed. The value or marginal utility of each additional increment of each factor of production is partly influenced by the institutional frame of rights, duties, privileges, immunities and exposures which circumscribe and relate to the role of each factor.

If one is to defend the institution of private property, one must look into the ingredients that constitute property. If one does not, one may generalize the problem out of existence. Property is not a word; it is a bundle of attributes. Ownership of property is always a bundle of stipulations and arrangements that the community is willing to back up that involve one's use and handling of a particular asset.

Professor John R. Commons wrote a book in which he organized those stipulations under the headings of Rights, Duties, Liberties, Exposures, Powers, and Privileges, and traced their changing content. The courts always deal with component stipulations when they deal with cases involving property rights. Property can be a tangible or an intangible item; it can be wheat and automobiles, or it can be goodwill and debt obligations.

When you own an automobile or a note, for example, you possess certain rights, certain privileges, certain liabilities, etc., in your handling of the property item. These are always in process of being added to or subtracted from by court decisions. They are always being modified. By modifying them, the courts change the value of your automobile, your rifle, your home, your mortgage, etc. Private property is a bundle of stipulations around some tangible or intangible item that you control within limits that the community first sets and then enforces.

The state often tailors the bundle for maximum equitableness so that the community mores will help with the matter of compliance and enforcement. But it often fails to do so. Today, for example, we seem to give too broad an ownership over the U.S. air waves to our national broadcasting stations. In contrast, we probably give inadequate ownership content (i.e., property rights) to the owners of factory facilities. We tolerate sit-ins, strikes, damage, barricades against even the owners entering and using their own buildings.

One aim of this book, I repeat, is to cancel a certain disruptive property attribute which unobservedly crept into our monetary system when checkbook money superseded commodity money—and gradually accrued to a disruptive degree, to the advantage of the savers of our medium of exchange.

The guide to the wisdom of today's enveloping rules is *whether the rewards are so well-balanced* in relation to one another that they tend to induce the savers both to save and to invest promptly, the entrepreneurs to initiate, the employees to work so their wages provide adequate end markets for the full operation of the country's facilities? If we do not, then it would be well to change the distribution to better advantage; that is, make distribution more functional and "fair" by changing the enveloping rules of the game. Just as the forward pass improved the game of football, and new rules could improve the sluggish tempo of baseball, so ingenious rules might improve the game of production as carried out by free market means.

A few imaginary institutional arrangements are given below under which the percentage reward distributed to workers, savers, entrepreneurs, etc., for producing a product might be changed for better and for worse through bargaining in a free market.

## In Regard to Wages

1. If the community were to get rough and were to treat all idle and unemployed workers as being vagrants, then workers' wages, as a percentage of the total reward for producing a product, would undoubtedly decline.

2. In contrast, if the workers were given the privilege of forming unions and given immunity from the monopoly provisions of the antitrust laws, their percent of the reward for producing goods would go up.

3. Again, if the government were to permit workers to form national unions in both the public and private sectors,

to permit them to strike the whole nation at one time, and then were to provide them with unemployment relief payments while they strike, wages would rise and float at still higher levels. (The two charts on pages 12 and 14 show how changes in the laws in the U.S. during two recent decades affected bargaining in the labor market.)

These three hypothetical changes in the rules for influencing wage rewards would all be crude devices. Still supply and demand, persuasion, and free agreements would be operating under them to give workers very different rewards for their efforts. In no case, however, would the various rules necessarily insure "justice"—that is, provide a functionally balanced wage reward as a percentage of the value added. Nonetheless, as Chapter 7 (Proposal #1) showed, there is a simple change in the rules which could provide for such a functional or "fair" wage return for labor.

### In Regard to Interest

Interest rates, the return to savers for the use of their money, is also influenced by the rules of the game which precede the haggling in the market place.

If, as in medieval times, when the Church forbade the charging of interest as usury and as being sinful, interest rates were probably dampened.

If on the other hand, a country goes in for embalming the value of all the claims handed out in payment for current production—so that the claims can retain their full value when used for the output of later years, interest rates will be on the high side.

So it is also with profit and rent. If corporations are required to pay large pensions to employees, or if they are required to share the management function with the unions etc., profit—other things being equal—will tend to shrink.

Similarly, if the Henry George form of land taxes were to be levied, rent would tend to run at lower levels.

The reader can use his own good imagination and think of hypothetical changes in those rules of the free market which precede the haggling that occurs in the market between the producing participants. The ideas presented above are merely theoretical suggestions.

The rules of the game on the demand side are today so defective that they prevent functionally balanced rewards from being made to the various factors of production as a result of haggling in the market. Chapter 7 showed how such a functional or more "fair" balance in bargaining can be achieved than is now the case.

The paragraphs above are also intended to highlight the intellectual futility of those widespread textbook approaches into economic problems of the free market which do not concurrently zero in on the many rules of the game which society first sets up to influence the distribution of income between wages, interest, rent and profit—as well as the overall tempo of business. As it is, the whole world chooses to play a hobbled free market game with hoardable money— and then says nothing about it.

# Chapter 11

## Major Benefits from the Proposed Plan

I F THE demand deposit accounts of depositors (which are also the debt obligations of commercial banks) were scheduled to lose value at a two percent per year rate, the outlook would put pressure on the depositor to entrust his money to some savings institution for investment in return for a two percent smaller interest reward than he had been able to obtain before. That means that he would be just as willing to accept, say, a three percent interest return on his money after the legislation goes into effect, as he had the five percent return before the legislation was enacted. Those who would insist on holding money in the form of demand deposits would have to pay for their liquidity at a rate equal to the interest that they forfeit, plus the demurrage loss.

Home builders, corporations and state and local governments would be able to borrow funds at much lower rates —say four to six percent—instead of six to eight percent. It follows, too, that if builders, corporations and state and local governments were able to borrow already existing money for two percent less than before, then commercial banks would also be forced to accept two percent less than before for creating new money for the borrowers. The rate paid by borrowers for new money is always competitive with the rate paid to savers for existing money. Thus, under the new legislation, the rate of interest paid to both lenders of old money and to bank lenders of new money would decline, while the cost of money to the dynamic entrepreneurial users would recede.

The net result would be that the investors, the real suppliers of capital facilities to the nation, would be under pressure to pay two percent more to those workers and entrepreneurs who help them to construct their new capital facilities.

A by-product of the lowering of the interest rate, with tremendous significance for business cycle stability, would be that all savings institutions could afford to invest in paper carrying, say, a two percent lower yield. That fact would have the far-reaching benefit that it would operate automatically to reduce significantly the long-term rate of interest on business loans—which has been one of the historic dream goals of economic theory. Money savers would find themselves investing in endless projects that earlier had seemed unattractive.

A period of rapid economic growth would follow, real, wholesome growth, rooted in the private sector of the economy. Such growth, which relies on the competitive drive of selfish entrepreneurs, who are restricted to earning their money by rendering superior service competitively to the community, probably tends to bring forth more sensible output than when the growth is directed by government officials who merely disburse tax revenues as the revenue comes in.

If people "oversave" occasionally—in the sense of withholding more income from consumption than is needed to build the plant for turning out the goods that end markets can buy—does it not follow that interest rates have been more than high enough to induce people to save adequate sums for facilities? Obviously, the inducements that are inadequate are those which should have insured that that money which is not spent for goods and services is induced either to hurry back into the channels of consumption or to accept a lower return on investment.

### *Tariff Discrimination against the U.S. Would Be Weakened*

The possibility exists of maintaining a high level of balanced trade between the large free trade area of the U.S. with the restricted trade area of Europe by using boomerang money as U.S. medium of exchange.

In the last analysis, the only place where Germans, for example, get goods and services for their dollars – directly or indirectly – is in the United States. So the Germans would have to window-shop our markets and select from among our goods – all of them perhaps produced at higher prices than in Germany – what consisted of the relatively "best buys."

The lowering of our tariff walls could be a fine action if at the same time we put a carrying cost on our money to insure its speedy use in rehiring into the surviving and expanding U.S. industries those workers who are laid off in the doomed industries.

In particular, if all world monies were made subject to a carrying cost, it would be far easier politically to lower the tariff barriers and to remove the trade restrictions that now exist between nations. Such an arrangement would insure the prompt re-employment in all countries of all workers who lose their jobs in each country as the relatively high-cost producers in each area are forced to close down, and the relatively low-cost producers are favored with expanded trade.

## As an Aid to Growth in Undeveloped Countries and As a Plan for When Socialism Fails

During the years since World War II, many poorly developed countries have tried unsuccessfully to install "welfare states" and socialistic forms of government. In several of these countries, as the breakdowns occurred, military men have taken over—sometimes reluctantly—the leadership of the government. They did this in the hope that industrial activity could be restored quickly, and that a viable government could be quickly reconstructed. For such military leaders, a recourse that would forestall tardiness in the use of their country's money would be a godsend. Thus, even well-meaning dictators, if any, could at least insure full employment for their people until parlimentary procedures had time to take root.

In our long-drawn-out contest with Communism for the minds of men, it will avail us little to work harder, to save more, to invest more—to outproduce Communism in material things by more and more. So long as our own producing millions—and the world's onlookers—observe our anarchy in private monetary demand, our chronic fear of business recession, and our unemployment of unskilled workers, whom our market appraises as not being worth our unrealistic minimum wage rates, so long will unsophisticated people in many lands choose the grim and plodding procedures of governmentalism over our free and efficient but erratic ways. Too many nations are already disposed to regiment their people and to sacrifice present generations in the naive belief that they can thus speed the future.

If we are to instill the leaders of aspiring nations in Africa, Asia and Latin America with a knowledgeable confidence in our own system, we must convince them that if they merely arrange for a continuity of private monetary demand at home,

they can pull themselves up by their own bootstraps, as did
the people of medieval Europe during the age of the Gothic.
Our current efforts to lift these nations with billions of dollars
of government-to-government aid — while we shut our eyes
to their expropriation of those foreign investors who helped
them both to start their industrialization and to install a few
free market institutions — are doomed to fail. We must export
not only our dollars, but our free market institutions, too, if
we are ever to induce the undeveloped nations to imitate
the free world's historic methods of advance. Adoption of a
nondeferrable money could provide all the emerging nations
with a dynamism under which they themselves could empirically experiment with a multiplicity of goals and programs.

### *The Split between Consumption and Investment Would Be in Better Balance*

What kind of split do we want? What criteria are we to
use? Economists know that the American standard of living
rises and can rise only if more and more investment per
worker is made in capital facilities. Economists also know
that the volume of money savings seeking investment in
facilities periodically become so large in relation to the
buying power of the end markets that the yield outlook per
dollar of investable funds becomes dimmer and dimmer. At
that point, industry after industry concludes that it has
excess capital facilities. (See page 141) Economists would,
of course, like to see savings invested in facilities as promptly
as money income is withheld from consumption channels.
But a still larger issue exists: What fraction of our national
income should we divert into new plant and equipment
year after year, even if money savings are invested promptly?
Should it be, say, ten, twenty-five or fifty percent? Socio-
logical criteria suggest an answer.

The first requirement is not that the amount of investment
should equal the volume of savings. It is that the spending

of all income claims should be prompt and continuous, whether they are spent for consumption goods or for investment. As earlier pages made clear: if we are to have a society of specialized workers, then we must have a prompt and continuous exchange of their specialties. It is more important that the recipients of income respend it for consumption, even silly consumption, than that they delay in spending it until they can find profitable investment opportunities. The longer they delay, the more do the end markets sag and make investment opportunities less attractive. As Chapter 23 brings out, workers would probably, if they felt convinced that high private monetary demand would continuously insure against unemployment, choose to work fewer hours and receive lower income than keep their income high and buy silly consumption goods.

To pose clearly the question of how much income should go annually into capital formation, let us picture what would happen to our pattern of life if we spent only fifty percent of our income for consumption goods and services year after year and actually invested the second fifty percent in capital goods.

We would then have a society in which men would be building an ever better physical plant to which the money savers would be acquiring title. Workers would then be but drones, not living life to its full in their own time but working away at capital goods activity, making whatever plant ever more efficient and excessive for the benefit of unborn children who, in their turn, might continue to use their economic machine to the same end as their forebears. To merely move money savings — whatever their amount — promptly into investment can thus be a silly solution too. The big trick in political economy is to get an enlarged portion of our national income diverted (during the initial bargaining that occurs in the market place) into the hands of recipients who are disposed to use large portions of it for consumption or leisure, and not to get an excessive portion of it diverted into the hands of those who will use it for capital facilities or for nothing at all. That is something that the carrying charge on money is uniquely designed to do.

A demurrage cost on today's tardily used money would be an empirical aid to public confidence. Heretofore, because of the institutional flaw in the free market mechanism, it has been needlessly difficult to maintain adequate confidence during periods when adjustments to business miscalculations were being made. Just as the Federal insurance of bank deposits was and is an institutional device for underpinning the confidence of people, and just as unemployment insurance, the amortization of mortgages, social security payments, etc., all constitute institutional underpinning for consumer confidence — and for the disposition to disburse income continually at adequate rates — so a demurrage charge on money, which would insure to all of us a continuous demand for our services, would be one additional powerful support to confidence.

What follows now is essentially a prefatory note to the immediately ensuing three chapters, 12, 13, and 14.

Instead of diagnosing correctly the monetary cause of our system's shortcomings, well-meaning but incompetent critics succeeded in inducing Congress to support two presumed correctives which, instead, worked out to undermine the free enterprise system further. These were:

1. National labor unions, to be assisted in their growth and bargaining by government.

2. Compensatory government spending.

From 1932 to 1939, ever more generous labor legislation was passed. It operated to raise union membership from about two and a half million members in 1932 to about twenty million members in 1972. On net, unions with government assistance were given the powers, privileges, and immunities which enabled them to lift wages much faster than man-hour productivity could be increased. A severe upward pressure on employers to lift their prices was thus built into the system.

Concurrently, Congress decided to maintain aggregate monetary demand by means of government deficit financing (whenever rising prices began to reduce demand), and—if need be—to accompany that recourse with a bureaucratic redistribution (via transfer payments) of whatever national income was generated.

The chart on page 194 shows how wage increases have been outrunning productivity increases in recent years. This upward trend is now occurring in all free market countries. Government spending, largely compensatory, has been accelerating in the U.S. and elsewhere. Before World War II, federal, state and local government disbursements totaled only about $10 billion per year. In 1971 they were $340 billion.

Had nonpostponable money been continually in use during the 1900s, serious unemployment and recessions would not have occurred. As it was, the two recourses relied upon have together driven all Western nations into inflation.

*To save the free enterprise system today, therefore, it is also necessary to neutralize the two disruptive recourses just mentioned.* It will not be easy to do so because both are firmly institutionalized. However, a shift to hot potato money from sanctuary money would facilitate such neutralization. This is explained in the next three chapters.

As a beginning, it is necessary to understand the process of cost-push inflation, and how government compensatory spending is a contributor to it.

# Chapter 12

## The Process of Cost-Push Inflation

E VEN though the free market system has for a hundred years severely handicapped itself by use of sanctuary money, it has lifted the living standards of its people sensationally. Moreover, it did this commendably by relying on persuasion rather than on coercion. Even so, the market system could have done much better. For it could in addition have generated a far more equitable distribution of income and performed without generating periodic recession and depression.

As it was, the version of the free market known as Capitalism was, as this book has shown, loaded against the worker and in favor of the money saver until about 1940. Income distribution was so unbalanced that recession and unemployment were unavoidable.

Instead of diagnosing correctly the cause of the system's shortcomings, well-meaning but incompetent critics, like the Fabians of England, sought to replace the market system in its entirety with a governmentalist system of central planning. Their success in expanding physical output has been impressive in both Europe and the United States. A major feature of their system, however, has been the maintenance of aggregate monetary demand by means of direct government spending accompanied by a controlled bureaucratic redistribution of the national income generated. (We frequently call this expanded governmentalism, "New Economics" or "Welfarism.")

Figure 3, shown here again, makes clear, that the many devices of the "New Economics" succeeded in holding

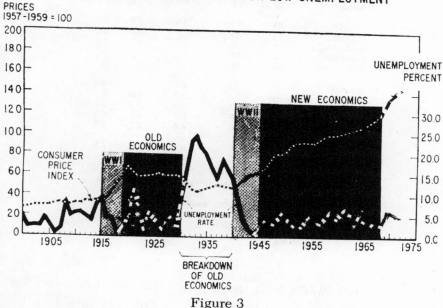

Figure 3

unemployment near the five percent rate ever since World War II ended. But it also shows that price inflation continuously accompanied that success. Not only has steady inflation been one of the prices paid in the U.S. for low unemployment under the new system, but this same price has also been paid under that system everywhere in the Western world.

Congress today legislatively transfers to the lower income

| | Industrialized countries | | | | |
|---|---|---|---|---|---|
| | Indexes of value of money (1961=100) | | Rates of depreciation of money | | |
| | 1966 | 1971 | '61-'71* | '66-'71* | '72† |
| United States | 92 | 74 | 3.0 | 4.3 | 3.2 |
| Greece | 89 | 80 | 2.2 | 2.2 | 3.8 |
| Japan | 74 | 56 | 5.6 | 5.4 | 4.1 |
| Luxembourg | 87 | 74 | 2.9 | 3.2 | 4.4 |
| Canada | 90 | 75 | 2.8 | 3.6 | 4.4 |
| Italy | 79 | 66 | 4.0 | 3.4 | 4.5 |
| Belgium | 85 | 72 | 3.3 | 3.4 | 4.9 |
| Germany | 86 | 74 | 2.9 | 2.8 | 5.2 |
| France | 83 | 65 | 4.2 | 4.7 | 5.3 |
| Sweden | 80 | 64 | 4.4 | 4.5 | 5.3 |
| Austria | 84 | 70 | 3.6 | 3.7 | 5.5 |
| Iceland | 56 | 32 | 10.7 | 10.6 | 5.8 |
| South Africa | 88 | 73 | 3.1 | 3.8 | 5.9 |
| Denmark | 76 | 55 | 5.7 | 6.0 | 6.0 |
| Switzerland | 83 | 69 | 3.7 | 3.7 | 6.1 |
| Norway | 81 | 62 | 4.7 | 5.2 | 6.2 |
| Australia | 91 | 76 | 2.7 | 3.6 | 6.5 |
| United Kingdom | 84 | 64 | 4.4 | 5.4 | 6.7 |
| Finland | 76 | 59 | 5.1 | 4.9 | 6.8 |
| New Zealand | 87 | 64 | 4.4 | 6.0 | 7.3 |
| Spain | 68 | 52 | 6.4 | 5.2 | 7.5 |
| Netherlands | 80 | 63 | 4.6 | 4.9 | 7.7 |
| Ireland | 81 | 59 | 5.1 | 6.1 | 8.0 |

*Compounded annually. †Based on average of monthly data

September 1972 · First National City Bank · 11

Figure 21

groups some of the high income that the well-to-do—as the chief possessors of sanctuary money—are able to obtain by bargaining in a market loaded in their favor. The government takes income from the rich with progressive income taxes and hands it out bureaucratically through transfer payments to the poor and the distressed.

In this chapter we shall investigate why price inflation is necessarily a built-in accompaniment of the "New Economics." We shall investigate why every society, so long as it uses hoardable money as its medium of exchange, must experience recession and other shortcomings and put pressure on its confused politicians to resort to governmentalist spending and handout programs — the only means politicians can think of for blotting up unemployment and for relieving distress.

Inflation can, of course, be caused by many disruptive actions and conditions. In the following pages we shall emphasize those major arrangements which induce price inflation today in the U.S. and other major countries.

Almost all economists premise that price inflation results from only two causes: (1) an excessive availability of money and (2) the excessive demand for goods and services which grows out of that availability.

Top policy makers, advisers and economic analysts everywhere have believed that a balanced budget along with credit restraint would be adequate tools for cooling the economy and for inducing the higher unemployment which, in their logic, would cure inflation.

Their orientation is succinctly reflected in this statement by a former chairman of the Council of Economic Advisers: "The plain fact is that the only way to deal adequately with inflation is through limits on Federal spending, higher taxes and tight money. And these restraints must be sufficiently stern and continued long enough to actually dampen the demand and slow the economy down." Ironically, major nations find themselves wedded to the brutal contention that balanced budgets and tight credit will cause the evil of unemployment to cure the evil of price inflation.

It is true that exuberant fiscal spending can by itself induce price inflation. It did so on a shocking scale in fiscal 1968 when the Federal government ran a twenty-five billion dollar deficit. That added fagots to the fire of inflation. But after the budget was put into balance, prices ran away nonetheless.

It is also true that an exuberant monetary policy of easy credit can even by itself induce price inflation. During 1967 and 1968, the Federal Reserve expanded its reserves to member banks at an 8.8% rate. And the money supply rose by twenty-seven billion dollars during those two years alone. In 1969 and 1970, both of the disruptive exuberances mentioned were calmed down, but inflation proceeded at a record rate regardless.

In free markets, where the relative strength of supply and demand determines prices, price inflation can occur when either physical supply or dollar demand changes quickly. Prices are especially apt to surge upward in response to large injections of new money into the spending streams of the nation.

During World War II, for example, the Federal government monetized billions of dollars of its debt obligations at the banks and spent this money in addition to the money that it obtained from taxes and from the borrowing of current income. Again, after the war, when civilian production resumed on a large scale, many American consumers spent billions of dollars out of their liquid savings in addition to what they spent out of current income. Then came Korea and Vietnam.

Most price inflation has historically been of the "demand-pull" kind, but price inflation can occur as a result of so-called cost-push too. It can result if pressure groups, with the aid of a servile government, lift business costs too rapidly.

Unfortunately, there are causal factors behind inflation which almost all analysts have disregarded. Those factors are our (1) legislated cost-push privileges; (2) a pervasive illusion among union members (and almost all other people) that corporate profits are several times higher than is employee compensation — and the unreasonableness that grows out of that illusion, and (3) the "permissive revolution" of the 1960's which makes unusable the Federal Reserve's tool of tight credit for restraining attempted price inflation.

The composite of the three causal factors just mentioned

has become an exogenous variable. It needs a thorough functional review. In order to understand how the three factors work and how they came to be, we must examine a few economic fundamentals and some institutional actions that Congress has resorted to over the years.

In order to insure business stability in every society in which workers sell the surplus of their specialty to someone else, it is necessary — as an overriding proposition in political economy — that each recipient of money income turn around and disburse it at about the same rate at which he receives it. Otherwise, one has unemployment for the difference. Also, the income generated by business activity should be so divided that the portion flowing to workers for consumption must be large enough to provide an adequate end market for the income that flows to money savers for investment. If this is not done, there will not be enough income to provide markets large enough to run profitably the capital facilities into which the money savers had put their money. Investment will stop and activity decline under such circumstances.

These two basic arrangements are not automatically assured by the laws and arrangements that envelop the bargaining powers in the market. And until about the 1930s — when legislative correctives were employed to reverse the situation — the bargaining power of the workers was drastically eroded and their share of the income generated reduced inequitably. (See Figure 1, page 12.)

Until checkbook money became dominant and commodity monies like silver, furs, tobacco and warehouse receipts (such as silver certificates) predominated, all monies had a preservation or ownership cost. It cost the owner some small sum merely to own it. This cost of protection needled the possessor to use it rather promptly before it whittled itself away. That pressure helped to maintain the community's aggregate monetary demand for goods and services. Under such conditions workers could also bargain very well in the labor market against the money savers and investors—their employers. These two basic arrangements have not, during recent decades, been automatically assured by the laws and rules that enveloped the market.

The change occurred because checkbook money possesses the characteristic of being a "sanctuary"—an island of safety—at which money recipients can stay without fear of much loss when they wish to slow down their disbursements and lengthen the interval between transactions.

Commodity money was in effect a "boomerang money" which placed a pressure on its holders to use it with adequate promptness as medium of exchange in buying something else. Checkbook money, in contrast, is "sanctuary money." (Chapters 4 and 5 described at length the subtle process by which the modern demand deposit acquired its tremendous store of value.)

The writer has tried to make clear that it was the introduction and use of sanctuary money that undermined the otherwise adequate bargaining power of employees with employers. But even if some other development had eroded that power, the fact of the matter is that drastic erosion did occur—as is shown in the chart, Annual Changes in Output and Wages in Manufacturing on page 12 and reproduced again here.

Note (Fig. 1 opp.) that average manufacturing wages were the same in 1930 as in 1920. Under such conditions profits were, of course, very large. Fortunately for business stability and employment, the profit recipients were on an investment binge, and all through the 1920's disbursed their profits for new plant and equipment. Unfortunately, however, the balance between investment and end market buying power was precarious. Because the income distribution of the 1920's did not adequately provide for synchronized growth in end market buying power needed to purchase the total output of the new plant and equipment, the economy

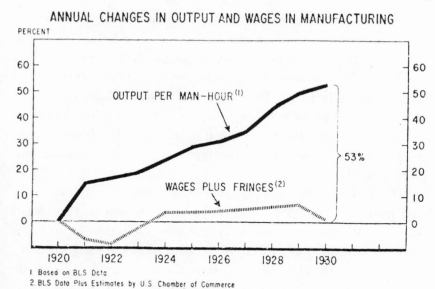

ANNUAL CHANGES IN OUTPUT AND WAGES IN MANUFACTURING

1 Based on BLS Data
2. BLS Data Plus Estimates by U.S Chamber of Commerce

Figure 1

was doomed to collapse. The collapse came in 1930. For a decade thereafter, the U.S. had between fifteen and twenty percent unemployed. (See Figure 3, page 15, Inflation Is Today's Price For Low Unemployment.) The distorted income distribution of the 1920's contributed heavily to the debacle of the 1930's.

A floundering public sensed during the 1930's that the workers had for a long time been shortchanged under the bargaining forces of the market place, but it did not understand the subtle monetary disrupter of the worker's bargaining power that had evolved in the free market. So instead of zeroing in on the excessive store of value of the monetary instrument, Congress tried to help the bargaining power of the worker with special legislation by granting him specific powers, privileges, and immunities.

The monopoly power of the unions developed largely as a pendulum reaction to the bargaining disadvantages that labor endured prior to the depression of the 1930's. But the labor union movement incorrectly diagnosed the reason for the workers' subnormal reward in the market place, and then drove single-mindedly for ever higher wage rates and special bargaining privileges. In so doing, it incidentally helped to generate continuous price inflation. The graphic frame of reference below helps to portray historically how wages, prices, money supply, velocity, and money creation are intertwined.

*Interdependence.* Wages, prices, money supply, velocity and money creation all intertwine. As shown in the chart, we are all consumer-workers (a) who sell our man-hours (b) to a firm (c) that produces goods and services. In return, we receive wages (d). We spend (e) these wages for the goods and services (f) turned out by producing firms. By exchanging man-hours for wages, we create an exchange ratio (g),

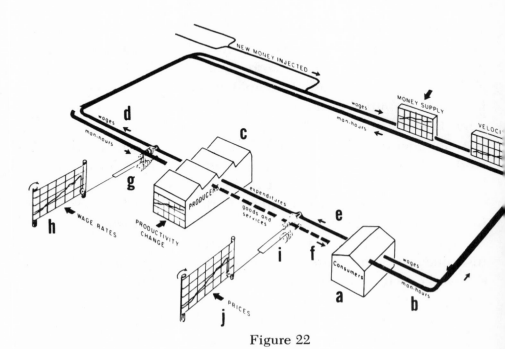

Figure 22

called the wage rate (h). Just as producing firms pay varying wages for man-hours of effort, so do they charge varying prices (i) for their goods and services. These varying charges, called market prices, are represented by (j).

In an effort to lower unit production costs and expand or maintain profit margins, most producers improve the efficiency and productivity of their establishments. During recent decades, U.S. producers have increased output per man-hour by about three percent per year.

Historically, as productivity and output have increased, the gains have usually been distributed, partly in lower prices, partly in higher wages and partly in larger profits. Figure 23 shows the trends during the 1920's.

Suppose employers increase the productivity of the man-hours employed and of all the other factors of production (sketched for simplicity in the chart on page 166) as con-

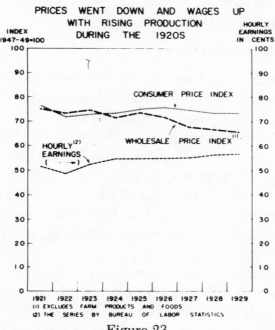

Figure 23

sisting of man-hours only) by three percent per year. There are three ways in which consumer-workers can participate in this improvement in productivity. Prices can be cut by, say, three percent a year, and the entire gain given to them in their roll as "consumers." Or prices can be left alone and wage rates increased by, say, three percent a year. Or prices can be cut by one and a half percent a year and wages increased by the same amount.

But what would happen if wage and other business costs were lifted by, say, six percent year after year, while the productivity gain remained at only three percent?

Since 1946, wage costs have risen much more rapidly than has efficiency. On the whole, the result has been that employers have had no efficiency cushion left after paying for wage increases, and have not usually been able to cut the prices of their goods. Instead, they have had to raise prices steadily in order to obtain a margin for profit. And, as we shall see, the banking system has been forced to dilute the money supply as a result.

## To Get a Larger Share

Both Congress and the public had been led by the universities and the unions to believe that collective bargaining and nationwide industrial unions could, if assisted by government, help workers get a larger portion of the income generated. So Congress passed the Norris-LaGuardia Act in 1932, the Wagner Act in 1935, the Walsh-Healy Act in 1936 and the Fair Labor Standards Act in 1938. Congress lavished rights, privileges, and immunities on the unions and exempted them from duties, liabilities, exposures, and responsibilities in general.

But even though the government helped the unions to increase their membership from 2,700,000 in 1933 to 8,700,000 in 1939, such grants of power were relatively worthless under the severe unemployment conditions of the 1930's.

With fifteen to twenty percent of all workers unemployed, the workers still had to bargain from their knees.

It was only when unemployment declined to the three to five percent level — under the vast government compensatory spending programs since World War II — that unions have been able to demand and obtain annual wage increases that far outrun productivity increases.

When Congress passed the Wagner Act in 1935, it in effect granted labor leaders the monopolistic privilege of combining, for bargaining purposes, local unions into large national unions, plus the privilege of shutting down or seriously inconveniencing the nation until they were awarded large wage rate increases. Through legislation, Congress in effect delegated to union leaders considerable sovereign price-fixing powers over the nation's wage rates.

This legislation was largely a pendulum reaction to the distress conditions that workers suffered during the 1930–1939 depression, when the possessors of money lowered their rate of use of money from about forty times a year in 1928 to about twenty-five times per year in 1933. (See Figure 5, page 19.)

Economists, politicians, and labor leaders did not understand the real cause of the workers' distressed condition. So instead of correcting the causal monetary situation, they turned to political power. They resorted to wage rate lifting via labor union pressure. This was a social tragedy of a very high order.

When unions use their great work-stoppage powers to raise wage rates by, say, about five to eight percent per year — and when employers can increase their productivity by only about 3 percent — the latter are obviously unable to reduce the selling prices of their goods. In fact, if they are to maintain their usual profit margins, they must try to recoup the new excessive wage costs by hiking their prices.

But the employers' recourse to price hikes of this kind

raises a monetary issue that usually goes undiscussed: The recouping process can work only if the nation's money supply is continuously increased.

The routine — maintained from the end of World War II until 1964 — of lifting wage costs by about four and a half percent a year, buffering the rise with a three percent annual increase in productivity, and then lifting selling prices by about one and a half percent a year, worked only because the nation's money supply also was increased so much that the majority of consumers could obtain enough additional money to buy the goods at the new and ever rising prices.

It is obvious that if wages and prices are doubled over a period of decades, the nation must as a practical matter also double its money supply. Otherwise a vast number of consumers will be priced out of the market. Only if that portion of price increases that outruns productivity increases is "validated" by adequate increases in the nation's money supply will modern leapfrog inflation be prevented from dampening the overall demand for goods and from bringing on unemployment.

It follows, therefore, that for the nation to be tolerant of cost increases that outrun productivity increases, and then to insist occasionally on credit policies that prevent prices from rising, is to imperil the very survival of what is left of the free enterprise system.

So long as business costs are administered upward by legislative and union pressure more rapidly than productivity goes up, we have no choice but to roll with the punches and to accept some price inflation in the hope that we will eventually come to understand how to increase workers' bargaining strength without invoking governmentalism and monopoly unionism. This is one of the basic situations with which this book attempts to deal.

By passing the Employment Act of 1946, Congress made it difficult to restrain unions. The act helped to destroy the possibility of using the particular restraint on wage hikes which increases in unemployment might otherwise exercise. Congress in effect told the unions that it would resort to any number of programs to pick up unemployment, however caused. By doing this—after granting unions enough power in the 1930's to bludgeon industry into granting annual wage rate increases of five to ten percent—Congress made the nation vulnerable to an inflationary process far more powerful than exuberant fiscal and monetary policy.

In addition, Congress' legislation in the 1960's emphasized permissiveness, tolerance, and appeasement of wrongdoing, while at the same time it increased the number of recipients of government largess to seventy-two million people. These recipients with their votes have tremendous political power. By means of protests, demonstrations, sit-ins, riots, etc., they often induce legislators to approve fiscal measures which negate the possibility of the Federal Reserve cooling the economy to the six or seven percent unemployment rate needed to restrain excessive wage increases. (See Fig. 25, page 177.) The tool of inducing an unemployment rate of adequate size to dampen price inflation—a tool which the Federal Reserve was able to use successfully in 1957–1958 was not therefore usable, for example, in 1969–1970—as almost all economic analysts had premised that it would be.

Court decisions of the 1960's also showed an overriding concern for the miscreant. Weak law enforcement characterized the decade. All three U.S. attorney generals of the 1960's took appeasement positions. One even tried to testify in Judge Hoffman's Chicago court in 1970 in favor of the "Chicago Seven" who were dedicated to the destruction of the judicial process.

*The above composite of 1930 laws and 1960 pressure tactics and tolerance of lawbreaking go practically undiscussed as a cause of inflation.* Now that fiscal and monetary restraint have been tried and found wanting, however, the public is beginning to suspect that unrestrained demands for government aid, and excessive union power in particular, are the long-term inflationary forces. That realization will spread, and Congress will have to face up to the actions and attitudes of the 1930's and 1960's which are having their belated impact today. Although earlier Congresses were the ones guilty of giving unions the power to vote themselves quart drinks out of pint bottles, it is up to the current Congress to put the cork back in the bottle.

Unfortunately, Congress has boxed itself in and cannot easily zero in on those institutional causes of price inflation which persist after both exuberant fiscal and monetary policy has been becalmed. First, union power has been permitted to freewheel even in periods when fiscal and monetary restraints were relied on to cool the economy. Second, Congress has provided for the steady transfer to lower income groups of large portions of income which the well-to-do are able to obtain under the lopsided bargaining rules that still envelop the market. It is through progressive income taxes that government takes billions of dollars of personal income from the rich and disburses it bureaucratically — by way of transfer payments — to the poor and the distressed.

The workers' weak position of the 1930's has, of course, turned full circle, which Figure 3 (page 15) brought out. As noted, union pressure for higher wages, along with special group pressure for fiscal expansion, have been intensified under the institutional arrangements set up by the New Economics since World War II. The key arrangements were: The Employment Act of 1946; retention of the progressive income tax legislation of 1942; the egalitarian programs of the 1960's; the government as "employer of last resort"; the 1960's tolerance of violence; the massive employment programs, such as urban renewal, demonstration cities, "health, education and welfare," interstate highways, antipollution, and flights to the moon. The net result has been that powers kindheartedly given to organized labor during the 1930's — and of negligible value to them at that time — are diabolically effective today. They are effective because government spending programs, along with public attitudes, assure such a tight labor market that the unions can demand and obtain wage increases that far outrun productivity increases.

Meanwhile, legislators and law enforcement officials also expand the strike privileges of union members, grant them unemployment benefits while they strike, and assure them of no punishment if they break the laws and contracts which forbid the strikes.

Even government workers have been permitted to strike in recent years, despite the fact that federal, state, and local governments expressly forbid it. Title 5, Section 7311 of the U.S. Code states:

> An individual may not accept or hold a position in the government of the United States . . . if he participates in a strike, or asserts the right to strike against the government of the United States . . . or is a member of an organization of employees of the government of the United States . . . that he knows asserts the right to strike against the government of the United States.

Title 18, Section 1918 of the U.S. Code states:

> Whoever violates the provision of Section 7311 of Title 5 . . . shall be fined not more than $1,000 or imprisoned not more than one year and a day or both. . . .

But lawbreaking by government workers is tolerated everywhere. In all lands academic and government leaders believe — or give lip service to the view — that collective bargaining and nationwide industrial unions are desirable. They have all given unions the privilege of increasing wage rates faster than productivity and allowed them to strike against the government. All have experienced inflation as a result. Afraid politically to tackle the problem head-on and to reduce the union privileges legislatively, they rationalize and maintain that restrictive fiscal and monetary policies will do the trick. So they adopt policies that slow the growth of their economies. When unemployment rises noticeably, however, they quickly resume exuberant (or at least accommodating) fiscal and monetary policies in order "to get their economies going again."

## A World-Wide Disease

Governments label their restrictive programs differently. Britain has an "income policy," France an "austerity" program, Germany a "stabilization" program, and the United States a "game plan." All of them try periodically to contract activity and employment in efforts to restrain the unions from exercising all the power that they kindheartedly gave them in the past and now lack the nerve to reduce. The U.S., like all the rest, has caught the Fabian disease of

### Prices in Major OECD Countries[1]

|  | 1958-1968 Average | 1969 | 1970 |
|---|---|---|---|
| United States | 2.1 | 4.7 | 5-¼ |
| Canada | 2.5 | 4.7 | 4 |
| Japan | 4.5 | 4.5 | 5-¾ |
| France | 4.0 | 6.9 | 5-½ |
| Germany | 2.8 | 3.5 | 7 |
| Italy | 2.5 | 4.1 | 6-¼ |
| United Kingdom | 3.1 | 5.1 | 6 |
| Total of above excluding U.S. | 3.7 | 4.8 | 6 |

[1] GNP/GDP deflator

Source: OECD Economic Outlook, December 1970

Figure 24

governmentalism. The light at the end of the tunnel is far away.

## A Silly Routine

The inflation process is a silly procedure. In my 1962 book, *Money In Motion,* I wrote:

> To understand the process of wage-push inflation—under a do-nothing policy about using sanctuary money—we must understand its several sequential steps:
>
> First, is the legislation that grants to union leaders the privilege of aggregating the bargaining power of all the local unions of an industry into one big monopoly so that leaders can bargain for all the local unions at one time.
>
> Second, is the government denial of adequate police protection to plants and workers who might try—as is their privilege under the law—to operate their plants when the union leaders withdraw the union workers.
>
> Third, is the union insistence on wage rate increases that outrun productivity increases.
>
> Fourth, is the employers' recouping of the new excessive costs by raising prices.
>
> Fifth, is the insistence by Congress and the Federal Reserve that, even though the government helps wages and other costs to rise faster than the productivity increases, prices must not rise because of the damage that price inflation inflicts upon the economy. The Federal Reserve Authorities then check the money supply by constricting bank reserves in order to prevent the money supply from increasing to "validate" the employers' higher prices.
>
> Sixth, is the contraction in the demand for goods that tight money induces, production then contracts, followed by unemployment, public fear and distress.
>
> Seventh, are the panicky efforts of Congress to relieve the unemployment by sponsoring public works programs, relief programs and subsidy programs.
>
> Eighth, is the resort—by deficit financing at the banks—to pay for the sudden expansion of government spending. Congress, using the Employment Act of 1946 as its justification,

throws monetary restraint to the wind, steam-rollers the
Federal Reserve's wishes and monetizes tremendous sums of
government securities.

Ninth, is the belated effort of the Federal Reserve to relieve
the induced unemployment by easing credit for private activity
through open market operations and the lowering of reserve
requirements.

It is a silly cycle. But it will continue so long as Congress
permits money-loitering, does not scale down the privileges
to union leaders which enable them to raise wage rates excessively.

Until annual wage increases are no larger than the annual
productivity increases will we have periodic credit restraint,
periodic unemployment and tardy boosts in the money supply.
Politically, the Federal Reserve is too weak to maintain credit
restraint in the face of severe unemployment. At such times
Congress pushes the Federal Reserve aside and resorts to
deficit bank borrowing.

As policy the Federal Reserve should loudly proclaim the
unfair position that excessive wage-cost increases place it in.
It should blare to the nation that if cost increases exceed
productivity increases, the economy will grind to a halt unless
the money supply is increased to validate the induced price
rises.

Insistence on price stability by Congress, the Administration and the public while all three supinely tolerate both
tardy reuse of money income and wage cost increases that
outrun productivity increases is to invite first the closing of
plants and unemployment, and then deficit financing as an
attempted means for undoing the damage.

The whole effort of Congress and the public to divert a
larger share of current income to the low income workers
by means of "collective union bargaining" and excessive cost
lifting is a fruitless approach. It leads inevitably to steady
price inflation, to tortuous interpretations and violations of
law and to expanded governmentalism. Not until Congress and
the public nullify the privilege to disburse income tardily
will the low income workers genuinely increase their bargaining power and share of a genuinely larger national output.
Only then will price inflation end, the pie get rapidly larger

and the worker and entrepreneur receive a portion of that reward which now goes as a bribe to money savers for not loitering in the markets.

Monetary and fiscal authorities will neither quantify their estimate of how much unemployment it will take to restrain price inflation, nor state how much unemployment they are willing to tolerate before they ease their restrictive policies. Historic U.S. data could have guided them.

Figure 25 shows vividly how unemployment rates in the U.S. during past years affected the wage rate increases and the Consumer Price Index. It shows that when the U.S. unemployment rate is less than about six percent, American workers are able to obtain annual wage rate increases that far outrun the increases in man-hour productivity. Seemingly union workers have the opportunity to use their vast powers irresponsibly only when the labor market is tight enough to

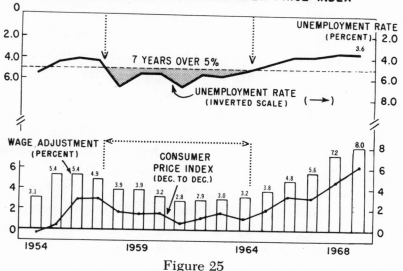

Figure 25

hold the unemployment rate below five and one-half percent to six and one-half percent.

Unemployment rates during the six year period 1958–1964 throws light on the restraining power that unemployment as such has on the rates of increase of wages and prices. The unemployment rate hovered between five and five tenths percent and seven and four tenths percent during those years. That rate acted as a tremendously effective restraint on the cost-push process. The average annual union wage increase was only three and one half percent over that six year period. Because the increases in output per man-hour during those years buffered most of that rise in labor costs, the average annual rise in the Consumer Price Index was only one and four tenths percent. Americans felt that they could live with that much inflation.

## How the Pie Was Sliced

The chart, How Claims Of Recipients Of U.S. Output Have Changed, shows how gross national product, as measured in current dollars, has changed since 1929. It shows how much went to all the factor groups that contributed to production. The chart shows the whole history of income distribution so vividly that readers can see for themselves the relative rewards that over a long period of years have gone to wages, salaries, and benefits on the one hand, and to corporate profits on the other.

It is clear that since about 1965 the portion for "corporate profits after taxes" has been relatively flat. The portion for wages, salaries and benefits, in contrast, has been escalating rapidly. Despite this verifiable record, the nation has been systematically heavily propagandized that "profits inflation" is the root cause of the price increases of recent years.

The AFL-CIO News on January 31, 1970, for example, editorialized: "Profits, rather than wages, are the culprits in the current inflation. The time has come to explode the myth of the wage-price spiral."

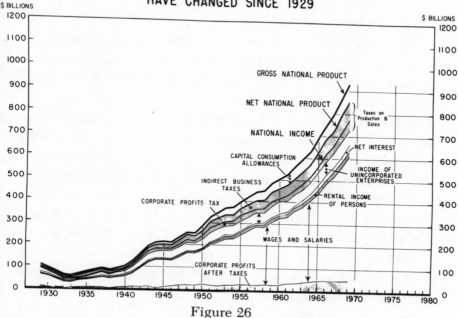

HOW THE CLAIMS OF PARTICIPANTS TO U.S. OUTPUT HAVE CHANGED SINCE 1929

Figure 26

Because monetary restraint will not be permitted by the public to induce the high unemployment rate needed to reduce labor's high wage demands, and because our inflation has its roots in the cost-push process which has the egalitarianism and permissiveness of the 1960's as its accomplice, the control of inflation, if it is to be undertaken at all, now becomes an educational project which the Administration and U.S. corporations themselves will have to carry out.

By now it is clear that price inflation is a built-in feature of the U.S. system because of a composite of three situations:

1. The awesome power and immunities of organized labor.
2. Lax law enforcement and public tolerance of pressure tactics by both labor unions and recipients of government largesse.

3. The illusion, harbored by almost all Americans, that corporate profits are many times as large a percentage of corporate income generated as is actually the case.

The permissive revolution of the 1960's, when added to the revolutionary labor legislation of the 1930's, has now made it impossible to use again the restraints on inflation used during, say, 1958–1964.

We have now lived through two recessions that did not grow out of serious unbalances and excesses in the private economy, but grew out of a credit garroting that was based on a mistaken analysis. During those periods the Administration did not review the role of disruptive labor legislation, riots, and demonstrations. It merely relied with blind faith on an inadequate monetary theory. The unanimity among monetary authorities at the time merely attested to the extent to which institutional economics was ignored in favor of simplistic monetary theory.

Since we are doomed to have price inflation during the next few years regardless of what is done about fiscal and monetary restraint, the awful choice now is between inflation accompanied by more pointless garroting and recession and inflation accompanied by an accommodating monetary policy that permits relatively full employment.

If inflation is to be licked at all, it will be done by resort to a recourse which the monetary authorities do not currently even discuss. (This recourse will be taken up in Chapter 14.)

The "cost-push" process has by now become an exogenous variable — that is, a factor originating outside the economic system — on the American scene. Suppose that the facts of today are these: that nothing less than a continuous six percent rate of unemployment can prevent unions from obtaining annual wage increases of, say, seven or eight percent. Suppose also that the public, our legislators, and our monetary authorities do not have the emotional strength to endure six percent unemployment without resuming again the expansion of the money supply and federal relief expenditures.

## Unions Call the Tune

If that is so, then this sequence takes over: Armed with the power to impose partial general strikes in key industries like autos, railroads, steel, etc., and to pepper the whole nation with local wildcat strikes, unions are able to call the tune on U.S. cost-price policy. Fiscal and monetary policies merely dance to that tune.

The rules of the free market could be modified so that the income that flows to workers primarily for consumption would be continuously large enough to provide an end market for the portion that flows to the money savers for investment. Since this is very unlikely to be done, we shall probably have to learn to live with price inflation until we have the wit and wisdom to repair the free market mechanism so well that the laws and rules that envelop the bargaining in its markets automatically stabilize the aggregate private monetary demand for goods and services at high levels and, at the same time, automatically distribute pretax income more equitably.

Today, economic analysts everywhere take an unfair advantage of the Federal Reserve authorities. The laws and rules in which our legislators have enveloped the economy have brought on continuous price inflation. Now that it is here, the Federal Reserve is being asked to correct the situation. That is patently unfair. The Federal Reserve should blare to the nation that there is a limit to the amount of unwise and disruptive legislation that Congress can pass and then expect the Federal Reserve to correct its evil results. Legislation brought on the current mess. Then Congress passed the buck to the Federal Reserve. And as of now, the Federal Reserve is the fall guy.

## The Fed's Proper Role

The Federal Reserve should proclaim to the nation that its proper function is not to act as a gyroscopic stabilizer of prices and business stability that have been thrown into turmoil by poor legislation. The Federal Reserve was set up and beautifully designed to provide for the monetary needs of the nation. It was not designed to provide specifically for price stability. While its design is such that it can — with an exuberant credit policy — induce both boom and price inflation, and also can, with a garroting credit policy, induce both depression and price deflation, it was not designed primarily to do either. But as it is, Congress, the courts and the Federal administrators ladle out powers, privileges, and immunities to many groups in the economy and then reduce the normal restraints on their demands and behavior. Afterwards, Congress expects the Federal Reserve to put the economy back on an even keel.

The monetary powers of the Federal Reserve are tremendous. In theory it could constrict and reduce the money supply to the point where it could force the economy into a big recession and even into a level of unemployment like that of the 1930's. But that is not its proper function. Nor is it even its proper function to cool the economy to that level of unemployment that would check cost-push inflation.

## Doomed to Failure

Today, the Federal Reserve is asked to do this in a climate of anarchy and lawlessness. The permissiveness and disruptive behavior which Congress, the courts, the colleges, the press and the TV have fanned during the 1960's has made it impractical for the Federal Reserve to impose again the heavy corrective unemployment tactics that it used in 1957. Consequently, the Federal Reserve's efforts of 1969–1970 have failed — and were doomed to fail — even at the very beginning when the "game plan" for restraining inflation was first announced.

Can nothing then be done? The next two chapters present two recourses: How price inflation can be basically and permanently overcome (a rather long-term project), and how price inflation can be seriously *dampened* under a crash program without a legislative cancelling of the unwarranted privileges of the unions, without wage and price controls, and without inducing unemployment rates in the five to seven percent range.

# Chapter 13

## How to Overcome Price Inflation Permanently

*Corrective Labor Legislation Is Also Needed to Forestall Cost-Push Inflation under Full Employment Conditions*

If aggregate private monetary demand were lifted and stabilized at higher levels — by either of the two monetary methods recommended in the previous chapters, and full employment and strong bargaining power for individual workers were assured by the new working rules — there would be no justification for the many special monopoly and disruptive privileges that Congress has given to the labor unions. The new milieu would provide more real income to the workers than unionism could ever give them. Under full employment conditions it would clearly be out of order to continue to give to the unions those special monopoly powers, privileges, immunities, and liberties which enable them to raise wage rates more rapidly than productivity increases.

If we modify the monetary laws and rules that envelop the bargaining in the market between labor and capital so the workers, through bargaining, get a functional and equitable share of the income generated, we will have repaired the key defect of Capitalism, as we have known it. And we will have obsoleted the presumed role of labor unions as a means for lifting the income of workers. Moreover, by providing for a curative Welfare Market we will also have obsoleted a presumed justification for the Welfare State.

If special union privileges were terminated, the nation's annual gains from increases in productivity would probably again be diverted to the people, partly in the form of lower prices to consumers, and partly in the form of higher wages to the workers.

If we changed our operating rules so that employers were always bidding for workers under nonbludgeoning conditions, instead of workers always bidding for jobs, we would be providing workers with more job security and real bargaining power at each local job and firm than they had ever had before. Under such conditions, we should alter those rules in equity pertaining to collective bargaining which now enable national labor unions to inflict inflation upon the nation.

The proposals presented here would continuously provide workers with a more stable demand for their services and with real confidence that there would always be a continuing demand for their services over the long term. Consequently, if either of the proposals in Chapter 7 were put into operation, it would be desirable — after the new plans had proved their effectiveness for a few years — to repeal special U.S. labor legislation (the Norris–LaGuardia Act, the Wagner Act, etc.) that were passed in efforts to help the working man to bargain more effectively. If that were not done, after aggregate private monetary demand for all labor had been rigorously provided for, continuation of monopoly privileges for labor unions would enable them to impose price inflation upon the nation.

In order to cancel or remove the unions' "wage-rate-fixing" powers, it would not be necessary to unravel one by one the many laws, court decisions, and labor board interpretations that have given the unions their vast monopoly powers. It could be done very simply.

If and when a carrying cost is imposed on the ownership of money, it would be advisable to stipulate simultaneously that if after, say, a four year period, total U.S. unemployment has been reduced to between two and two and one half million and held there for two full years, our courts will thereafter enforce only union contracts relating to wage rates and employment costs that are made between *local* employers and *local* labor unions, but will not enforce such contracts made between employers and unions with more than, say, 5,000 members. The wage rates of small local operations would closely reflect the worth of an employee's services in a free market, the second might not.

The government could also—if union stampedes are going on which lift annual wage rate increases by from 8% to 15% per year—decide not to protect union property, such as cash and pension funds, of those unions which extract increases of, say, over 6% per year. No bureaucratic enforcement machinery would be needed to make such an outlawing plan effective. The plan could be relied on until the more basic plan of Chapter 14 is in force.

Congress would not be driven periodically by the unemployment that arises when increases in business costs outrun productivity increases to resort to deficit financing through the banks. For the government does this now mainly to provide enough more money in the economy so it can move the nation's output at the new and higher prices made necessary by excessive cost increases.

An ownership cost on money would cause the nation's money savers to accelerate their search for those entrepreneurs who can use their funds most profitably, and cause entrepreneurs in their turn to seek and bid for those workers who can help them with their projects. In order to hold and attract their workers under such conditions, employers would be under continuous pressure to bid for workers and to be as generous to them as their competitors make necessary, or as their revenues permit. The labor union movement as we now know it—spurious as it is in logic for improving the workers' standard of living, and often ruthless in its means— would be a thing of the past.

The termination of the money saver's opportunity to slow down his use of money, and of the labor union's privilege to dominate both the worker's wage rates and his right to work, could be terminated simultaneously. The two big evils which have distorted the free market system would thus be gone. Such terminations could be achieved by the simple recourse of the government's modifying two types of contracts which today it is willing to enforce. Such action would also remove the government from its hopeless administrative concern with both wage rates and union operations on the one hand, and from its other awesome chore of trying to shore up demand (after hoarding privileges have first been extended).

## Price Inflation Would Cease

Price inflation, as well as periodic unemployment, would be a thing of the past if one of the new plans were adopted. Prices rise—other things being equal—when production is low and goods are in short supply, when the dollar demand rises either because more money is being created and put into circulation, or because of a faster rate of use of the existing money.

The intensified demand for goods which is proposed under both Proposals 1 and 2 above would of course—other things again being equal—raise prices at first, but only if the existing production facilities were already fully in use. If they were not, then the intensified demand would bring forth more output and a slow upward pressure on prices.

But even under these conditions there would be a limit to

tarists face up to or deal realistically with the goliath power of the labor unions, which has been institutionalized during recent decades. Several major developments have come to pass: The privilege of union organizations to operate as national unions, compulsory union membership, "collective bargaining," public tolerance of massive use of union funds to influence political elections, and compensatory spending.

When federal spending rises from the five billion dollar per year rate of the 1930s to over the 250 billion dollar per year rate of today, political candidates and policy makers are naturally tempted to use their discretion over vast dollar disbursements to win the endorsement of both union members and recipients of government largess.

Keynes seemingly did not foresee developments under which officials were driven to be permissive and meek when faced with militant and lawbreaking demands of the millions of Americans receiving government checks — who, as policy, simply demand more and more. Permissiveness, weak law enforcement, and accommodating expansion of the money supply are built-in features of the fiscal approach. Inflation has been practically ignored by the fiscalists, not as a hazard, but as a functional, built-in component of compensatory spending.

The monetarists, unlike the Keynesians, have been deeply concerned over inflation. But they have an unrealistic and myopic approach for overcoming and preventing it. Grant that restraining the growth of the money supply to about three percent per year (or to the rate of increase in real national output) would eliminate inflation. But such restraint is based on two or three institutionally unrealistic premises. One is that such tightness will cause enough unemployment — as began to happen in 1965–67 and in 1969–70 — to bring down the cost-push demands of the unions to a bearable two to three percent per year rate.

The other premise is that the economy would continue

to operate at full speed indefinitely with no increase in unemployment even though deferrable money would continue to be relied on to maintain an adequate private monetary demand. There is the further premise, too, that if unemployment increases as a result of a contraction in the rate of growth of the money supply to only three percent per year, the unemployment would be endured by our protesters long enough for reasonableness to enter the wage demands of workers and union leaders. The institutionalized laws and privileges of today make such premises very unrealistic.

The thesis of this book constitutes a counterrevolution. The composite of theories of the post World War II period — each inadequate because of its blindness to the disruptive role that debt-obligation money plays in societies of specialized workers — has failed to stop the Juggernaut of governmentalism. This book sets itself against the theories of the Keynesian fiscalists; the Friedmanite monetarists; the inadequacies of the Marshallian equilibrium approach; the mathematical formulations with their loose institutional premises; and the noninstitutionalism of the Austrian marginal utility school. All of these approaches premise that it is acceptable to continue to use a form of debt obligation as money which I maintain is functionally disruptive.

Our times have reached a moment of truth. All the accepted orthodoxies are ludicrously incapable of meeting the realities of today. One outstanding champion of the free market system, for example, in apparent frustration, even recommends a program of "negative income taxes" and of dispensing the revenues to the bottom income groups. Another well-known economist — at the other end of the intellectual spectrum — simply disparages both the reality of competition and the need for seasoned corporate managers, gives up on the free market system, and, like a nonschooled person, simply advocates "mandatory wage and price controls."

It is patently clear that prevailing orthodoxies cannot solve the social and economic problems of our time. This book hopefully presents a recourse that accepts many valid elements of traditional theory, and then attempts—by means of a unique analytical tool—to point the way to solving those problems.

Despite the fact that both the fiscalists and monetarists sponsor inadequate approaches for overcoming inflation, for example; and despite the fact that Congressmen are today politically too weak to curtail union power with remedial legislation, there is something very practical that can be done, even under the warped institutional conditions of the 1970's. There is a recourse which the accepted authorities and opinion makers do not even discuss. The next chapter reviews it.

# Chapter 14

## We Can Restrain Inflation without Controls

D ESPITE the fact that the analysis of inflation in Chapter 12 is institutionally very pessimistic, there does exist a realistic recourse for *dampening* inflation. It is a recourse that receives practically no publicity. Fortunately, it does not involve wage and price control, new labor legislation, or resort to the damper of additional unemployment. It involves education in a completely overlooked area. It is, moreover, a recourse that has been successfully tested in two major U.S. corporations.

The educational procedures employed in those two companies went on slowly but tenaciously for many years. In this chapter, I wish to present an ingenious means for carrying out swiftly the education which in the past took a long time to effect. The method employed is easily comprehended by laymen. It is both quantitative and self-substantiating, and has the great merit of instilling belief instantaneously.

### Political Unacceptability of Monetary and Fiscal Restraint

Tight credit and lower federal spending during 1957–1958 had checked the price inflation of 1955–1957 by lowering production and raising unemployment from a 4% rate in 1957 to 7.4% in 1958. But by 1969, institutional priorities in the U.S. had changed so drastically that the inflation control procedures of the earlier period had become politically unacceptable for use in 1969–1970.

By 1965–1969, the political power of unions and of the recipients of government largess had grown so much that higher unemployment rates, ten percent surtaxes, and cutbacks in federal spending became politically unacceptable. The power balance in the economy had shifted. The recourse which had worked so well in 1957–1958 could not be used again. As Figure 27 shows, the "First Year Wage Rate Increases In All Industries," for example, which rose from a 3.2% rate in 1964 to a 7.2% rate in 1968, kept right on going upward during the game-plan period to an 8% rate in 1969, an 11.7% rate in 1970, and to an 11.6% rate in 1971.

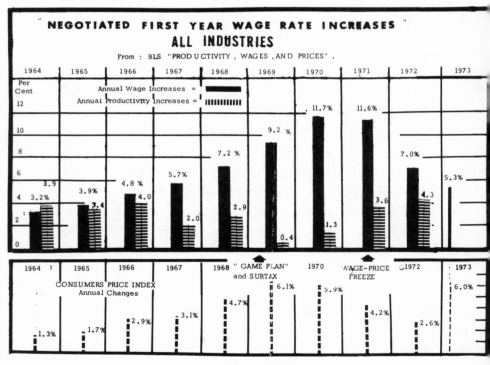

Figure 27

By that time, a stampede of wage demands, militancy and permissiveness seemed to be on in both unionized fields and in federal, state, and local government. By December 7, 1970, Arthur Burns, chairman of the Federal Reserve Board, said that the type of inflation under way was of a kind that could not be stopped by fiscal and monetary restraints alone. Yet something had to be done. So on August 15, 1971, President Nixon invoked wage and price controls.

The whole plan was, of course, a desperate gamble. It jeopardized the very incentive machinery of the institutions that had brought the U.S. to affluence. And yet the Administration's gamble seemed to pay off.

Phase I of the freeze was for ninety days. Phase II was to continue until inflation was brought down to tolerable levels. No bureaucratic planned society was contemplated—the aim was only to break up the psychological stampede.

The inflationary process since 1965 seems to have contained such a stampede factor. Other factors, of course, were also powerful. Historically, labor legislation may have given national unions excessive power and immunities; the banking system may have provided a vastly excessive supply of money; the public may have tolerated beyond reason illegal strikes by public servants; and Congress may have been far too ready to disburse payouts to organized pressure groups and to carry on a spending spree for far too many "priority" programs during a time of war. But while such situations had their impact, almost everyone's attitude came to be "to get mine while the getting is good."

To the extent that such an attitude had been built up, "temporary" controls did have a dampening effect. They cooled the greed factor which had reached stampede proportions.

But what will the Administration do that will have long-term effectiveness? Fortunately, there is something realistic and startling that it can do.

*Massive Illusion about Profits*

Union members naturally bargain "for all that the traffic will bear." Unfortunately, as surveys of American opinion show, the statistical illiteracy of union members (and of the whole American public for that matter) is such that they generally believe that corporate profits are routinely far larger than total "Wages and Benefits." *NAM Reports* of April 19, 1971, published a 1969 survey made by the Opinion Research Corporation in which a cross section of Americans were asked what they thought the distribution of available corporate income was in 1968 between employee compensation and net profit. The average answer was that of that income which is left after paying taxes and other costs (and thus available for taking care of payroll and

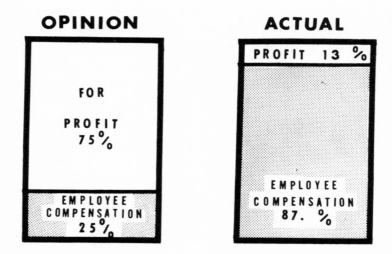

**OPINION**

FOR

PROFIT
75%

EMPLOYEE
COMPENSATION
25%

**ACTUAL**

PROFIT   13 %

EMPLOYEE
COMPENSATION
87. %

OPINION OF AMERICANS POLLED IN 1969 WAS THAT EMPLOYEES OF
U. S. CORPORATIONS RECEIVE ONLY 25% OF THE INCOME THAT IS
DIVIDED BETWEEN EMPLOYEE COMPENSATION AND PROFIT. THE
FACTS ARE THAT IN 1968 EMPLOYEES RECEIVED 87.2% OF THE
INCOME THAT WAS DIVIDED BETWEEN THEM AND SHAREHOLDERS.

* Opinion survey as reported by Opinion Research Corporation.

Figure 28

profit) profit gets seventy-five percent and employee compensation twenty-five percent.

The illusion is worldwide that the percentage going to profit is larger than the percentage going to payroll. The illusion has been systematically fostered by labor unions, leftist teachers, and Communist and Socialist writings. In South America, where data is scarce, the Communists have so successfully instilled the belief that the profit-payroll split in U.S. corporations is eighty percent–twenty percent that most South Americans fervently believe that almost all U.S. corporations are "exploiters." They chant "Yankee Go Home," and, as we know, increasingly expropriate Yankee petroleum, copper and other facilities. Against such beliefs, multibillion dollar Latin American aid programs turn out to be very ineffective.

In his recent book, *Dividing The Wealth,* Dr. Howard E. Kershner reports how surveys of public opinion in fifteen of the largest cities of the world regarding how that particular portion of U.S. corporation income (which is available for profit and payroll) is divided between owners and employees. In none of the cities did the respondents believe that the profit portion was less than sixty percent.*

## How Such Hard-to-believe Ideas Came About

An almost unbelievable dereliction in education on income distribution has historically occurred. And it is still occurring in our schools, in our corporate annual reports, and in our government releases.

Americans have been forced to fly blind regarding the ratio of profit to payroll. Few people know what that split is, and they do not know where they can lay their hands on the necessary statistical information. Textbooks, corporate annual reports, and government releases do not show in

---

* Howard E. Kershner, *Dividing The Wealth* (Old Greenwich: Devin-Adair, 1971, pp. 13–20).

easy juxtaposition profit-payroll comparisons. Corporate
profits and corporate "wages and benefits" are reported in
separate publications by government agencies. Percentage
comparisons are missing. They have been missing for
generations. Under such conditions, it has been easy for
critics of our economic system to convince people that employment costs are a niggardly portion of the pie available
for distribution—and that profits are unconscionably high.

*The Facts*

"Corporate profits after taxes," as reported by the Department of Commerce, averaged about forty billion dollars
during 1961–1970; corporate profits as a percent of the total
income generated by corporations averaged about 11%
during 1961–1970; and profits as a percent of sales in manufacturing averaged about 4.1% during 1961–1970.

The profit percentage hovers between ten percent and
fourteen percent year after year, and employment costs

**SEVEN YEAR COMPARISON
BETWEEN PROFIT & PAYROLL**
*(In Billions)*

| PROFITS | PERCENT FOR PROFITS | PERCENT FOR PAYROLL | COMPENSATION |
|---------|---------------------|---------------------|--------------|
| 1964 $38.4 | 14.2 | 85.8% | $231.4 |
| 1965 $46.5 | 15.7 | 84.3% | $249.0 |
| 1966 $49.9 | 15.4 | 84.6% | $275.5 |
| 1967 $46.6 | 13.7 | 86.3% | $291.8 |
| 1968 $48.2 | 13.0 | 87.0% | $319.2 |
| 1969 $48.5 | 12.2 | 87.8% | $349.7 |
| 1970 $43.8 | 10.7 | 89.3% | $365.6 |

**SOURCE: U.S. DEPT. OF COMMERCE**
Figure 29

between eighty-six percent and ninety percent. Figure 29 (opp.) highlights the stability of the percentage over a series of recent years for all U.S. corporations.

One can easily check on the prevalence and degree of ignorance about this ratio between payroll and profit. Ask, say, fifteen of your closest associates their opinion of what that ratio is. Unless they have worked deeply in the statistical field, they will not make even reasonable estimates. No publications have delineated the split for them.

Even college students are not knowledgeable on this matter. In 1971, the First National City Bank of New York asked a sampling of its employees, "How do you think that total wages compare with net profits for most business firms?"

Those who have never taken economics answered 55%.

Those who have taken some economics answered 49%.

The percentage split is a key issue that is argued about in almost all union bargaining negotiations. Yet one cannot find the percentage comparisons in textbooks or in corporate annual reports. Almost all corporations utilize a nondisclosive accounting convention which tends to mislead themselves and others.

### Corporate Accounting is Nondisclosive

In the intricacies of accounting there is also a very understandable explanation for the practical nonexistence of the percentage information. Confusion arises from the fact that corporate accountants usually relate corporate disbursements for major costs — such as payroll — to total corporate *sales revenue* and *not to what is left* after outside purchases and tax payments have been made.

Of their sales revenue U.S. corporations as a whole disburse about one half for materials, supplies, light, heat, power, etc., — items that they buy from outsiders. The other half they disburse to those who help them transform the purchased ingredients into their own unique products and services. After payroll, state, and local taxes, interest and federal income taxes are paid out, the net percentage for profit is about ten to fourteen percent.

## All Corporate Purchases from Suppliers Become in the End Mainly Payroll and Profit

All the payments of the single firm to others for materials and supplies turn eventually into (factor) income payments, too—such as rent, profit, wages, interest and taxes. Failure to emphasize that most of the disbursements to suppliers also ends up as payroll causes it to appear that outpayments to employees are only in the range of twenty-five to thirty percent to sales, rather than eighty to ninety percent of what there is to divide between payroll and profit.

Auditing firms, in preparing corporate annual reports, relate payroll—when they report it at all—to total sales. (About one half of *Fortune's* list of the 500 largest U.S. manufacturing corporations do not disclose the payroll in their annual reports.)

Even the occasional "pie chart" depictions of a corporation's disbursements to payroll do not help much. They too implicitly relate payrolls to total sales revenue (which is usually shown as 360 degrees of a big circle), and not to what is left to the corporation for payment to the combination of payroll and profit after the corporation has paid its large outside costs such as for supplies and taxes.

For example, the press sometimes reports how very large salaries and bonuses are often paid to corporate officers. Because such payments are included in the total employee compensation figure, critics may believe that the compensation to officers accounts for a large portion of the total. But compared to the total payment to employees and to total sales revenue, that compensation is almost infinitesimal.

For General Motors, the figures recently were as follows:

|  | 1970 | 1969 |
|---|---|---|
|  | ($ millions) | |
| Total worldwide payrolls:<br>(From the Annual Report) | $6,259.8 | $6,928.3 |
| Total Salaries, fees and bonuses of<br>officers and directors. (About sixty<br>men). | $5.2 | $15.0 |
| Amounts paid to all officers and<br>directors as percent of total. | 0.08% | 0.22% |

Seldom do top salaries plus bonuses in the large corporations amount to as much as one percent of total employee compensation.

Advertisements also tend to mislead people about the size of profits. A barrage of advertising offers merchandise at twenty-five percent off, fifty percent off, etc. People reason that, since no one is in business for his health, prices must be providing for adequate profit despite the big markdowns.

## Corporate Annual Reports Usually Bury the Payroll Figures

The corporate auditors' practice of combining in their annual reports most of the corporate payroll with the corporation's outside costs for supplies, etc., in their annual reports and then relating that sum to total sales revenue buries the payroll figure. The sample table below illustrates how it is done.

By burying the payroll figure in the "Cost of Products Sold" entry, or combining most of the company's payroll costs with the payments to other businesses for supplies, power, etc., corporations do not let the employees, public or stockholders get a realistic picture of the large percentage that wages and benefits are of that dollar value that corporations add to the ingredients that they purchase — that is, to the "value that they add" by their activity. So the public guesses that the payroll percentage is a niggardly twenty-five percent, when in fact it averages (after cor-

McCORD CORPORATION
AND SUBSIDIARIES

**Consolidated Statement of Operations**
YEAR ENDED AUGUST 31

|  | 1970 | 1969 |
|---|---|---|
| **INCOME** | | |
| Net sales | $114,988,000 | $127,924,000 |
| Other income | 745,000 | 614,000 |
|  | 115,733,000 | 128,538,000 |
| **DEDUCTIONS FROM INCOME** | | |
| Cost of products sold | 94,986,000 | 104,469,000 |
| Selling and administrative expenses | 11,355,000 | 11,603,000 |
| Interest expense | 918,000 | 566,000 |
|  | 107,259,000 | 116,638,000 |
| EARNINGS BEFORE INCOME TAXES AND EXTRAORDINARY CREDIT | 8,474,000 | 11,900,000 |
| Income taxes | 4,190,000 | 5,960,000 |
| EARNINGS BEFORE EXTRAORDINARY CREDIT | 4,284,000 | 5,940,000 |
| Extraordinary credit—net | 204,000 | — |
| NET EARNINGS | $ 4,488,000 | $ 5,940,000 |

Figure 30

porate taxes have been paid) about eighty-seven percent annually year after year of *what there is to divide between payroll and profit.* By adhering to their nondisclosive accounting conventions, corporations injure their image seriously with both labor and the public.

### Social Turmoil Is Caused by Nonreporting, Ignorance and Misinterpretation

*It was in this practice of relating payroll to total sales revenue instead of to what the corporation has left after paying for its outside purchases of components, materials, and taxes that the massive propaganda campaign—to the effect that corporate owners exploit workers—had its roots.* Standard accounting practice led long ago to a miscalculation that has bred anger and disruption over the whole Western world.

In *Dividing The Wealth,* mentioned earlier, Dr. Howard Kershner reports the historic repercussions of such a miscalculation made over sixty years ago. He relates how in

September, 1905, Daniel DeLeon—a noneconomist professor of philosophy at Columbia University—made a speech
in Minneapolis which changed the course of history.

DeLeon displayed a chart, prepared by the Republican
National Committee for use in the campaign of 1904, which
showed that for census years workers received the following
percentages of the sales revenue from manufacturers' production:

| Year | Value Produced | Workers Compensation | Workers Percent |
|------|----------------|----------------------|-----------------|
| 1860 | $1.9 billion   | $400 million         | about 20%       |
| 1870 | 4.2 billion    |                      | 18%             |
| 1880 | 5.3 billion    |                      | 17%             |
| 1900 | 13.0 billion   |                      | 17%             |

DeLeon, a socialist and a cohort of Eugene Debs, sum-
marized that in America owners receive about eighty percent
of the wealth produced while workers get only about twenty
percent. He ignored the amounts that the owners paid out
for materials, supplies, light, heat, power, interest on borrowed money, state, local and federal taxes, etc., and then
assumed that the owners pocketed all of the sales dollars
that were not disbursed directly to workers. DeLeon's
misinterpretation went around the world. Dr. Kershner
writes:

DeLeon created a political and economic whirlwind that developed into a veritable hurricane. . . . His address was put
into booklet form. . . . The speech, "Socialist Reconstruction
of Society," was printed in many languages . . . German,
French, Yiddish, Spanish and Italian. . . . Its picture of the
division of income between the owners and workers of American industry was never questioned in any foreign country,
and the effect on foreign public opinion of the American
economic system was volcanic and disastrous to us.

Lenin, a decade before he became the dictator of Russia, was
so impressed with the DeLeon speech that he declared it to

be "the only real contribution to socialism since the Marx Manifesto". . . . It gave "Seven League Boots" to socialism and communism. . . .

Arnold Peterson, National Secretary of the Socialist Labor Party . . . in the preface of the 25th anniversary printing of the noted speech, said that . . . "It stands today (1930) as a monument of Socialist Science . . . and a terrible indictment of capitalism. . . .

The fact remains that the economic remarks in the speech that changed the course of history . . . constituted an unchallenged hoax of devastating magnitude.

## Union Members Lack The Facts That Might Make Their Wage Demands More Reasonable

Unfortunately, we have in the U.S. today the sad situation where union members, with hallucinations in their heads, are equipped with vast power to stop business operations in efforts to obtain what in their illiterate opinion the traffic will bear.

This is all the more tragic because employees are basically as reasonable as other people – and tend to keep their wage demands within rather sensible limits when they are effectively made aware of what the real income distribution is in ways that they can understand and believe.

On July 1, 1970, *The Wall Street Journal*, for example, reported the following:

### Bright Note

You would hardly think it could happen any more, but some 450 production workers at an Aluminum Company of America subsidiary have actually voted to forego wage and benefit increases due them in this year of their labor contract.

The decision of the men at Wear-Ever Aluminum, Inc. in Chillicothe, Ohio, was not entirely disinterested to be sure. There were indications that in the absence of such action the subsidiary might have to cease operations.

When all that is said and done, however, the workers displayed a commendable realism; all too often, labor unions insist on getting more, even in the face of common sense.

Two large American billion dollar corporations which operate worldwide have effectively made their employees aware of the true relationship within the company of the relative return to profit and payroll, and as a reward have (1) maintained fine employee relationships without strikes in the U.S. for twenty years, and (2) experienced smaller inflationary wage increases than generally prevail. The companies relied on the premise that their employees would be reasonable when given the truth in an understandable, convincing, and believable manner.

Unfortunately for the inflation jam that the U.S. is in, the companies' procedure of inducing reasonableness by dripping the water of truth continuously on the stone of disbelief for many years is simply too slow an educational process. Something much faster is needed.

## A Means for Spreading Information and Belief Quickly

To that end, I developed a unique flow-chart technique for showing dramatically what happens to both a corporation's total sales revenues and to the dollar value that it adds to what it purchases. The technique is immediately comprehended and believed by both schooled and unschooled people. These financial flows are so well-integrated, and so easily understood that they have the effect of being self-substantiating. The result is rapid education and rapid viewer belief. The diagram below is an illustration of this technique.

Because the diagram regards all U.S. corporations as one, and charts their consolidated financial flows as one, all intercorporate flows are, of course, implicitly taken into account. So no intercorporate disbursements for materials, supplies, and interest are shown. By consolidating, we get a vivid

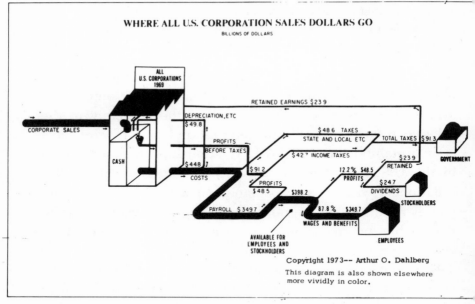

Figure 31

look at how income left to be split between payroll and profit is divided. The diagram is almost self-explanatory and self-substantiating because the portrayal is both quantitative and integrated.

In the diagram, total corporate sales revenue (a) flows into the cash bin (b). Costs must then be taken care of. These total costs in 1969 (in excess of the intercorporate purchases— which, as was explained, cancel out) amounted to $448 billion (c). The particular costs, which did not cancel out— such as the cost allowances for replacing facilities that were worn out in turning out the product (d), the cost of state and local taxes (e), and the cost of payroll (f)— constituted the $448 billion (c).

The largest of these costs was for payroll (wages and supplements) (f). If the sum of the above enumerated costs totals less than the total revenue into the cash bin (b), revenue spills over into profits before taxes (g). This spillover must be shared with the federal government as corporate profit taxes (h). In 1969, the profits before taxes totaled $91.2 billion, corporate profit taxes, $42.7 billion, and profits after taxes (i), $48.5 billion.

Thus in 1969, owners and workers together received $48.5 billion plus $349.7 billion or $398.2 billion (j) for carrying out all U.S. corporate operations. Owners received 12.2% (k) of what there was to divide, and employees received 87.8% (l).

Of the profits generated, the owners disbursed $24.7 billion to themselves as dividends (m), and the remainder, retained earnings, (n), they left in the business, mostly for expansion purposes.

Diagrams drawn in perspective for use in slide projector presentations are even more convincing than the diagram shown above. Every corporation can show its Income Statement and Balance Sheet concurrently in a single diagram. Such integrated depictions of corporate disbursements and performance could instill belief promptly.

### Retained Earnings Are Usually Reinvested and Increase Productivity

By reinvesting such earnings in up-to-date facilities, corporations are able as a general rule to increase the output per employee by about 3 percent per year. This improvement contributed heavily to their ability to increase real wages by about that same percentage year after year without increasing their selling prices. Unions with their great market power may occasionally be able to force their nominal dollar wage rates to go up more rapidly than three percent. But the real buying power of whatever nominal increases they do obtain are locked into the real three percent engineering increases. Gains in excess of that percentage are merely deceptive gains which help to push prices up into inflationary levels.

A tremendous educational opportunity lies before us. The

new and dramatic educational tool just described for fighting inflation is now available for use in books, in the press, in corporate reports, in government publications, and in television presentations.

During the 1960's, an opinion climate was built in the U.S. which probably makes it politically impossible to reduce by legislation the vast privileges union members have to insist on disruptive wage demands. The only hope, consequently, is to correct rapidly the misinformation in the heads of the members themselves. Misuse of power by recipients does not necessarily follow when power is granted to them — if, concurrently, they possess facts in believable form.

Western pioneers were privileged to carry guns on their hips. But — except in the movies — they did not routinely kill one another. The restraining forces were the values in their heads.

In the Ozarks, in contrast, the feuding Hatfields and McCoys — who were also privileged to carry guns — routinely misused their privilege. They shot one another on sight. The values in their heads were weak restraints.

We have a situation today in the labor union world that parallels the situation in the Ozarks one hundred years ago. Legislated privileges, court interpretations, weak law enforcement, and pampering in the press and TV have placed enormous power in the hands of unions which they often misuse on sight.

As it turned out, it was much easier in the Ozarks and more enduring to stop hillbilly manslaughter by spreading education and values than it was to legislate away the feuders' privilege of carrying guns. Similarly, it would probably be easier today to restrain possessors of union power with economic facts presented in believable form than it would be to try to curtail their special privileges with legislation. Corrective reform legislation will come only after current illusions about the profit-payroll split have been destroyed.

The only hope—and it is a very real hope—lies in the common sense and fairness of union workers. They would not be doing what they are doing if they knew the true size of profit and payroll, and the customary ratios between them. Labor leaders often know such facts, but will not risk their leadership by passing such information on to the union members. Still, if the needed facts were well and dramatically presented, bargaining could become a realistic process, because the affluent workers of today would quickly grasp how the inflation which they help to create recoils to hurt them. Knowledgeable workers do not act against themselves.

The greatest crime that management commits today against its workers is its failure to let them know how their own company's profit and payroll compare. The depth, extent, and magnitude of the ignorance depicted in earlier pages is alarming. But the ease with which the ignorance can be quickly dispelled by an integrated self-substantiating type of chart with supporting data is most encouraging.

Nationwide ignorance of simple facts has created an apparently insoluble national problem. Still, if every company undertook the problem of educating its own people—its own employees and managers—the problem might quickly disappear.

# Chapter 15

## The Old Economics vs. the New Economics

YOU HAVE now had a glimpse of the economic and social disruption caused by the free market system's historic failure to use some form of nonhoardable money as medium of exchange.

Over the years, countless men have seen the evil fruits of postponable money without associating the evil results with the underlying cause. And over the years countless men have advanced hundreds of plans for overcoming the unsatisfactory performance of the market system without giving attention to the cancerous defect at its heart. None of them noticed how the seemingly innocent practice of bank customers giving to bankers collateral for their borrowings (collateral worth much more than the face value of their borrowings) made the new deposits that were created against their notes and mortgages into disruptive deferrable money. They didn't notice how the new deposits were subtly, unintentionally, and accidentally given an excessive store of value.

Recipients of such money are and have been in a position to disburse it without penalty more slowly than they received it Possessing this deferral power, the money savers chronically weakened the bargaining power of workers. When the deferral power was used to the full, as it was in the 1930's, the workers had to bargain at a big disadvantage in the market. As a result, an inequitably low income flowed to the workers, and unemployment and slow growth occurred. (See charts, pages 12 and 14.)

During the 1920's, business activity had seemed to be booming along nicely, but as it boomed the deferrable money in use loaded the free market against the worker and pampered the providers of capital — the money savers. The resulting income distribution that occurred in the market place channeled so much income to those who insisted on investing it in facilities, or in spending it tardily, that what was left to go to those who used it mainly to buy the current output of the facilities did not obtain enough to induce the plants to run full blast. After a decade of such unbalanced distribution, during which the savers invested their large sums profligately in both the U.S. and abroad, they drastically reduced the tempo of their spending for U.S. plant and equipment. And the sad decade of the 1930's began. The bank holiday of 1933 recorded the collapse of one of the monetary systems based on sanctuary money.

Our economists did not know how to repair the free market system. So they improvised several recourses which collectively constitute the New Economics of today. They have succeeded with deficit financing in devising a bureaucratic and administrative machine for achieving a relatively stable monetary demand. And by resorting to heavy taxes on the rich and handouts to the poor, they have obtained a relatively balanced income distribution. But in the process of doing so, they have introduced new major evils.

In retrospect, Americans have lived under two different economic systems since 1900. The diagrams that follow will make this clear. Prior to World War II, the role of government was far more limited than it has been since then. Its role then was mainly to preserve the peace, to prevent violence and misrepresentation, to protect persons and property, and to enforce contract. Since 1945, the role of government has been expanded to deal directly in a centrally planned way even with the redistribution of income.

Until World War II, the U.S. was essentially a free market economy. The state thought it was enough to write the rules of the game, and then stand by to enforce impartially the agreements arrived at. It sought not to inject its own judgment on what the resulting market values ought to be providing, of course, that the agreements stayed within the circumscribed rules and community values. It did interfere legislatively with the market's answers with tariffs and other special legislation occasionally, but that was the exception.

As stated earlier, the state depended greatly on price competition and wage competition to control both the intake and outgo prices of business and the resultant distribution of income. The state gambled that the "hiring price competition" among entrepreneurs, in their efforts to hire employees and to purchase materials and supplies, would keep their outgo high, and that, moreover, in disposing of their products the "selling price competition" among them would keep their intake low. As a consequence, the profit return, for example, in the economy as a whole would never be more than just enough to induce businessmen to undertake socially desirable projects. This reliance on competition to settle prices made the role of the state a very simple one. For when forces of competition work as intended, all state interference with the fairness of prices becomes unnecessary. Everyone bargains and haggles with everyone else, and in the process of doing so all goods are disposed of, all transactions are cleared, all spheres of industrial activity are correlated, and all goods are produced in the order of their desirability as seen by those who have buying power or capital. Once the rules of the game are written, the state simply stands by impartially enforcing the price agreements arrived at, but never injecting its own opinion as to what the exchange ratios ought to be. At least that was the theory.

But after diagnosing the rules that have enveloped the free market, I was forced to conclude that ever since credit banking became dominant, the bargaining rules have been loaded against the workers and in favor of the money savers. The rules were not planned that way. The favoritism toward money savers and against workers developed accidentally as money evolved from the early barter and commodity money stage into the checkbook money stage of today. (See Chapter 3.)

Inadvertently, the bargaining power of labor was weakened, while that of the money savers increased. Such favoritism did not, however, necessarily insure a breakdown in aggregate monetary demand, but it did make the free market system ever more vulnerable to breakdowns—because the money savers acquired larger percentages of the income generated than they could sensibly invest to serve the end market buying power of the worker-consumers. Capital spending booms tended to occur in waves (See Figure 20, page 141) and periodically to be excessive as expanding profits induced excessive expansions of the money supply. During the latter half of the 1920s, for example, a pronounced credit and capital goods boom was under way. In order that money savings could find sensible outlets, they had to flow beyond American frontiers and into foreign countries. This they did—into Latin America in particular.

Money savings must be disbursed at the rate at which they are saved out of current income, even for silly capital or consumer goods, or we get unemployment for the difference. By 1930, through bargaining in the market, the money savers were still obtaining more investment funds than it was sensible to invest promptly in more U.S. facilities. End market buying power had not risen rapidly enough. And the investment boom collapsed.

The unbalance was so severe that the free market system broke down for a decade. Concerned men did not know how to repair it. The tools relied on by classical economists for reactivating tardy investment spending—such as sags in wages and prices—did not work. For the whole decade of the 1930's they did not work. As Figure 3 showed, the rate of unemployment stayed in the range of fifteen-twenty percent for ten years. The Old Economics died during that decade. It was gradually replaced by a new system of vast governmentalism, the "New Economics" of today. For a few years the government military demand of World War II relieved the situation. But during the 1930's, the design of the new system was begun. Let us in the next few pages diagram that revolutionary system and contrast it with a diagram of the "Old."

Today it is orthodox doctrine in our schools to maintain that our relatively free market system cannot continually and automatically maintain an adequate monetary demand for goods and services. Consequently, many people—including the author of the economic textbook that dominates the college field today—contend that a supplementary monetary demand, rooted in government spending, is needed to maintain full employment. They stress the need for more governmentalism as the corrective, and ignore the need for changes in the rules that envelop the free market system. Unfortunately, under today's warped conditions, when the property rights that envelop checkbook money are still permitted to give it an excessive store of value, they are correct. The working rules that envelop today's supposedly free market simply are not designed to insure that aggregate private monetary demand will be strong enough to maintain full employment continuously, or that the distribution of income will be equitable. Because that is so, civic leaders have tried to devise bureaucratic or administrative means for obtaining a better result. Since 1930, three massive movements of questionable sociological merit have grown out of their efforts. One has been Compensatory Spending, another Collective Bargaining and Compulsory Unionism, and a third—for want of a better name—"Welfarism."

Figure 32 outlines the major spending circuits of the "Old Economics," the system that has been drastically modi-

THE OLD ECONOMICS

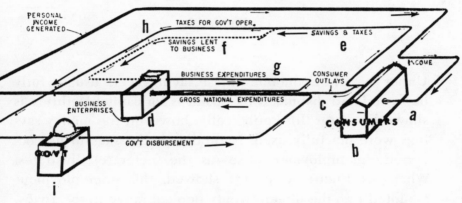

Figure 32

fied since the depression of the 1930's. Figure 32 shows how part of the income (a) that flowed to all consumers (b) went out again as consumer outlays (c) to flow over the counter to Business Enterprise (d). The remainder consisted of Savings and Taxes (e). The Savings portion was normally lent (f) to Business which then expended it (g) for plant, equipment, and inventory. The Taxes portion flowed on (h) to the Government (i) which then also proceeded to disburse the money in the market for goods and services.

Figure 33 highlights that consumer savings (a), as a percent of consumer income, is relatively stable year after year.

## THE OLD ECONOMICS

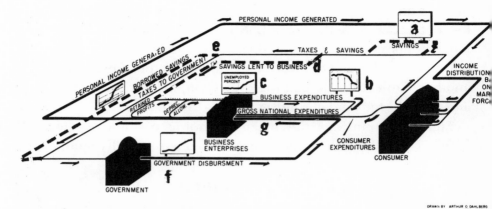

Figure 33

Under the Old Economics, these savings were usually fully borrowed and disbursed by business for capital facilities as shown by meter (b). Periodically, however, the money savings were not fully used. Naturally, as the sags in use occurred, unemployment rose — as the meter (c) illustrates. When, as Figure 3 (p. 15) showed, this unemployment mounted into the fifteen-twenty percent range in the 1930s, drastic remedies were proposed.

Under the Old Economics, people had the privilege of spending both for *what* they wanted and of spending *when* they wanted. When private spending sagged, government at first did nothing about it. It relied on the premise that if and when wages and prices sagged far enough, the owners of sanctuary money would come back into the market again. Such an adjustment procedure was so severe that people would not stand for it. In rebellion, they jumped from the Old Economics frying pan into the New Economics fire. They resorted mainly to these five recourses:

1.  Compensatory Spending.
2.  Massive "Collective Bargaining."

3. A Practical Guarantee of full employment under The Employment Act of 1946.
4. Increases and decreases in the money supply.
5. Welfarism.

The first step toward "Compensatory Spending" occurred in 1934, seemingly in response to the recommendations of John Maynard Keynes. Keynes had correctly observed that when business activity dipped and unemployment increased, the demand for goods — even when prices declined — did not respond upward automatically as classical theory had maintained it would. He observed that the private aggregate monetary demand for goods could stay down for years at a time even after prices had tumbled.

For such periods, Keynes recommended not that taxes be increased to provide for government spending, nor that wages and prices be induced to be flexible downward, but that taxes be cut in order to help expand demand. In addition, he recommended that the government accept as inviolate the striking power of the labor unions so that it could prevent wage rates from being lowered flexibly downward.

He recommended that the government make up for inadequate private monetary demand by borrowing the sluggishly used private funds, or by monetizing new government debt and then disbursing the new monies into the markets.

His recommendation consisted of a rather modest spending program. He proposed to borrow income and to pay it back when business activity was back up to normal. From 1934 to 1939, the U.S. tried to do this on a homeopathic scale. It borrowed and disbursed only about three to four billion dollars per year. Figure 33 (p. 216) illustrates how this amount of savings — which was not borrowed at (d) by business — was borrowed by government at (e). The government injected (f) this sum into the market (g). But this small injection of monetary demand from the public sector did not rid the U.S. of unemployment.

Compensatory spending was invoked mainly in an effort to keep people alive. The subtle disruptive rules of the free market were never modified to make the market system fully viable. Instead, the U.S. gradually invoked more and more governmentalism. It still tries one desperate statist expedient after another in its understandable effort to sustain full employment and to lift employee income. As sags in production, employment and income result from declines in private spending, it expands government spending as a neutralizer. It spends sensibly or foolishly, economically or unprofitably, on almost anything: highways, leaf-raking, new post offices, bridges, schools, rent subsidies, income maintenance or public welfare.

When the working rules of society are not designed to insure that current income is redisbursed by its private recipients as rapidly as the matching goods are produced, a popular case can be made for injecting a substitute stream of buying power—even if the buying power must be created out of thin air. In that case, such buying power is only a neutralizer of the unemployment that would otherwise occur.

As it turned out, the modest volume of compensatory spending during the 1930's did not get the economy going again.

In financing its needed spending, the New Economists realized that if they resorted to increased taxes, they might absorb some of the very private funds that might be spent anyway, and that no net uplift would result. They likewise realized that if they borrowed the sluggishly used private funds, that particular money would not be available to come forth later to make purchases. The seemingly obvious recourse, therefore, was to create a new batch of money and to inject it as substitute spending for the delayed and sluggish private spending that did not come forth.

So during the 1930's, the government created new money annually by putting about three billion dollars worth of

Federal obligations into the portfolio of the banking system. It spent some of this money for new worthwhile bridges, post offices, and highways—for products about as worthwhile as private contractors might have built, but large portions of the new money were spent on unproductive make-work, relief and sustenance.

### Progressive Income Tax Rates

In 1942, in its efforts to finance the war, Congress legislated very high progressive income tax rates. These taxes yielded vast revenues. In 1944, for example, personal and corporate income taxes yielded $34.6 billion. In 1939, they had yielded only $2.1 billion. These taxes were too lucrative as sources of revenue to let go of when the war was over—inasmuch as Congress was still intent on maintaining aggregate monetary demand governmentally. (In 1967, the individual income and employment tax plus the corporation tax yielded $135 billion.)

Very high personal and corporate income taxes became one of the major tools of the New Economics system.

In rising, they contributed heavily toward financing the direct pocket-to-pocket transfer of government funds to selected pressure groups. These "Transfer Payments" amounted to $2.4 billion in 1939, and to over $80 billion in 1971.

When World War II was over, Congress was determined not to live through the trauma of the 1930's all over again. So it voted the Employment Act of 1946. Under this act, the key desideratum of government came to be the policy of maintaining fiscal and monetary programs that would insure "growth" and relatively full employment. Government compensatory spending was thereby given additional legal justification.

So during recent decades the New Economics has gone far beyond the proposals of John Maynard Keynes. Not only

has it borrowed current income (c) and disbursed it into
the gross national expenditure stream (f) as Keynes recommended, but it has also resorted to taxing (d) and handout
recourses (m) which operate to hold up aggregate monetary
demand.

The New Economics trys to correct through bureaucratic
discretion the free market's lopsided income distribution
by taxing large portions of income away from the rich and
giving it to the poor. It uses bureaucratic judgment to alter
the unacceptable results of a free market that is permitted
to function under hoarding privileges that load the bargaining situation against the worker.

The revolutionary implications of trying to use bureaucratic discretion as a corrective are partially highlighted by
Figure 34 below.

Figure 34 shows how Government (b) resorts to three
sources of revenue: it borrows current savings (c) in exchange
for its E bonds, F bonds, etc. It taxes personal and other

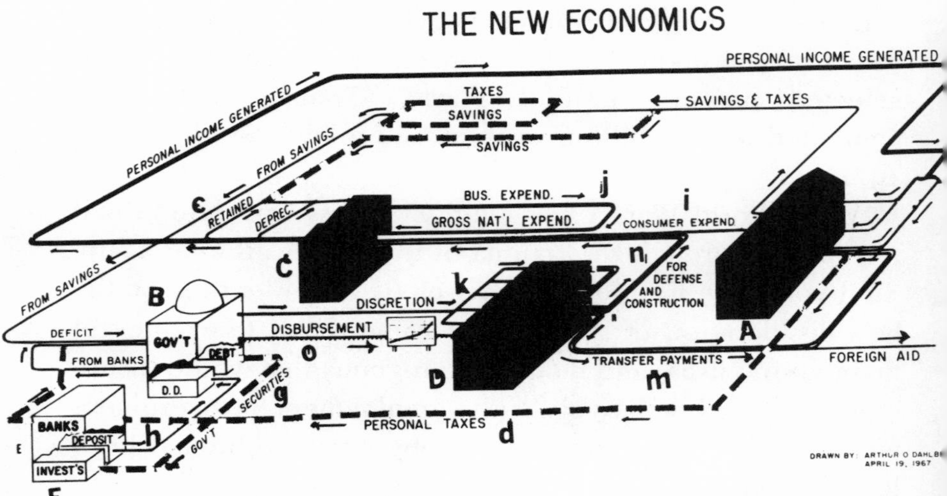

## THE NEW ECONOMICS

This diagram is also shown elsewhere
more vividly in color.

Copyright 1974 by Arthur O. Dahlberg.

Figure 34

income (d), and it "borrows" from the Banking System
(f). When a government's tax revenues are insufficient to
finance its budgeted or programmed disbursements (o), it
is privileged not only to borrow current income, but also—
being sovereign—to exchange its debt obligations (g) for
new money (h) at the banks. Since the end of World War II,
the federal government has borrowed very heavily—and
raised the federal debt to over $400 billion.

Figure 34 also highlights the startling contrasting sociological implications of spending that go on in the private
sector and those which occur in the public sector. Note
that when spending occurs in the private sector, Consumers
(A) and Business (C) spend as they please—at (i) and (j).
Note, too, that when Congress spends money it must necessarily do so through its many departments and agencies
(D): such as the Depts. of Defense; Health, Education and
Welfare; Agriculture; etc. In the process of doing so, note
also that Congress must delegate (k) vast discretion to the
administrators in charge of each of the programs. There are
over one hundred fifty federal agencies with their own budgets. Each is necessarily entrusted with considerable discretion.

Congress sets up some controls over the more than $260
billion that it disburses annually to recipients. But vast
latitude remains. Bureaucrats are permitted to add their
own not inconsiderable conditions; subsidized farmers are
subject to special controls over their acreage, accounting,
production, and prices; welfare recipients are subject to
family review; government contractors are required to maintain an acceptable racial mix in their employment practices,
etc. As shown at (n) and (m), bureaucratic discretion rides
along with every government dollar that is disbursed,
whether it is spent for goods and services (n) or for Transfer
Payments (such as for medicare, education, family aid, etc.)
as at (m).

## *"Welfarism"*

In 1939, the federal bureaucrats had the power to disburse Treasury funds of only about five billion dollars per year. Today they have discretionary power to disburse over two hundred billion dollars per year. That power is so great that a new nonclassical system of political economy has come into existence as a response to it. The classical economists of old had never even thought to delineate such a system as a possibility. A major component of that system is called "Welfarism."

Welfarism is the growing practice of using the political powers and financial resources of the state to provide economic, educational, medical, and other benefits to people in the lower income brackets. To obtain the money for these benefits, the government usually taxes the people in the upper income groups ever more heavily. Welfarism strives to control revenues and disbursements governmentally so that not only equality of opportunity is provided to all citizens, but also equality of living conditions regardless of their contributions to production. "Need," not the productive contribution of goods and services, merits an ever larger portion of the national income.

Because federal, state and local government officials today annually disburse into the market directly or indirectly over $420 billion of the nation's more than $1,200 billion of expenditures for goods and services, they naturally exercise vast economic power over all contractors, corporations, etc., who seek government contracts. Their power in placing orders and giving jobs is tremendous. Their power is even greater in making the recipients of government largess beholden to them. The recipients of checks for medicare, education, welfare, unemployment, relief, social security benefits, etc., now number over seventy-two million — a high percentage of the electorate. And millions of them can vote.

(Adam Smith and John Stuart Mill never contemplated such an organization of political power.)

The well-meant recourses of compensatory spending, welfarism, collective bargaining and easy credit—which constitute the basic rationale of the New Economics— necessarily call forth the breakdown of law and order. The riots, demonstrations, sit-ins, burnings and revolts against social values and controls, which went practically unpunished and uncriticized under the Kennedy-Johnson administrations in particular, are, as we shall see, logical accompaniments of an ever expanding direct pocket-to-pocket governmental distribution of income to selected groups of citizens.

Thinner and thinner pretexts are used by the rebel leaders to justify factory and student strikes. Student rebels tear down what they do not like, but offer no outline of what they would put in its place. They reject a capitalism they do not even understand, and flaunt the pictures of Marx, Lenin and Mao on university walls while they chant the clichés of communism.

Ignorant of the subtle machinery of the free market that provides them with their cornucopia of goods and the liberty to fulminate, their criticisms of that machinery are usually childish. Seemingly unaware that individual reward is at least somewhat related to personal effort and contribution, they merely bawl, scream, riot and burn. Fortunately, because they have very fuzzy ideas of what they want, no program is likely to survive them when their lawlessness has spent itself. They will merely have prepared the way for the more effective attacks of the communists, who craftily use childish liberals as their pawns.

A new kind of political candidate caters to their massive political power and demands. Political candidates compete with one another in telling the recipients of transfer payments about all the fine things they would do for them with ever more of the taxpayers' money. In the process, they carefully avoid criticizing the occasional misbehavior of the recipients of welfare. If the recipients riot, demonstrate, or burn, politicians do not even slap them on the wrist.

Since the 1960's, lawlessness has even accelerated. The quotations below highlight how, during the mid-1960's, many top ranking political leaders expressed themselves as highly tolerant of misbehavior.

Adlai Stevenson in a commencement address at Colby College, June, 1964: "Even a jail sentence is no longer a dishonor but a proud achievement. Perhaps we are destined to see in this law-loving land people running for office not on their stainless record but on their prison records."

John F. Kennedy, 1963: "In too many parts of the country, wrongs are inflicted on Negro citizens for which there are no remedies at law. Unless the Congress acts, their only remedy is in the street."

Hubert Humphrey, July, 1966, in New Orleans, saying that if he lived in slums, "I think you'd have more trouble than you have already, because I've got enough spark in me to lead a mighty good revolt."

Robert Kennedy, March, 1968: "The more riots that come on college campuses, the better the world for tomorrow." *

Everywhere, police officials are restrained by court decisions, administrative timidity and public confusion. No longer is it enough simply to "maintain law and order"; now we must maintain law and order "with justice." The implication is that we must first establish justice before we venture to insist on law and order. Unhappily, the world is so full of economic, racial, and political injustice that it will take ages to eradicate it. In the meantime, if we do maintain law and order we at least have a chance to eradicate the old wrongs bit by bit.

---

* *National Review*, April 23, 1968.

Only if property is protected while it is being produced will individuals willingly produce the surpluses that enter into exchange — or invest in the plant and equipment which increases the community's output. Selfishness can only be lured into specialization and harnessed to perform service competitively for the community by a meaningful protection of the property of individuals.

"Property rights" and "human rights" are but two sides of the same coin, for without property rights there can be few human rights. It is difficult to see how a man whose produce and property are not protected can provide for himself, or how without property he can avoid being dependent on the charity or sufferance of others. A man without a reserve of property who is even temporarily unemployed is soon a dependent, a slave, or a ward of the state. He has no reserve cushion of wealth to tide him over from day to day, or from job to job. When completely dependent, he cannot be said to possess human rights. For if he is not permitted to own, he is implicitly not permitted to live except by sufferance and gratuity. From a functional point of view, human rights and property rights are thus complementary; they are not competitive or alternatives. One is not "good" and the other "bad." Both are essential for human survival with liberty.

To understand functionally the nature of property, one must look into the ingredients that constitute property. Unless one does that, one may generalize the problem out of existence. Property is not a word; and it is not an absolute. Property is a bundle of attributes. The ownership of private property is a well-defined bundle of stipulations and arrangements that the community is willing to back up involving one's handling and use of particular assets.

Professor John R. Commons wrote an illuminating book in which he organized those stipulations under the headings of Rights, Duties, Liberties, Exposures, Powers and Privileges. The courts deal eternally with these component stipulations and arrangements when they deal and rule on cases involving property rights. Property can be a tangible or intangible item; it can be tangible wheat or automobiles, or it can be intangible goodwill and debt obligations.

When you own an automobile or someone's note, you possess certain rights, duties, privileges, exposures, etc. These are always in process of being added to or subtracted from by court decisions—always being modified. By modifying them, the courts are continuously changing the value of your automobile, your home, your mortgage, etc. Private property is a bundle of stipulations around some tangible or intangible item over which you personally have control within the limits that the community first sets and then enforces.

This book seeks a scaling down of a certain disruptive property attribute which unobservedly crept into our monetary system as checkbook money superseded commodity money—an attribute which accrued to the advantage of the savers of our medium of exchange. It does not seek to subtract from the other warranted attributes of checkbook money.

The pervasive regulations of the centralized state reach far beyond the material world. They control not only our food, but also our minds and our hearts. For the centralized state—in order to obtain compliance with its plans—must necessarily use force and propaganda in controlling our views. It must even deny us that somewhat religious behavior which looks toward our serving of others. This is the setting:

A newborn child knows nothing, absolutely nothing. Consequently, the parents must control its adjustment to the world for many years. Parents must have authority and rule by command. Papa and mama know best. But the parents' goal is emancipation, adjustment and maturity for the child. Parents first delineate the goals and then outline how to reach those goals through the maze of obstacles that will line the path.

This process of *parentally* providing both goals and guidance is one that the Centrally Planned State cannot utilize or even tolerate. For in order to assure compliance with its intricate centralized plans, it must keep its aging youngsters forever in statist apron strings. The centralized state must enforce its centrally selected values and dominate its people from the cradle to the grave. It cannot even permit parents to imbue their children with the impulse to help their fellowmen. There is an economic reason for this.

Because of its controlled production, the state must control and limit the citizens' income, food, clothing, opportunity and property. And when it restricts the amounts involved to mere survival proportions in order to make its central plans workable, the individual is able to obtain a surplus of neither time nor goods for use in generously or religiously serving others. He is not permitted to produce an economic excess which he can big-heartedly give away in ways which satisfy his mind and heart. His latitude of action is squeezed to nothingness. The state effectively pre-empts his soul.

In the United States, individuals are still fairly free to make large contributions toward the ends they value most. This fact has enabled us to build a system of cooperative effort out of which flows—almost as a by-product—a volume of earthly goods and services that astounds the world. But this system is being eroded by political programs that revolve around the recourses reviewed above: wage and price fixing, compensatory spending, cost-push inflation, and income redistribution under progressive income taxes, all four leading to more and more government regulation. In many countries, the free market system is already destroyed. In our country, that system is still dominant, but

it is being steadily eroded. Too many men in government
and in our channels of communications have statist orienta-
tions. They seek to solve almost all economic problems with
government interference. College faculty members are by
their own identification predominantly "left or liberal,"
as the survey results charted below bring out.

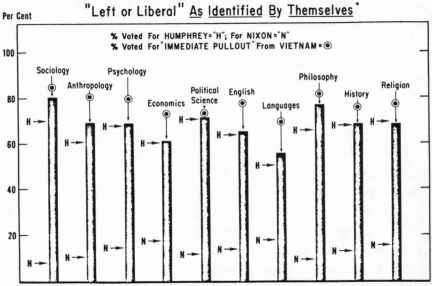

**THE ORIENTATION OF COLLEGE FACULTY MEMBERS**
"Left or Liberal" As Identified By Themselves*

Figure 35

The economists, the most conservative group in the liberal
arts college, with a twelve percent self-identification score,
are nonetheless so anti-free market in attitude that their
professional organization, The American Economic Association, elected as its president for 1972 a Harvard professor
who loudly advocates bureaucratically ordained *mandatory*

wage and price controls—the very antithesis of the free market—as a permanent arrangement.

So our cultural future is dim indeed.

## All Major Countries Have the Same Disease

All major countries have contracted the Fabian inflation disease. They all try—the U.S. slightly less than the others—to retain just enough of the free market mechanism to provide a carrot incentive to businessmen, and then to superimpose on that fragile arrangement a set of almost sovereign rights for labor unions to raise labor costs faster than productivity increases. (See Figure 27, p. 194.) Fabian societies also accompany their grants of power over wage rates with almost unlimited privileges to unions to use their dues money to influence political elections. Then they strengthen labor power still further with a compensatory spending policy that tries to insure full employment and a tight labor market.

Even so, all governmental efforts to help employees obtain a theoretically larger and desirable share of the income generated (during the initial bargaining in the market) does not enable employees to accomplish this because the use of deferrable money frustrates the effort, and continues to enable the savers of money to obtain a functionally excessive portion of the income generated. Periodically, the excessive savings pour themselves into new plant and equipment—which turn out to be excessive in relation to the portion of income that flows to consumers to provide end market demands for the new facilities. As the investors gradually realize that the facilities are excessive, they cut back their appropriations and capital disbursements. They do not shift their spending into the purchase of big ticket consumer items to maintain equilibrium. They simply slow down their spending and lengthen the interval between their transactions. (See Figure 6 on p. 20.)

So, as a supplementary recourse, Fabian governments

establish a myriad of programs to achieve a more even distribution of income. They do this by transferring income
bureaucratically from top income groups to the lower ones.
In fiscal 1971, for example, the U.S. government disbursed a
total of $210 billion. Of this sum, $80 billion constituted so-
called "transfer payments" — pocket-to-pocket transfers of
federal receipts to favored groups. All over the world, progressive income tax collections become ever larger, while
transfer payments become ever more generous. As policy
everywhere, all major governments — by means of taxes —
skim income from the free market's producers who are
successful (under rules and arrangements that are partially
loaded against the workers) and transfer it in the name of
egalitarianism to people in the lower income brackets, some
of whom do no work at all.

Millions of recipients of government largesse possess the
vote and become forceful advocates of ever larger governmental disbursements to themselves. In all Fabian societies,
apparently, political representatives cannot resist such
pressures.

The disheartening depiction above roughly portrays the
economic structure of the Western world, of which the U.S.
has recently become a full-fledged member.

### Planning the Rules Versus Planning the Details

A few men still wish to repair our free enterprise system
by paring down the privileges, powers, and immunities
which hamstring its full operation, and by modifying rights,
duties, liberties, and exposures so as to make the system into
a rationally integrated machine. Such actions could obviously
be thought of as being "planning," too.

But those who have usurped the word "planning" mean
something very different thereby. They do not aim to create a
climate of laws and rules to which producers — by freely
attuning themselves to it — automatically generate full

production. These self-styled arrogators do not seek to set up rules which tempt everyone to do his best, to look over his own potentialities, appraise his neighbor's needs, consider his world's technology, etc., and then, by applying his efforts to best advantage, to service the needs of his fellows. Instead, they would banish the "disorderliness" which only superficially characterizes the everyday behavior of our more than two hundred million people. In Olympian fashion, they would "plan" all work arithmetically from the top.

Advocates of centralized government planning stress their well-intentioned goals. But they conveniently ignore revealing their means for obtaining enforcement of and compliance with their "directives." Nowhere do they outline the means needed to coerce those who would differ with the values implied in their directives; never a word on whether they would impose fines or jail or death on those who would try to exchange goods and services on a free basis in the black markets of the centrally planned state.

Slighting as they do the discussion of enforcement and compliance, it is not surprising that they have not portrayed the grim controls which totalitarian states must impose if they are to have an integrated economic machine. "Planners" do not mention the arbitrariness needed when determination of jobs, services, products, and mandatory wages and prices lies not in the individual but in the presumptious and arrogant philosophy of the planning officials.

"Planners" naively believe that, with the help of statisticians, planning can be perfect. So when their system bogs down, they blame the cussedness of human nature, the lack of police power and the incompetence of helpers. They fire their assistants and concentrate power in their own hands. Martial law tends to be set up.

"Planners" imply that the ruling of their Central Planning Boards on employment, investment, wages, and prices will be obeyed without the use of purges, slaughter and secret police. They vaguely maintain that centralized power will be restrained by elections. "Democratic socialism" is the contradiction on which they rely. They simply ignore the fact that republican government cannot function without free speech.

The planners blithely dismiss the possibility of adequately improving the free enterprise system. I maintain that they have failed to isolate the key maladjustment within the capitalistic system, and that in their anger over the system's shortcomings they have been throwing the baby out with the bath.

Since World War II, the craven acceptance of central planning has become a part of the milieu of our times. Even many advocates of civil liberties endorse it. Still, the recourse is basically reactionary because it is functionally inoperative unless civil liberties are suppressed.

# Chapter 16

## The Federal Reserve System and Its Limitations

*It Lacks the Tools for Offsetting the Damage Caused by Sanctuary Money*

Because the Federal Reserve System is well designed for attuning the money supply to the needs of the nation, but not for maintaining the prompt reuse of the money that exists, the description of the Federal Reserve System that follows below is only tangential to the main theme of this book. This chapter is included to show that despite the Federal Reserve's great powers and its fine design for a limited purpose, the exercise of all of its powers cannot provide us with the economic equivalent of boomerang money.

The actions and policies of the Federal Reserve authorities are extremely important, even though the design and technical operation of the System may be rather boring to explore. Unless one understands the mechanics of the system, however, one cannot appraise the limits of its power to intensify or dampen monetary demand.

In recent decades, the Federal Reserve has attempted to do more than provide for relatively simple things like the elasticity of the currency. Consequently, many people believe that it can, with its controls over credit, maintain relatively full employment under free market conditions. This writer believes that its control tools are too weak for that purpose. When wisely and opportunely applied, its controls can helpfully influence the level of activity—particularly to dampen booms—but they cannot deal with the two or three basic maladjustments which steadily push us toward unemployment and statism. For these maladies, its controls are too homeopathic and tangential. We must examine the design and mechanics of the Federal Reserve System to see why this is so.

Before the days of the Federal Reserve System, the money supply was inelastic. Smaller banks usually kept their legal reserves in the form of cash with big city banks. When the demand for credit expanded, even seasonally, as was usual every fall, the big banks were often forced to sell securities, call loans, and raise interest rates. Business contraction and disruption tended to follow. Crises were chronic. The Federal Reserve Act of 1913 was designed to provide a means for dealing smoothly with a fluctuating demand for money and credit.

Although commercial banks were required by law before the establishment of the Federal Reserve System to hold as reserves an amount of uninvested funds equal to a designated portion of their deposits, no effort was made to insure that the aggregate reserves of the member banks were at desirable levels. No one was responsible for checking whether banks were creating or contracting their deposits excessively.

An agency was needed to pass on whether the overall money supply was adequate to meet the needs of a growing economy; whether it was elastic enough to meet the fluctuating needs of business; whether it was fluid enough regionally; whether it could suffer the ups and downs of the business cycle; whether the banking system would fully anticipate and allow for the actions of the U.S. Treasury in shifting funds around, and whether the banks as a group were liquid enough and had aggregate reserves of adequate size.

Because banks incur an obligation to redeem their customers' checks with legal money, they do not increase their bank loans and investments without limit. And the fact that they do not do so, unless they have adequate legal money within easy reach for meeting reasonable cash drains, makes the size of their reserves of legal money a matter of major importance to them. Because the Federal Reserve was given power to vary the size of these reserves as ratios to the volume of loans and investments made, it obtained great power to control the volume of credit extended and money created. Instead of the member banks modifying their own reserves and money supply in response to business demand, the Federal Reserve was given power to modify them in an effort to stimulate or restrain demand.

Most new money reaches people by way of the member banks, because borrowers must first monetize their debts there, and then send the new money on its way. By controlling the availability and cost of member banks' reserves and thus indirectly the amount of debt the member banks can monetize, the Federal Reserve influences the amount of new money that banks can create against loans and investments.

The amount of money that people in the aggregate possess is a major factor influencing how much they will disburse for goods and services. But because it is not the only factor, all that the Federal Reserve authorities can do when they seek to stimulate spending is to make money creation easy. However, when they seek to dampen spending they can do it positively because they can make the supply of money inadequate and turn it into the limiting factor.

Because, historically, too many banks maintained inadequate reserves and sought income at the expense of safety, laws were passed that required banks to keep "adequate reserves," that is, a volume of readily reachable money in some minimum fixed ratio to their liabilities to depositors. But such fixed requirements tended to freeze the availability of the reserves in times of trouble—when they were needed the most. For banks could not draw on their reserves when the reserves fell below the legal minimum. At such times, banks had to reduce their outstanding loans—just when they should have been expanding them to help business out of trouble.

After several tight-money panics, like the one of 1907, it became clear that, although minimum reserves should be provided for by law, they should nonetheless be elastic and not fixed and frozen so that lending banks could obtain additional reserves at a price when sorely needed. The Federal Reserve System was set up to provide such flexibility. It aimed not only to insist on the maintenance of prudent reserves, but also to provide for additional reserves at a price in times of trouble.

The Federal Reserve System's means of doing this was to permit member banks to convert certain selected assets rather easily into cash or currency in time of stress. Just as nonbank borrowers can go to member banks and in effect convert their debt obligations into member bank deposits, so member banks can go to the Federal Reserve and convert their own debt obligations (or certain kinds of other assets) into Federal Reserve deposits.

After elastic reserves had been provided for and banks were able at a moment's notice to convert selected assets (such as commercial paper and government bonds) into money form, they were, of course, able to operate with smaller reserves than before. This eased situation could in itself have led to excessive credit expansion and inflation. But the Federal Reserve System was established to forestall that possible abuse of credit, too.

For the Federal Reserve authorities were directed to use their power not merely to assure elastic and ample credit for the needs of commerce, industry and agriculture, but also to curb the use of credit for speculation. Under these circumstances, control over the reserve requirements took on a new significance. For it gave to the Federal Reserve authorities both the power to curb the tempo of activity when they thought "excesses" were current or imminent as well as the power to squeeze the economy into recession if their analyses and forecasts should turn out to be wrong. As we shall see, a good central bank system requires that its central authorities be expert quantitative analysts of business pressures and unbalances, both good short-term forecasters of business change and able analysts of institutional change.

When the Federal Reserve System was established, a primary requirement for membership was that all member banks transfer to the Federal Reserve banks all the reserves that they had on deposit with the big city banks or in their own vaults. By aggregating all the reserves of member banks in a single place, the Federal Reserve authorities were, by means of the powers given to them, able to immobilize the reserves or to stretch their use as a basis for credit.

The System was not designed entirely to fit our functional needs. To a modest extent it also reflects political compromise. Twelve regional banks were set up, not one. The fact that 13,500 commercial banks of the United States are classified as National Banks, State Banks, Member Banks, and Non-Member Banks reflects this compromise.

Only about 6,200 of our 13,500 commercial banks are members of the Federal Reserve System. Fifty-six years after the creation of the system, 7,300 commercial banks choose to remain outside of it.

As a rule, the larger banks are members. As a result, the deposits of the member banks, as of December 31, 1968, constituted eighty-three percent of the total deposits of all commercial banks, while only seventeen percent of the deposits were in non-member banks.

Some of our commercial banks operate under state charters and others under national charters. As of December 31, 1968, 7,300 banks operated under state charters.

All three of the means which the Federal Reserve has for influencing the volume of credit that its member banks may extend to customers, work by modifying the size of the reserves which the member banks must maintain. But there are also random and anarchic changes that are always going on in the economy which have nothing to do with credit policy, and these also influence the size of member bank reserves. The Federal Reserve first tries to adjust member bank reserves to what the random and anarchic disrupters are doing to them, and then it changes the reserves some more through open market and other actions to make them conform to its idea of a desirable credit situation.

On its performance to date, the Federal Reserve System has successfully provided for an elastic currency. Basically, this problem was met by an arrangement under which the banks in the System could always create more deposits or currency for customers by borrowing reserves from the Federal Reserve Banks at a modest cost.

But the Federal Reserve also took on the task of maximizing at stable prices the overall demand for goods and services within the economy. Tragically, as we shall see, the Federal Reserve System is not designed to cope with certain institutionalized disrupters, such as 1) the privilege to disburse income much more slowly than it is received, and 2) cost-push inflation. (See Chapter 12.)

Practically the sole means by which the Federal Reserve has sought to stabilize the overall monetary demand for goods has been to make credit more or less rapidly available to bank borrowers. For this reason, its tools have really not been adequate. It does, however, have adequate tools for restraining demand when demand begins to run away. Moreover, when production and employment are subnormal — and the subnormality is actually caused by tight credit — the Federal Reserve is able to lift activity by making credit more readily available. But when the declines in activity and employment have not been due to tight credit but to basic unbalances in the economy, such as excessive inventory accumulation and excessive capital formation, its efforts to stimulate activity have only a minor effect.

# PART 3

## International Exchange Problems

# Chapter 17

# International Exchange Problems

W E HAVE now seen how the use domestically of Sanctuary Money instead of Boomerang Money gradually impaired the bargaining power of workers in the free market and distorted the distribution of income between consumers and investors so severely that slow growth, unemployment, and general dissatisfaction became so pronounced that a "New Economics" system was adopted.

It remains a great misfortune that the economists of the past and present all overlooked the basic cause of the impairment and dissatisfaction, and to date have concerned themselves only with the symptoms of the trouble. Their historic failure to realize that all societies utilizing specialized production must arrange — if full employment in a free market is to prevail — that the claims to the goods, which they turn out concurrently with the goods that they produce, are funneled promptly into the market as a private monetary demand, has also led to vast floundering in the international monetary field.

Because all countries today use some form of hoardable money as their medium of exchange, international trade between them is necessarily subject to ceaseless variation and occasional disruption. Even when a single country's aggregate monetary demand is not stabilized—and its activity, wages, inflation and productivity swing up or down —its thrashing about with its own problems gradually throws its fixed exchange rates out of line and transmits trouble to other countries.

Several systems for achieving stable international trade under fixed exchange rates have been tried. The full gold bullion standard, which had its final breakdown in 1933, was one. This was followed by the interim and unplanned flexible exchange rates of the 1930's. Then we had fixed rates again under the Bretton Woods arrangements of 1944 and the subsequent Bretton Woods improvisations between 1968 and 1971. All of these systems have had their breakdowns. None of them has operated to induce positive corrective action by countries in surplus, as well as by the countries in deficit, nor to intensify domestic private monetary demand in all of the trading countries simultaneously. After rigging and freezing their exchange rates, all the systems have called for austerity and a lowering of activity in the deficit country as the main corrective to its balance of payment deficit (which is the cost to the deficit country—in reserves or borrowings—of trying to hold to its chosen exchange rate). We shall examine each of the systems mentioned. Sad to say, each one could have worked better if the trading countries had used nonhoardable money as its medium of exchange. As it was, each was doomed to have recessions and trade troubles for lack of it.

Today, U.S. policies for stabilizing its foreign trade are confused because U.S. monetary authorities—ever since they chose to use gold as a reserve control over the volume of U.S. bank credit extended—seemed not to have adequately understood the relative value of the commodity, gold, and the checkbook dollar, which is a debt obligation. They did not understand how an ounce of gold was and is functionally and quantitatively related in value to our major monetary unit, the checkbook dollar. (This relationship was explained on page 100.) Without that understanding they cannot understand or deal sensibly with the role of gold or the role of the demand deposit dollar as an international monetary unit.

The world needs some kind of an international monetary system. Made up as it is of many countries which trade with one another, the world needs some system that will give the trading countries a reasonable idea of what the relative future values of their currencies will be. Because almost all trade relates to future delivery dates, traders, manufacturers and bankers would not import or export readily if exchange rates fluctuated so widely that the risks growing out of currency changes alone could seriously hurt them.

If exchange rates fluctuated daily with the supply and demand for the various currencies, there would, of course, be no balance of payments problems. But there might also be a greatly reduced volume of trade. In theory, flexible exchange rates with broad future markets and absence of bureaucratic controls would eliminate the problem of deficits and surpluses in the balance of payments. But, after considerable experience with flexible rates, such as from 1933 to 1944, manufacturers and bankers in foreign trade rather unanimously prefer, whether rationally or not, to have fixed exchange rates for operational or emotional reasons.

International monetary crises occur when huge funds flow from one country to another in expectation of likely changes in exchange rates. Then monetary authorities focus on such crises issues. Because all countries today use sanctuary money, the authorities try to use government spending programs and credit and fiscal programs as corrective tools. They also maintain that a satisfactory international monetary solution must zero in on the role of the dollar and the price of gold. It certainly must. Serious as such issues are, however, they are very subsidiary problems (in political economy) to the overruling ones of stabilizing domestic prices, and of intensifying and stabilizing aggregate private monetary demand domestically and internationally.

Undoubtedly, the most fundamental issue is to design a monetary system or instrument in which the *instrument itself* guarantees that the recipients of money income—both domestically and internationally—exercise their claims to goods and services at approximately the same rate at which the goods and services themselves are produced—whether the exchange rates are rigged out of line with supply and demand or not. A monetary instrument is needed which in the normal course of its use assures, among other things, that countries with surpluses in their balance of payments promptly patronize the countries in deficit. An instrument is needed which will match the beseeching for sales by deficit countries with a beseeching for goods by surplus countries. With such an instrument in use—under either fixed or flexible exchange rates—a country could not experience deficits or surpluses of any significant size in its balance of payments.

Until such a monetary instrument has been designed, monetary leaders will have to resort to one irrational improvisation after another in dealing with the role of the dollar and the price of gold. The world needs a system that will not only eliminate the balance of payments problem without invoking tighter credit and other deflationary controls, but one that will put specific pressure on countries in surplus to hurry their monies back into the deficit country's markets for goods. Such a system should also concurrently intensify the aggregate monetary demand for all goods and services, and do all this without relying on either of the major disruptive recourses of government: compensatory spending and credit restraints.

Let us premise that two island groups agree on a fixed parity ratio: that two monetary units of one country shall exchange for one unit of the other. If the carrying cost of owning these monies were larger than the average carrying cost of owning the products of the islands, neither island would find it advisable to build up a surplus of checkbook claims against the other—in the event that one island wanted to buy more goods than it sold. Neither island would want to accumulate claims against the one in deficit when the latter's slowly deteriorating money, given in payment for what was obtained, made it costly to delay using the claims for a long time even if fixed parity ratios existed. The island in surplus would buy something—the best buy that it could make on the basis of "comparative advantage." Deficits in balance of payments that normally accompany island trade would as a result be very small and temporary.

The world seems to want fixed exchange rates. This requires, of course, that the trading countries possess central bank reserves. These reserves could be relatively small if the deficits themselves were relatively small. (And they would be very small if all surplus countries, which today grant to recipients of income the privileges of respending their money tardily, were set up to operate with nondeferrable currencies that would push money holders to speed up the tempo of their return into the markets for the goods of the countries in deficit.)

# Chapter 18

## The Full Gold Bullion Standard and Its Limitations

Throughout history, gold has been valued highly because of its beauty, scarcity, and indestructibility. Consequently, when trade grew to require the use of a medium of exchange, gold was early selected to serve as money. Each nation placed a value on its gold coins on the basis of gold's domestic buying power and on the value attributed to it in foreign lands. Every country engaging in international trade had its own currency. These countries therefore amicably decided on the relative value of their currencies for trading purposes. They decided on what were called the parity ratios.

If each country permits free markets and permits its foreign exchange dealers to buy and sell currencies, the dealers — in touch with the bids and offers for currencies all over the world — would normally change the parity ratios a little from day to day. Under such circumstances, each country would in effect be operating under floating exchange rates, fixed by the changes in supply and demand. Countries have often had such floating exchange rates, but traders, merchants and bankers much prefer to have fixed ratios, believing that such ratios remove a major risk from future commitments. Traders want stable rates on which they can rely as a basis of contract, trade and long term investment. For a long time, the world's major countries managed successfully to provide for relatively stable parities by relying on the use of the full gold bullion standard.

In about the year 1800, Britain, at the vortex of world trade and the possessor of a worldwide banking system, provided a bench mark of value for gold—a worldwide offering price for gold—which enabled traders to plan on stable rates for both long- and short-term commitments. Someone had to provide such a value gauge by implying that gold had an intrinsic value. Britain provided the first bench mark by making its own currency convertible into gold at a fixed rate and by offering to buy and sell other currencies at fixed known exchange rates. All currencies thus became exchangeable for gold. By that action, the gold standard and the British pound became the world's unit of account.

Then about 1890 a uniform worldwide value of $20.67 per ounce was assigned to gold in terms of the major currencies of the time. A mark, for example, was defined as being worth 1/87 of an ounce of gold, the pound sterling as worth a little over 1/4 of an ounce, the dollar as worth nearly 1/20 of an ounce, etc. All the major countries related the value of their currencies to the arbitrary agreed upon value of gold at $20.67 per ounce. This price was not a "free market supply and demand" price. It was an internationally administered price-support price. Because there was no black market for gold in which people were offering even as much as $22 per ounce for it, the $20.67 offering price in the U.S. was probably on the high side. In the U.S. until 1933, Congress attributed this value of $20.67 to an ounce of gold.

Some nations used their gold coins as everyday currency and most of them used their gold as a limiting control over the volume of credit extended by their commercial banks to bank borrowers. Moreover, they used their gold as reserves for settling deficits in their balance of payments. As a result, the flow of reserves between countries operated fairly well as a stabilizer of exchange rates between countries.

Because countries in international trade do not, over the short term, have their sales equal their purchases, they need a reserve of acceptable currencies or other assets for settling deficits in their balance of payments when the deficits occur. Naturally, the countries that related their currencies to gold were willing to accept gold as a prime reserve asset and to settle their payment deficits by shipping gold to one another. So by relating the value of their currencies to gold, and by using gold as their reserve asset, they placed themselves on the full gold bullion standard.

For several decades, the gold bullion standard worked fairly well. It did stabilize exchange rates, although—as we shall see—it had serious shortcomings. In time it became inoperative for three major reasons: (1) assorted internal domestic developments within the trading countries such as inflexible wages and prices—which the movement of gold between countries could not correct—caused the parity ratios to go out of line, (2) the tardy respending of foreign currencies that countries in surplus obtained, and (3) the holdings of gold in the world's central banks became gradually inadequate to serve as the entire reserve for settling deficits in the balance of payments. Before we examine how those three disrupters worked, let us review how the full gold standard worked when at its very best.

The full gold bullion standard was intended to work automatically to maintain parity ratios between currencies. It was designed to control credit conditions within countries so well—by shifting the gold base for credit between countries—that little discretion over credit was left to the managers of the central banks. The mechanism involved was designed to work approximately like this:

When the money supply in any one country expanded as a result of enlarged gold reserves and easy credit, the price level rose in that country. The rising prices baited an inflow of foreign goods and induced an outflow of domestic gold to pay for the goods brought in. As the gold flowed out, however, the base for bank credit contracted in the gold-exporting country and operated to contract its money in circulation and to lower its prices, relative to those in other countries.

The gold outflow, of course, expanded reserves abroad and accommodated easier credit in the country receiving the gold, tended to lift its activity, and to increase its prices. This price rise, in its turn, baited an inflow of goods from the country which had just lost gold, expanded gold payments to that country, eased that country's credit and lifted its prices. Thus prices and parity ratios tended to be stabilized through gold movements between the trading countries.

This gold yoyo stabilizing mechanism worked fairly well for several decades. All the while, Americans and others believed that governments should, as policy, accumulate gold. To some extent, too, they seemed to believe with the classical economists that the use of paper money and bank deposit money as medium of exchange could only be justified if such monies were convertible — at least internationally — into gold at some fixed exchange ratio.

Before World War I, when the gold standard prevailed so fully that any American could obtain gold coins on request for his currency and checkbook money, the gold standard did help to achieve a few worthwhile economic goals. But in retrospect, these goals were mainly of secondary importance.

The fact that all governments related the value of their currencies to the value of an ounce of gold did knit together the currencies of the world. These currencies could fluctuate only a little way from the "mint parities" or gold would be exported. There was little opportunity for bureaucratic meddling. Exchange rates were relatively stable, and even paper currencies were convertible for one another and for gold. Still, these favorable contributions were not enough.

Booms and depressions, cyclical unemployment, and vast swings in the buying power of currencies occurred nonetheless. Some people thought the gold standard even got in the way of what might have been corrective actions. They even accused the gold standard of being a transmission belt for both deflation and inflation.

Superficially, the stabilized exchange conditions which the shuttling of gold from country to country induced did seem to justify a useful role for gold. But a Spartan acceptance of deflation in the country losing gold was part of the adjustment process — part of the automatic mechanism required — if the shuttling of gold reserves from country to country was to stabilize the exchange rates.

But, even Spartan austerity would not stabilize the exchange rates unless the wages and prices in trading countries were flexible both downward and upward. In the end, people came to regard both the domestic downward adjustments in wages and prices and the increases in unemployment as intolerable, and too high a price to pay for merely stabilized exchange rates.

When people began to realize fully that among the prices for stabilizing exchange rates — by shuttling gold reserves away from the country with the boom and rising prices — there was the austere requirement that they contract their own country's credit, lower their own wages and prices, and increase their unemployment, they concluded that they wanted a better monetary system than that — despite the help that gold shuttling gave to stable exchange rates. They wanted a system that would regard continuous full employment, continuous growth, full production, and stable domestic prices as being far more worthwhile objectives of government policy than the mere stability of foreign exchange rates and the convertibility of paper currencies into gold. They sought a system that would permit full blast exchange under conditions of sacrosanct wage rates and "full employment."

Incidentally, they have never found that system. This book is an effort to provide it.

## Altered Goals of Economic Policy

If proper goals of economic policy are to include — besides relatively stable exchange rates — (1) stable activity, (2) full employment, (3) higher worker income relative to capital income and (4) individual freedom, then the gold standard as it was operated (not as it could have been operated) got in the way of desirable social action.

The old-fashioned gold standard — as a balancing wheel for interlaced world economies — was not good enough. Gradually and subtly the critics did succeed in changing the monetary system. In 1934, Congress, for example, aimed at an entirely new rationale for the government management of domestic affairs. It began to regard full employment, vast privileges for labor unions, higher nominal wage rates for their own sake, altered income distribution, etc., as being more important than stable exchange rates. (What it did not see was that the two legislative recourses to which it resorted would necessarily lead, as we saw in Chapter 12, to price inflation; nor, as we have seen in Chapter 15, to vast expansion of bureaucratic discretion.

In the 1930s, the U.S. Congress, convinced that collective bargaining and compulsory unionism would help to lift the real income of workers, gave considerable sovereignty over wage rates to union leaders. For example, they legislated the Norris-LaGuardia Act in 1932, the Wagner Act in 1935, and the Walsh-Healy Act in 1936. One result was that wages and prices ceased to be flexible downward. Wage rates began to be raised steadily to outrun increases in man-hour productivity and to be fixed mainly through labor union power. This inflexibility helped to make the old gold standard inoperative. For several decades now, wage rates have been institutionalized to rise continually whether gold was flowing

out of the country or flowing in. The full gold bullion standard could not work under such conditions. The removal of
the needed wage and price flexibility was one major destroyer of the full gold bullion standard as a stabilizer of
exchange rates.

There was a second major destroyer: price inflation. In
the U.S., for example, Congress legislated the Employment
Act of 1946. In effect, Congress decided that the primary
duties of government were to prevent unemployment caused
by any reason whatsoever, and to blot up all unemployment
by resort to government spending if need be. Preservation
of price stability and prevention of price inflation were of
secondary importance.

All major countries permit or encourage labor unions to
increase employment costs more rapidly than engineers can
increase output per man-hour. Under such conditions, business survives by meeting the excessive costs by raising its
product prices. These price increases require more monetary
units to carry on the increased dollar volume of worldwide
trade. Pressure is therefore put on the central banks to
facilitate the creation of bank money at a much faster rate
than the output of gold could be increased.

All of the world's exchange media are being inflated. (See
Figure 36 opp.) During the past thirty or more years, the
whole world has institutionalized price inflation by resorting
to two devices — Nationwide Collective Bargaining and
Deficit Government Spending — which it naively believes
will tend to give the workers of the world a larger portion
of the claims to the goods produced, and to lift and intensify
the overall monetary demand for goods and services. Under
institutionalized price inflation, the full gold bullion standard
was clearly unworkable.

There was a third major destroyer: the volume of international trade began to increase far more rapidly than the
output of gold. World trade grows by about eight percent

ANNUAL RATES OF INFLATION IN MAJOR COUNTRIES

| | Indexes of Value of Money (1958=100) | | Annual Rates of Depreciation | | | |
|---|---|---|---|---|---|---|
| | 1963 | 1968 | '58-'68* | '66-'67 | '67-'68 | '69-70 |
| United States | 94 | 83 | 1.9 | 2.7 | 4.0 | 5.7 |
| Germany(Fed.Rep.) | 90 | 80 | 2.2 | 1.7 | 1.6 | 3.6 |
| United Kingdom | 90 | 74 | 2.9 | 2.4 | 4.5 | 5.2 |
| Italy | 86 | 72 | 3.2 | 3.1 | 1.4 | 3.7 |
| France | 80 | 69 | 3.8 | 2.6 | 4.4 | 5.4 |
| Japan | 79 | 62 | 4.7 | 3.8 | 5.1 | 7.5 |

*Compounded annually

Source: First National City Bank – September. 1969 **and September 1970**

Figure 36

per year in terms of the world's steadily inflated prices. Thus, other things being equal, the volume of reserves needed for settling international payments deficits should logically (while sanctuary money prevails) also grow at a parallel rate. Annual population growth of about two percent, plus annual average increases in output per worker of about three percent, plus average annual price inflation of about three percent, means that the annual dollar increase in the currency value of world trade increased by about eight percent per year. Under such circumstances, gold could not (unless its price was unpegged and floated freely) continue to serve as the sole international reserve currency. That disturbing situation has plagued the world.

Gold reserves have ceased to increase in volume. Since 1965, gold has even been drained out of the reserves of the central banks. Under such conditions, the existing volume of gold became too small to serve as the entire international reserve for handling international deficits.

The proposals that currently enlist most support in official circles for monetary reform are those which seek to create more international monetary reserves and liquidity—reserves of a nongold nature. In my opinion, that is not a basic approach.

During the huge government debt financing and general inflation of World War I, the gold standard first broke down in several European countries. For a time the warring countries no longer expressed the value of their currencies in terms of gold. Still, after World War I was over, some countries made an effort to return to new or prewar parities. Germany, France and England did succeed in doing so for a time, but the domestic deflationary credit policies that were required in each country to bring this about caused so much internal unemployment and stagnation that many banks were forced to close. By 1933, Britain devalued its pound in relation to other currencies. This helped to cause both American exports and U.S. domestic prices to collapse. In 1933, the U.S. also went off the full gold bullion standard. The disruption gradually forced the abandonment of all efforts to return to prewar parities.

The gold standard, when it was working at its best, had put pressure both on the country in deficit and on the one in surplus—pressuring the one to install contractive policies and the other to install expansionary ones. *It did not, however, tend to stimulate concurrently the aggregate private monetary demand for goods in both countries.* (Chapter 22 will show how the adoption of nonhoardable money would do that, and in addition would place pressure on both deficit and surplus countries to adjust their balance of payments promptly.)

If in the 1930's the U.S. Treasury had been lowering its offered purchase price for gold by, say, two percent per year, people certainly would not have been disposed to purchase gold, even though it was available.

It follows that if, say, a two percent annual decline were to prevail in the Treasury's offering price for gold (when and if the offering price is above the free market price), a country would not in normal times need to possess large gold reserves in order to remain on the full gold bullion standard.

Clearly, the old-fashioned gold standard helped nations to achieve only secondary goals. As stated, it ignored or overlooked the major economic goal of contributing to an intensification of aggregate private monetary demand. So even if we could go back to the old-fashioned gold bullion standard (under the old sanctuary money conditions), it would not solve the basic monetary problem. We need something better. Moreover, even if it were generally desirable in theory to return to it, the output of gold in recent years has been too low to make the return feasible under conditions of wages and prices that are inflexible downward, where price inflation is built into the system, where the volume of world trade expands at an eight percent per year rate, and where the whole world uses collateralized bank obligations — which facilitates the safe deferral of spending — as its medium of exchange.

While gold is too scarce to be used again as a medium of exchange under today's sanctuary money conditions, there would, however, even today be enough of it to serve as adequate international central bank reserves *if* the U.S. Treasury began to lower its offering price for gold by two percent per year and thus impose a dissuader on the ownership of it.

In 1929, the world was on the full gold bullion standard. Anyone wishing to do so could then exchange his currency or checkbook money at the bank for gold coins and put them in his pocket. It was possible to do this in practically all countries even though the total gold reserves of the world's central banks were then only about $31 billion. The reason was that there was no buying power advantage in owning gold rather than checkbook dollars.

Inasmuch as the value of gold at the time was legislatively

tied to the value of the U.S. checkbook dollar (20.27 of such dollars for each ounce of gold until 1933, and 35 such dollars for each ounce of gold from 1934 until March, 1968) there was no buying power advantage in owning gold instead of bank money.

Not only has the value of gold been tied legislatively to the value of bank money, but gold has not even been an earning asset. It has cost money to own it and to store it safely. Moreover, it is a relatively clumsy medium of exchange compared to checkbook money. Thus, owning gold normally carried several disadvantages. In the 1920's, conditions were such that no one normally wanted to own it even though they could obtain it. Consequently, it was feasible at that time to remain on the full gold bullion standard.

## A Higher Price for Gold

Many people maintain that the U.S. Treasury price for gold is too low and should be raised. They stress that gold production costs, like other costs, have risen drastically since 1934 when the $35 gold price was first established, that many marginal gold mines have already had to shut down, and that as a result the world's gold reserves are undesirably low. They stress that if the price were, say, twice as high as it is now—$70 per ounce, for example—the current U.S. stock of gold would suddenly be worth twice as much, and that the U.S. would reap a tremendous windfall profit. Concurrently, the $40 billion of gold in the reserves of the world's central banks (which total about $100 billion) would jump in worth to $80 billion. Such a reserve of gold would suddenly reduce the need for some time to come for more dollars, pounds and "supplementary drawing rights" to augment gold as international bank reserve assets.

A high price for gold would undoubtedly induce billions of dollars worth of gold to flow back into central bank reserves. But would not a gradually lowered U.S. Treasury offering price for gold which began above the current free market price do the same thing?

Suppose that you were an European and had acquired a million dollar hoard of gold at thirty-five dollars or even seventy dollars per ounce which you were speculatively holding for the day when the U.S. would raise its offering price for gold still further. Suppose, then, that instead of Congress raising that price, it suddenly legislated a gradually lowering purchase price by the rate of, say, two percent per year from a beginning price slightly higher than the prevailing London market price. Such a legislated price change would induce you to turn in your gold dollars for more U.S. demand deposits. Speculators, too, would not want to hold gold under a gradually receding price. They would hurry to minimize their losses.

The gold standard was intellectually defective in concept, and would still be defective — even if the world's total central bank reserves consisted entirely of gold, and gold actually replaced all of the current holdings of dollars and pounds held as reserves. Even if we had one hundred percent international gold reserves, we would still have done nothing to the free market mechanism for resolving the problem of lifting consumer income (without the reladling of it by bureaucrats) in relation to the savings available for investment, or of intensifying and stabilizing aggregate private monetary demand, and at the same time curtailing governmentalism, stabilizing prices, and extending the borders of individual freedom. Later pages will tell how that could be done.

# Chapter 19

## Interim Monetary System, 1933–1944

AFTER the full gold bullion standard broke down during 1931–1933, and before the Bretton Woods arrangement was set up in 1944, a decade of monetary turmoil prevailed. We had floating exchange rates, competitive exchange rates, and a welter of governmental controls over money flows and trade. When politicians believe that exports are good and imports are bad, they impose tariff barriers to imports, border taxes, clerical foot-dragging, exchange controls, quotas, licenses, etc., even when a system of free exchange rates prevail. In the main, however, currencies were exchanged mainly on the basis of what they would buy in relatively free markets.

In 1933, when the U.S. price level was flat on its back, President Roosevelt was convinced by two university professors that if the Congress raised the U.S. Treasury's offering price for gold, the action would operate to lift the whole price level of the United States.

Congress did act on the President's recommendation and raised both the buying and selling price of gold from $20.67 per ounce to $35 per ounce. But the U.S. price level stayed on its back nonetheless. Congress returned us to a new limited gold exchange standard under which the dollar was arbitrarily defined as being worth 1/35 of an ounce of gold, 9/10 fine, instead of 1/20 of an ounce of gold as before. From then on, the U.S. Treasury offered to buy all the new and old gold of the world at $35 per ounce. It in effect established an *international* price support program for gold, just as it had earlier established a *domestic* price support program for wheat and corn. Concurrently, Americans were forbidden to own gold. So were the banks. And the U.S. Treasury commandeered the gold from the banks at $20.67 per ounce giving gold certificates to the banking system in return.

Because the $35 price was far above the prevailing $20.67 price — which probably was itself far above what a free market price would have been (since there had not been a black market price for gold above $20.67 per ounce) — an avalanche of gold rolled into the U.S. Treasury. And a windfall profit flowed out to the producers of Colorado, South Africa, Russia and others. New marginal mines were opened up all over the world. The value of the world's gold production promptly doubled. During the five years before 1934, the annual production of gold averaged $640 million. During the five years after 1934, it averaged $1,200 million. By 1946, the U.S. owned 57 percent of the gold of the whole free world.

The standing offer of the U.S. to buy gold from anyone and everyone at $35 per ounce was soon matched by other countries. They, of course, dared to pay $35 per ounce because they could always, if they so desired, unload the gold on the U.S. at that figure.

The up valuation of gold vis-à-vis the dollar and other currencies was, of course, nominally a devaluation of all the world's currencies in terms of gold. But this in itself did not affect the relative parity ratios of the many currencies at the time. World trade went on as before at approximately the old exchange rates.

Since the spring of 1933, the use of gold as medium of exchange in the U.S. has been prohibited. The gold certificates which the Federal Reserve System received for the gold that it turned over to the U.S. Treasury were used only in a nominal way after 1933 as a domestic central bank reserve and nominally as limit gauges to the volume of credit (demand deposit and currency) that the member banks could extend to their customers.

Realistically, the genuine controls over the amount of credit extended by the U.S. member banks have nonetheless been (1) open market operations, (2) the discount rate, and (3) changes in reserve requirements.

During the whole 1933–1944 period, the shifts from country to country that occurred in the ownership of gold did not affect the volume of credit that the member banks could extend. The yoyo ups and downs had no contracting or expanding impact on the nation's level of activity. Moreover, the shifts had practically no influence on the exchange rates during the entire period—which included the war period.

In retrospect, the U.S. price support program for gold during the whole support period was an intellectual aberration. If from 1933 to 1944, for example, the price of gold had remained at $20.67 per ounce, the reserves that the Federal Reserve would have made available to its member banks (through open market operations) would probably have had the same degree of adequacy, while the parity ratios of the world's currencies, and the price levels of the U.S. and other countries would also probably have remained the same.

Prohibiting the use of gold as money, and raising the offering price for it, influenced many people—including monetary authorities—into believing that the arbitrary U.S. support price for gold of $35 per ounce represented an intrinsic free market value. Many people naively believed that "the value of the dollar was tied to gold." They did not

see that it was the other way around—that it was the value
of gold that was tied to the dollar, in the same way that the
value of wheat and corn are tied to it with arbitrary support
prices. They did not see that the $35 value of gold was safe
only so long as the confused monetary authorities of the U.S.
wanted to offer $35 per ounce for it. Nor did they seem to
realize that the 1934 decision to pay $35 an ounce for gold
to all suppliers of gold was the innovation of an international
price support program for gold.

The academic and lay world are so mesmerized by the
age-old desire for gold that they have not even tried to
depict rigorously the relative value of the gold and the
banking system's "debt obligation," the demand deposit
dollar. (See pages 97–99.)

Gold has had a legal and a functional tie to the dollar, but
that nexus was widely misunderstood. When the world was
on the full gold bullion standard—before the prohibition on
owning gold—anyone could, as we have seen, exchange his
currency or checks at the bank for gold coins and put them
in his pocket. People could do this in practically all countries. Still, they chose not to do so, mainly because—to make
the point once more—there was no buying power advantage
in owning gold over and above owning checkbook dollars.
An illustration will bring that out:

If, say, you had owned one hundred dollars in gold in 1900
and another hundred in checkbook money, you would not
have been able at any time between 1900 and 1933—as
prices of goods and services went violently up and down—to
buy more goods and services with the gold than with the
bank money. Because the value of gold is tied to the dollar,
it loses buying power in terms of baskets full of goods at the
same rate as the dollar loses value. It therefore declines in
buying power year after year as U.S. built-in price inflation
proceeds. Again, as illustration: No one who owned, say,
one hundred dollars in gold in 1934 could at any time since

then have purchased any more goods in the open market place with it than he could have purchased with one hundred dollars in U.S. currency. Since 1934, the two monies have shrunk in lock step together. Despite that fact, and despite the fact that checkbook dollars can be invested for a three percent to six percent return, while gold holdings can earn nothing at all, many foreign holders of dollar currency have turned their checkbook dollars in for gold.

But the world seemed to want, at least nominally, to fix exchange ratios and to relate the value of their currencies to gold at a fixed U.S. price. They attempted to arrange that through the Bretton Woods Agreement of 1944.

# Chapter 20

# The Bretton Woods Monetary System, 1944–1968

IN 1944, World War II was ending. The monetary authorities of the major countries — unhappy over the monetary and trade controls that most countries had imposed during 1933–1944 while floating exchange rates had prevailed — decided to design a monetary system that would operate under fixed exchange rates. So, led by John Maynard Keynes and Harry Dexter White, the leading monetary nations met at Bretton Woods, New Hampshire, in 1944, set up the International Monetary Fund, and agreed on the rates at which they would exchange their currencies.

The basic aim of the system was to meet deficit imbalances, not by changing the parity ratios, but by shifting international reserves from surplus countries to countries in trouble until (1) the country in deficit either improved its efficiency and gave the world more goods for its money, or (2) lowered its domestic production costs and standard of living so that it could give the world more favorable prices. If all that failed, then devaluation was to be in order.

As business demand for currencies swings up and down, the parity ratios in London, Paris, Berlin, etc., tend, of course, to do likewise. But the IMF agreement of 1944 stipulated that no currency could fluctuate more than one percent from the agreed upon par. If it deviated or fell more than that, the country with the weak currency had to step in and, through its central bank, lift its weak currency by buying it with its dollar or gold reserves. If it ran out of reserves and could not borrow more reserve funds, it had to devalue its currency. All nations must bolster their currencies with reserve purchases, and to devalue if they run out of exchange reserves.

## Why Fixed Parity Ratios Break Down

The disparity that occurs between countries in their rates of technical advance, in their adoption of inflationary domestic policies, in nationalization of industries, etc., insured that the fixed exchange parities layed out at Bretton Woods could not endure.

Suppose that each of ten countries has a monetary unit of its own with a well-established buying power in terms of domestic goods and services. Then suppose that the monetary authorities of the ten countries agree on the relative value of their currencies—that is, on their parity ratios.

Suppose further that they agree to carry on trade among themselves at those ratios and agree to lend money to any of the ten countries whose currency becomes unacceptable to the other nine because of its decline in buying power. Slippage into such unacceptability can occur for three major reasons: (1) different rates of growth in output per man-hour in ten countries; (2) different rates of price inflation in ten countries and, (3) different degrees of risk of revolution in the ten countries.

Another drawback to the satisfactory operation of the Bretton Woods fixed parity system was politics. When conceived, the Bretton Woods Agreement premised more political flexibility in modifying parities than turned out to be realistic. The framers in 1944 did not foresee that countries with currencies that were sliding into fundamental disequilibrium would fight devaluation and parity changes as ferociously as they have done. To leaders of countries in deficit, such as Wilson of Britain and DeGaulle of France, for example, currency devaluation was regarded as such a pronounced public confession of failure that they would sooner impose severe austerity on their own people as an alternative.

Still another basic trouble tends to prevent fixed, agreed-upon exchange rates from enduring. With exchange rates frozen, countries in deficit—which buy more over the short run than they sell—are saddled with the entire adjustment problem of getting the countries in surplus to buy more goods from them. It is entirely up to the deficit country to attract more trade and customers. This they attempt to do by clumsy, Stone Age means such as direct controls over exports and imports (subsidizing one and taxing the other), or by deflating their domestic costs and standards of living. The recent exchange rate system as set up under the Bretton Woods Agreement had no direct means designed into the currencies themselves (as this book maintains could be done) for pressuring the countries in surplus—those that obtained more revenue than they were willing to turn around and disburse at the rates at which they received the revenue —to buy more goods from the country in deficit. (Later pages will show how this could be done.)

Figure 37 portrays the size and composition of the total reserves of the world's central banks. (See next page.)

Since World War II, both the U.S. and Britain have run large deficits in their balance of payments. Even so (probably because the real value of the dollar and the pound depended on the quality of the notes, mortgages and bonds in the portfolios of the U.S. and British banks—and these were deemed to be of relatively high quality), the deficit obligations of the U.S. and Britain have been widely acceptable as

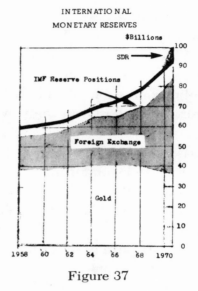

Figure 37

reserves. (The widespread acceptance of the pound as a reserve currency, however, has shrunk considerably since its devaluation and other troubles in 1967.)

The belief and hope of many monetary authorities in 1944 that the use of gold as the international monetary system's reserve would act in all countries, including the U.S., as a brake on the quantity of money created by the several banking systems turned out to be a dream.

In 1967, for example, a year when a two billion dollar avalanche of U.S. gold flowed abroad, the total reserves of U.S. commercial banks did not go down. The governors of the Federal Reserve System merely increased vastly the nonborrowed reserves of the member banks through open market operations that year and facilitated an increase in the U.S. money supply by about eleven billion dollars. According to the classical theory of the full gold bullion standard — which was obsoleted by the Bretton Woods system — U.S. prices should also have declined as the gold reserves flowed out. Instead they rose by approximately three and one half percent. So the large outflow of gold in 1967 exercised no braking action whatsoever on either the volume of money created or on the upward trend of prices.

It was the U.S. that wrote the rules in 1944 at Bretton Woods under which gold played its powerful role in international finance. Unilaterally, the U.S. linked the value of gold to the value of the dollar by saying bureaucratically that one dollar was to be worth 1/35 of an ounce of gold, 9/10 fine. From 1944 until mid-March, 1968, it continued to do this in the mistaken belief that the international value of its checkbook dollar was dependent — not on the quality of the assets in the portfolios of its banks — but on the integrity of the U.S. promise to exchange an ounce of gold for every $35 worth of checkbook dollars turned in.

In 1932, for example, the purchasing power of the dollar, considered in terms of the basket of goods that it would buy, was 2.41 times as high as it was in 1920, even though the dollar was on both dates redeemable in and worth 23.2 grains of gold. Historically and logically, stable dollar prices for gold at government treasuries have been (and are) unable to provide a stable purchasing power for the dollar. That stable buying power can be communicated to it only by insuring an adequate desire on the part of the public to move steadily from money into U.S. goods by insuring that only the debt obligations of successful producing borrowers are monetized into demand deposits by the banking system.

In 1967, foreigners began to request gold for their dollars at a rapid rate. By March, 1968, the large drain forced a vast modification of the Bretton Woods monetary system and caused the monetary authorities to spawn several inoperative adjustment proposals.

# Chapter 21

## International Exchange Arrangements after 1968

IN MARCH, 1968, the world's monetary system—midst closed exchanges and the panic buying of gold—had a preliminary breakdown. The major monetary countries, after deciding hurriedly not to supply the free London gold market any longer with enough gold from their reserves to hold the price down to $35 per ounce; but they then resuscitated the system, after a fashion. They agreed to a two price policy for gold. They agreed to a free market for non-monetary gold, and further agreed to buy and sell gold only among themselves and other IMF countries—at $35 per ounce—to settle their balance of payments accounts, but only on condition that no country sell gold to the London and other free gold markets where a higher price might prevail. Their action threw into relief the fact that the logic of the system was itself basically defective.

The U.S. monetary authorities believed that the gold drain would stop only if the U.S. could induce foreign dollar surpluses to come back into U.S. markets in larger volume. So the Administration, the Federal Reserve, the Congress, analysts, and commentators everywhere seemed willing to pay almost any self-induced deflationary price to lure laggardly used foreign dollars to return promptly into U.S. markets.

But they made no move toward the use of a monetary instrument which would put pressure on foreign held dollar surpluses to do so. Instead, they recommended assorted deflationary actions such as proposals to: Withdraw troops from Germany; Cut and run in Vietnam; Raise the price of gold; Raise interest rates in the U.S.; Deflate the U.S. economy; Impose interest-equalization taxes; Institute direct controls over labor costs and selling prices; Invent a new international monetary reserve unit, and let the value of the U.S. dollar fluctuate freely in relation to other currencies.

These assorted proposals indicated clearly that our monetary leaders had no integrated comprehension of the root monetary trouble and that they were merely improvising desperately. Blind dedication to continued use of "deferrable money" instead of to "nondeferrable money" was their basic error.

During the period after March, 1968, the fiscal authorities realized that the world's monetary instrument was out-of-date. Being oblivious of the merits of nondeferrable money, however, they merely discussed patchwork recourses of many kinds. Among them were these:

1. The creation and allocation of Special Drawing Rights.
2. Border taxes and subsidies.
3. An international central reserve bank. (Even if bank officials acted responsibly and prudently, considerable merging of sovereignty would be an initial requirement. What men and which country could be entrusted to warehouse all of the world's gold?)
4. Demonetize gold and adopt the dollar standard exclusively as the world's monetary reserve.
5. Expand the number and kind of "swap" agreements.
6. Adopt floating exchange rates.
7. Adopt a "crawling peg" — or slow changes in parity ratios.

8. Accept a wider permissible band of fluctuation in exchange rates—from the recent one percent from parity to, say, three to five percent.
9. Resignedly learn to accept worldwide price inflation, and then provide ever larger reserves by creating ever more Special Drawing Rights, etc.
10. Negotiate parity changes more promptly before any one balance of payment deficit becomes frightening in size.
11. Establish fixed rates under more flexible rules—rules that would change and be geared to relative rates of, say, growth and/or inflation.
12. Help the U.S. to improve its balance of payments either by helping it to run a large trade balance or by curtailing sharply its flow of U.S. capital abroad.

From March, 1968, until August 15, 1971, improvisations enabled the Bretton Woods system of fixed parities to hang together—mainly through vast loans to countries in pronounced deficit. But the flaws in the system were so basic that it was irreparable.

On August 15th, 1971, President Nixon decided not to ship U.S. gold in settlement of the claims of other countries against the dollar, imposed a ten percent surtax on U.S. imports, and decided to let the value of the dollar float.

The world wants stable or, at least, slowly changing exchange rates, full employment, domestic growth and personal liberty—all without resort to discretionary controls over business by government. But as yet the world has not designed such a system—and none of the proposals being resorted to tend in that direction. Until a monetary instrument like the one described in Chapter 7 has been designed, our monetary leaders are only spinning their wheels and will continue to resort to one irrational improvisation after another during the years ahead in dealing with payments deficits, parity ratios, and the price of gold.

# Chapter 22

## International Exchange under Nonpostponable Money

THIS SECTION presents a revolutionary plan for improving and stabilizing *international* trade regardless of whether trade is proceeding under inflationary or noninflationary conditions, or under fixed or floating exchange rates.

Preceding chapters have tried to make clear that the fundamental international monetary problem today is to design a monetary system or instrument *in which the instrument itself guarantees* that the recipients of money income —both domestically and internationally—exercise their claims to goods and services at approximately the same rate at which the goods and services themselves are produced.

Such a monetary instrument should also make it possible to adjust the balance of payments deficits without requiring that the country in deficit deliberately contract as policy the level of its domestic activity, that is, deliberately "cool its economy" by means of assorted deflationary programs.

Chapter 7 described two such monetary instruments. Resort to the use of either would place a demurrage pressure on the holding of money. Either would cause property held in the form of money to lose value about as rapidly as depreciation losses proceed—on the average—on all other kinds of property. Aggregate private monetary demand would be continuously intensified by such a pressure against loitering.

The money medium itself would place a penalty pressure on all recipients of income to disburse it at the rate at which they receive it.

Either recourse proposed in Chapter 7 would cause all of the world's sanctuary monies to become boomerang monies, and cause them to return more rapidly to their homelands in the form of a demand for the homeland's goods and services.

In contrast to today's approach whereby countries-in-deficit resort to self-induced austerity, I propose to modify the rules and pressures that bear on the use of all kinds of money so that all nations would avoid lengthening the interval between their transactions, and in that way be able to keep their international accounts in better balance. A small, controlled and known-in-advance reduction in the "store of value" of all monies—obtained by resorting to either of the two plans mentioned above would operate to generate that result.

Earlier chapters dealt with the likely domestic impact of the adoption of a boomerang money. This chapter will explain what the likely impact of a boomerang money would be on *international* trade if several—or even one—major country adopted a medium of exchange that had a gradual—but known-in-advance—receding value.

(Of the two feasible ways described for intensifying the pressure to re-use one's current income promptly, I indicated on page 100 that I preferred—only for an interim period—that Proposal No. 2 be adopted: that the U.S. return to the full gold bullion standard and concurrently lower steadily its offering price for gold by two percent per year. Proposal No. 1, however, would be more basic, but Proposal No. 2 would be easier to sell to the American public.)

The preferred solution would be to have Congress stipulate that the courts enforce no demand deposit obligations of commercial banks to depositors unless the banks and depositors jointly agree beforehand (when making their deposits and loans) that the principal sum of the bank's obligations to the borrower be lowered steadily by about two percent per year. Nonetheless, the solution of arranging for a slow and steady decline in the price of gold would be a very good recourse as an interim arrangement, so long as gold is used as an international monetary reserve.

As international trade goes up—in monetary terms— through increases in productivity, population growth, and price inflation, larger reserves are regularly needed (when countries operate under fixed or almost fixed exchange rates). The current annual growth tempo is about eight to ten percent per year. Gold alone is completely inadequate today to serve as the only central bank reserve. Consequently, central banks have had to supplement their gold holdings with dollars and pounds and to use all three kinds of assets in settling their deficits with one another. Total central bank reserves today amount to over one hundred billion dollars. The monetary authorities plan to add to them by creating about three billion dollars of "paper gold" per year for ten years, that is, about thirty billion dollars worth of paper gold during the decade ahead. Perhaps they should delay—because systematically lowering the U.S. Treasury's offering price for gold by two percent per year would reactivate a vast amount of hoarded gold. Such a lowering could probably continue for many years. It should begin from some newly established purchase price which is higher than the prevailing free market (providing it is at a time when South Africa is not withholding but is selling its high annual gold production to the free market). Only then would the "offering price" for gold come down to the new likely free market "supply and demand price." No one knows where that free market price would be.

Until some such lower price is reached, the receding

purchase price for gold would operate as a continuous pressure for intensifying and stabilizing the world's aggregate private monetary demand for goods and services and, in the process, for lifting the income of employees.

Suppose the U.S. were to revert to its pre-Stockholm policies toward gold, and to the policy before 1966 of maintaining a percentage gold reserve under the volume of federal reserve bank credit extended. Let us imagine that this situation is again established with a ten, five, or even three percent required gold reserve along with the additional arrangement of a resulting two percent demurrage charge on all money. (See Chapter 7 for how that would work.) By itself, a declining two percent purchase price would drive considerable gold out of hoarding. It would reactivate a vast supply of gold for use in trade and banking and vastly expand the size of the world's gold reserves. As of today, it is estimated that the free world possesses about eighty billion dollars in gold (at $35 per ounce). The hoarders hold about forty billion of it, and the world's central banks hold the other forty billion.

It would also make the realignment of exchange rates between countries easier to achieve, because the aggregate monetary demand for the goods of countries in deficit would be increased. It would, for example, induce American dollars — which had been spent rapidly abroad in buying foreign imports — to be under continuous pressure to come back promptly to purchase American exports and help us with our balance of payments.

### Cure for Deficits in Balance of Payments

Just as, almost by definition, a country "in deficit" has purchased more goods from other countries than it has sold to them, so a country "in surplus" has not exercised as large a demand for goods as it has had the power to exercise. In fact, a country in surplus is extending credit somewhere to countries that are in deficit. Europe's dollar surplus of over fifty billion dollars which she accumulated in recent years should come back with certainty to the U.S. at the same tempo at which the U.S. sent them out. So should the gift dollars and the tourist dollars – and the Eurodollars. So should the investment dollars. But, as we witnessed in February and March of 1968, many European nationals who then held dollar surpluses – after laggardly exercising a demand for American goods – suddenly chose instead to buy U.S. gold in volume through London and the other free gold markets.

I maintain that the need of the day is to design a *monetary instrument* that forces nations in surplus, along with those in deficit who have rigged their exchange rates too high, to help adjust the balance of payments problem.

Originally, the International Monetary Fund contemplated means for penalizing nations – with long continued payment surpluses – by discriminating against their exports. But nothing was done about it. I contend that it could be done easily if all countries, or even one major country (the others would have to follow suit), utilized a medium of exchange that carried a demurrage cost. A demurrage penalty would clearly constitute a continuing pressure on all nations in surplus to use their funds promptly, if not for imports, then for capital investment abroad.

Today, if market values permit Germany, for example, to sell and export more to the U.S. than the U.S. can export to Germany, Germany can "save" U.S. dollars – that is, add them to its reserve balances. Under the now defunct Bretton Woods system, as under the full gold bullion standard (which also tried to operate with deferrable money), the full responsibility for restoring – or evening out – the imbalance in trade falls on deficit U.S.; none falls on surplus Germany. If Germany chooses not to sell to the U.S., even when the U.S. tries to maintain an unrealistically high value for the dollar, she should nonetheless be kept under pressure to redisburse her dollar holdings. Her real option should be to patronize the U.S. or to use her dollars in buying goods from other countries which are willing to accept dollars on some terms — but not to stand on the side lines with her claims.

If the credit money that the U.S. disbursed had had a slowly receding value related to the length of time that it was held and not reused, the dollars would become worth less and less to the Germans the longer they delayed disbursing them. Just as much pressure would have been pressing on Germany to correct the payments imbalance as on the United States. Boomerang money would eliminate deficits in the balance of payments the same way that floating exchange rates would do it. Surpluses would not get out of line with deficits. On September 27, 1972, the Treasury Secretary, George Schultz, reflecting the Administration's views for improving and stabilizing international monetary exchange, proposed to the International Monetary Fund that sanctions be employed against nations that insist on running balance of payment surpluses. But he proposed no specific means. Unfortunately, all the assembled experts of the Fund seem completely oblivious of the potential possibility of invoking the writer's Proposals #1 and #2.

## Advantage of Boomerang Money over Floating Exchange Rates

A system using boomerang currencies would for a very basic reason be even superior to one using floating exchange rates. Under a money with a shrinking store of value, the *future value of the money — although declining in value at, say, two percent per year — would always be known in advance, could be anticipated in advance, and could be relied on far into the future for making future business commitments.* Business contracts could be made without uncertainty regarding future currency rates, as would be the case if floating exchange rates were being depended upon. Money would have a gradually contracting (but nonetheless a known-in-advance) store of value that would be related to the calendar. Although floating or flexible exchange rates could also clear the currency markets promptly, they would not insure that aggregate monetary demand would stay up in any one country, nor that the buying power of any one currency would hold up.

In 1938, for example, we had, in effect, floating exchange rates. But aggregate monetary demand in the U.S. and elsewhere declined so drastically that the U.S. had a depression with eighteen percent of its workers unemployed. Parity ratios were in continuous flux. It mattered less, however, that they were changing promptly under the floating rate conditions of the time than that the deferrable money in use permitted a slowdown in its rate of use and a lag in aggregate monetary demand.

The world wants, as we have seen, currencies with predictable future values. These values hinge considerably on the maintenance of aggregate monetary demand. Nonpostponable money would balance off trade without being subject to a major disadvantage of floating exchange rates — namely, the continuous fear of traders that monetary demand might sag and lead to discounted values for the currencies of the countries suffering recession.

### One Major Nation Could Pioneer the Adoption of Nondeferrable Money

Fortunately, if a single major country were to adopt a nondeferrable money, it would not only assure itself full blast domestic exchange and activity, but also put pressure on other countries to follow suit.

If a single bellweather nation such as Germany were to adopt nondeferrable money, other nations would quickly be under pressure to follow her lead. Countries receiving German marks for their exports, for example, would be under pressure to redisburse them promptly in trade. A new restraint would be imposed on the recipients of the marks not to build up surpluses.

If, while such an arrangement were prevailing in Germany the U.S., for example, were simultaneously trying to repair its deficits with the orthodox recourse of inducing domestic austerity at home in efforts to lure U.S. dollars back into U.S. markets, the American people, seeing Germany's action and boom results, would probably angrily insist that the U.S. follow Germany's lead and proceed to place a demurrage cost on the dollar.

Because the monetary systems of all major countries are basically alike, I believe that with a modest amount of work it would be easy to modify any one system to fit the logic of the two means described in Chapter 7 for stabilizing monetary demand. Financial officers of multinational corporations would probably quickly anticipate the needed modifications.

With a demurrage cost of, say, two percent per year on money, the deficits and surpluses between countries would be much smaller. Therefore, much less shoring up would be called for. The need for central bank reserves would probably be less than half of what it is today. All accounts would tend to stay in balance. The present forty billion dollar volume of gold reserves would probably be large enough, under the circumstances pictured, to constitute all the reserves needed for even higher levels of international trade than prevail today. Supplementary dollars, pounds and SDRs would not be needed as reserve currencies.

The use of demurrage money would not, however, eliminate the functional requirement that countries with subnormal annual gains in productivity and larger than average rates of price inflation would have to devalue their currencies, just as it was necessary for them to do under the Bretton Woods Agreement. Again, the only difference would be that countries under pressure to devalue would be under, say, only half as much pressure, because the countries in surplus—when possessing surpluses of demurrage money—would be under pressure to do half of the corrective work. Under the present international monetary system, the U.S. being a country in deficit, is expected to do all of the adjusting to the imbalance.

To that end, the U.S. proposed to entice foreigners who hold dollar surpluses to come and spend them here. It proposed to deflate the U.S. economy in Spartan fashion; to entice foreign tourists with lower U.S. prices, to devalue the dollar, to bait foreign investors with higher interest rates implicitly to lower the U.S. level of activity, and to accept more unemployment and a lower standard of living. The recourses and restraints mentioned were in themselves obviously evil. They constituted prima facie evidence of a faulty understanding by the monetary authorities of the basic essence of money (see Chapter 2) and of the disruptions necessarily caused by the historic worldwide use of hoardable money.

Under a receding U.S. Treasury purchase price for gold, an avalanche of gold would also probably return from the world's hoarders and speculators to provide an added monetary demand for goods. The disgorgers would probably promptly shift their cash into securities and investment.

### The Use of a Nonpostponable Money Would:

1. Automatically take care of the worldwide need for adequate central bank reserves.
2. Insure that exchange rates would be adjusted promptly and continuously.
3. Induce surplus countries to disburse their surplus reserves so promptly that they could not build up their liquidity by dampening trade.

4. Make unnecessary the resort to devices discriminating against imports in efforts to balance trade.
5. Lick the problem of price inflation (see Chapters 12, 13, 14) and by doing so eliminate the need for continually enlarging international reserves as world trade expands in nominal dollar terms. As of now, for example, price inflation during the postwar period alone has cut world liquidity in half.

In the light of the basic error of trying to operate international trade with sanctuary money instead of with boomerang money, it is a chronic mistake to concern ourselves myopically with the role of gold and deficits in our balance of payments as isolated subjects. That is not to start at the beginning. In order to understand how our many economic ailments are tied together, we had to begin, as was done in Chapter 1, with something as elementary as the processes of exchange in simple societies that utilize specialization of labor. Such a beginning made clear that the prompt use of claims to the output of others (claims which one receives for one's own contribution to output) is the *sine qua non* for both domestic and international stability in every society that relies for production on limited government and persuasion and makes use of a free division of labor.

It is shocking that the world's monetary authorities see no way out of situations where one country is in deficit and another in surplus, but for the country in deficit to deflate itself. The recourses they suggest include: tighter credit, curtailed spending, taxes on imports, subsidies on exports, reductions of buying power by way of personal taxes, prevention of investment abroad and curtailed travel. These are among the plebeian meat axe recourses. The basic idea is to seduce the tardily used dollars held abroad to come back into U.S. markets, but not to penalize them for staying away. The monetary authorities propose to do nothing about putting pressure on foreign held dollar claims to goods to come back home within the time period during which the American production (corresponding to the money creating loan) took place—the time period during which in economic theory they functionally should come back.

Thus, in summary, recourse to either of the proposals described in Chapter 7 would overcome the three most troublesome international monetary problems:

A) By maintaining prompt re-use of money surpluses everywhere, all national payments deficits would be so small that the *liquidity* problem would be overcome. With about forty billion dollars of gold reserves still on hand the age-old shortage of an internationally acceptable money would be over.

B) Because demurrage money would press countries momentarily in surplus to disburse promptly in world markets their accumulating foreign currencies—and make the best buys they can arrange for—the *adjustment problem* would also be resolved. Changing parities would not be accompanied to any large extent with hiatuses in international trade.

C) Monetary crises occur when, for a variety of reasons, holders of a currency lose confidence in its value relative to other currencies, and in panicky fashion flee to preferred currencies. If nondeferrable money were to stabilize the volume of private aggregate monetary demand in all lands and the volume of trade between all lands, parity changes would be as gradual as they would be under floating exchange rates. The *crises problem* would disappear because changes in confidence would at worst be gradual. Flights of business capital would not be induced. The worldwide availability of gold would also calm those who are driven by its shrinking volume in one country to seek the currencies of countries where the volume is increasing.

All efforts to date at a rational international exchange standard have failed. Floating exchange rates would come closest to providing a functional solution — but only if non-deferrable currencies were being used. Floating rates, when deferrable money is being used, provide no solution. They would still leave international trade vulnerable to disruptive slowdowns in aggregate demand, with accompanying unemployment and recession.

Inasmuch as the use of nondeferrable money would be a fundamental innovation and seems to be the only means for resolving the three most troublesome international monetary problems, why wait its adoption?

You have now seen the economic and social disruption that the use of deferrable money tends to create. Use of it has been a key barrier to obtaining satisfactory results from the free market system. It has also been a major reason for the resort to more and more governmental efforts to correct the shortcomings which necessarily characterize the free market system when it tries to function internationally with sanctuary money instead of nondeferrable money as its medium of exchange. Arranging for a nondeferrable money with a gradually declining price could stop the drift toward governmentalism in the international as well as in the domestic field.

# PART 4

## Socioeconomic Problems Brought on by Unreliable Monetary Demand

# Chapter 23

## How Our Fear of Declines in Monetary Demand and of Losing Our Jobs Blocks the Acceptance of Leisure

Use of "loitering money," and resulting uncertainty over the stability of private monetary demand, induces job insecurity in all of us. We live in constant fear that a downturn is always around the corner. We know from experience that the monetary demand for goods and services is so anarchic, and so unreliable that unemployment will arrive sooner or later. Owners of corporate stocks, for example, are always hoping to get ready for the next downturn. After witnessing recessions in 1969, 1966, 1961, 1958, 1954, and 1949, they know that recessions are a way of American life.

### The Sociology of Adjustment to Instability of Monetary Demand

The uncertainty deriving from "loitering money" is the major causal factor that drives workers to try to build up reserves of buying power for those slack periods when they may be unemployed, or for when they grow old. As a consequence, many workers make a practice of moonlighting, of working long hours, and of not relaxing.

This chapter will show that our reliance on a hoardable money that makes demand uncertain also makes the economy itself so vulnerable that it leads us into excessive and irrational work activity—while in effect it denies us the leisure that we could otherwise enjoy.

Why do we choose to produce endless elaborations of old products rather than to enjoy more of the leisure that machines make possible? Could it be that our use of a money form that occasionally defers demand for our services is the factor that frightens us into making that odd choice?

Suppose that some supernatural power had long ago decreed that (1) U.S. workers must work continuously for forty hours per week, (2) that their jobs would always be so uncertain that they would not dare to work less—and (3) that it had nonetheless endowed them with the ability to increase their output per man-hour by about three percent per year. Suppose that it were foreordained that those determinants were to circumscribe their lives forever. At least two of those determinants have been very stable ever since World War II. The increase in man-hour productivity has in fact been about three percent per year since then. And Figure 38 shows that the length of the working week of about forty hours has been with us in the U.S. for the last forty years.

Can it be that we are living under an institutionalized predetermination? Many facts suggest that we are. But it is not supernatural power that restricts us to a life of forty weekly hours of activity, and to relatively little leisure. Instead, it is we who lock ourselves into that silly preference.

We did it by installing uncertainty—fear for the job— among all U.S. workers by using a nondepreciating checkbook money which drives them to prepare for the worst by laboring without letup. We do it by using a money medium that enables money savers to use their money tardily and without cost to themselves for both consumer goods and capital goods. We have locked ourselves into a treadmill that requires us to busy ourselves in a massive amount of very low priority activity.

If, say, it took ninety percent of the working week to

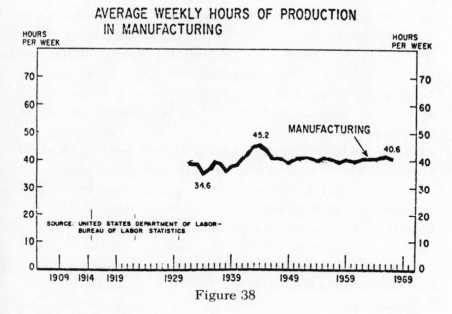

**AVERAGE WEEKLY HOURS OF PRODUCTION IN MANUFACTURING**

Figure 38

provide for our basic food, clothing and shelter two hundred years ago, and that it now takes only thirty percent of our time for that purpose, we have no choice but to fill in the remaining working hours by introducing and producing new kinds of goods and services—silly though they may be. Clearly, as less and less time is needed to produce goods and services that take care of high priority needs, U.S. workers have no choice—since the recourse of additional leisure, except for a dozen holidays, is largely ruled out by the forty hour week—but to design and produce new goods and services—or ever more variations of the old.

### The Impact of Output That Is Not Spontaneously Wanted

The nature of jobs and job opportunity necessarily changes as we maintain a constant length of working week while more machinery comes in. Just how do we adjust to the immigration of machines—of billions of mechanical slaves, who need no rest, who need no sleep, who neither dream nor love, who do nothing but compete? As they take many of our jobs away, we hurriedly, desperately, invent others. But many of these new jobs they also take over. Thereupon we try to make much of the few things that iron men cannot do. But our chronic unemployment testifies that we do not do this very well.

Machines have been displacing workers for two hundred years, and the displaced men have, in a rough measure, been reabsorbed. But is the reabsorption process a distorter of serenity, values, and rationality? What social effect does the retention of a constant length of working week have on our choices and activity when machinery is steadily injected *and the stability of the monetary demand for our services is not concurrently assured?*

During the past two hundred years, our productive capacity has increased steadily, and yet the cold facts of our society reveal that we do not have the additional job security and serenity which corresponds to the productive capacity of our age. Hardship, worry, unceasing toil still characterize the life of our multitudes. Uncertainty, moonlighting and ever more working wives all reflect this. Forethought and fear for the morrow characterizes our time. There seems to be a disruptive mechanism within the economic machine itself which automatically dissipates the major portion of what machinery makes possible for our world. This disruptive process is very different from any that has been outlined anywhere before.

Note that Bureau of Labor Statistics employment data report that there are very few more employees turning out tangible goods today than was the case fifty years ago, even though the U.S. labor force has almost doubled during that period. Almost all of the new workers have gone into the production of intangible items — mainly services. This despite the fact that the output of tangible goods has con-

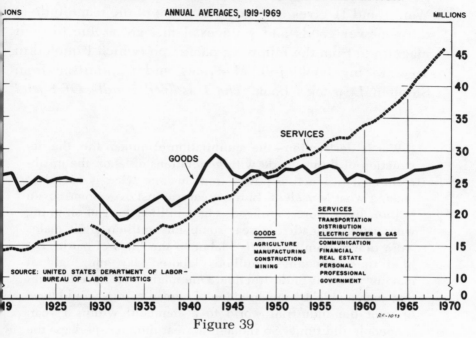

**EMPLOYMENT—SERVICES VS. PHYSICAL PRODUCTION**

ANNUAL AVERAGES, 1919-1969

Figure 39

currently also drastically increased. In 1919, there were only 6,770,000 automobiles in the U.S. Now there are over eighty million of them. In 1919, there were only seven million homes with bathtubs and only 2,800,000 with telephones. Now these numbers have risen into the tens of millions. (See Figure 39 above.)

Reckless indeed seems he who says that the adjustment process is defective. But this issue arises: Are the new types of jobs and goods and opportunities the economic equivalents of the old? Has there been a change in the nature of our newer consumption goods and services, a change large enough to impair and demean the free market system itself? The newer classes of goods and services do differ from the old in being less needed, in being more superfluous and in being less spontaneously wanted by the people with buying power. U.S. experience during World Wars I and II gives us a good measure of the magnitude of these newer goods and services. I first got a clue to their magnitude from the following paragraph (which I quoted in 1932 in my book, *Job, Machines and Capitalism*) from Stephen Leacock's book, *The Unsolved Riddle Of Social Justice.*

War is destruction—the annihilation of human life, the destruction of things made with generations of labor, the misdirection of productive power from making what is useful to making what is useless. In the great war just over, some seven million lives were sacrificed; eight million tons of shipping were sunk beneath the sea; some fifty million adult males were drawn from productive labor to the lines of battle; behind them uncounted millions labored day and night at making weapons of destruction. One might well have thought that such a gigantic misdirection of human energy would have brought the industrial world to a standstill within a year. So people did think. So thought a great number, perhaps the greater number, of the financiers and economists and industrial leaders trained in the world in which we used to live. The expectation was unfounded. Great as is the destruction of war, not even five years of it have broken the productive machine. And the reason is plain enough. Peace, also—or peace under the old conditions of industry—is infinitely wasteful of human energy. . . . War turns workers from making the glittering superfluities of peace to making its grim engines of destruction. . . . The economics of war, therefore, has thrown its lurid light upon the economics of peace.

I began my speculations with Leacock's suggestive point of view and gradually evolved the hypothesis that many of the evils of Capitalism—its unemployment, its very unequal distribution of wealth, its plant duplications, its wastes of production and distribution, and its commercialistic and materialistic standards—were basically rooted in the failure to insure stability of aggregate monetary demand and in the attendant failure to appreciably shorten the hours of labor. In 1932 I wrote the following in the book referred to.

> Only when all the people of a community, the very rich and the very poor, have wants which induce them to spend their incomes as fast as they receive them, will there be no unemployment. If . . . we had some arrangement under which dollars were dated — under which the claims to wealth flowing to people were somehow cancelled or automatically lowered after a period . . . should the purchasing power not have been exercised — then demand would always equal supply and the capitalistic process could not slow down or stop. . . . The relation, accepted almost as a truism in economics, that production creates its own demand, assumes that receivers of income spend it immediately, either for new consumption goods, or invest it immediately for new production goods. But we must remember that when human beings have incomes which enable them to satisfy their spontaneous wants, they will be in no hurry to spend for the new and often weird products and investments which the advertising men and bond salesmen extend to them.

I contend that many of the wastes and evils of Capitalism themselves result from failing to reduce per capita working hours while labor-saving machinery is injected (because of the fear of downturns in monetary demand and employment) — that many industrial excesses constitute the expedient and logical recourses to which displaced labor and capital can flee when driven out of old activity by technical invention.

We entered World War I with about forty million workers. The Secretary of War reported that for 1918 about thirty-eight percent were in the army and navy. Some of their work was undoubtedly productive, but by conservative estimate, at least twenty-five percent of the labor force was truly nonproductive. In an economic sense, we had in effect reduced the length of the working week by twenty-five percent.

Unemployment in 1916–1918 went down to record lows,

wages zoomed, overall output increased, the standard of living rose, and the workers, with jobs available everywhere, even took it easy. The FRB Index of Industrial Production rose as follows:

| | |
|---|---|
| 1913 | 100% |
| 1914 | 99% |
| 1915 | 108% |
| 1916 | 111% |
| 1917 | 117% |
| 1918 | 116% |

How could such a paradox occur: fewer workers turning out more products?

A powerful monetary demand eliminated unemployment and gave even nonunionized workers (unions were not needed) such great bargaining power that they changed the pattern of income distribution. Consumers could buy back what was produced—and production ran full blast.

Percent of Total Income Received by the
Highest 5% of the Income Receivers

| | | | |
|---|---|---|---|
| 1913 | 33% | 1916 | 34% |
| 1914 | 32% | 1917 | 29% |
| 1915 | 32% | 1918 | 26% |
| | | 1919 | 24% |

Source: National Bureau of Economic Research. Income in the U.S., N.Y. 1922.

Whenever the capacity of industrial facilities exceeds the capacity of the market, manufacturers try to diversify their products in efforts to get a second order from those who have the buying power. They must do more than merely satisfy tangential wants; they must first create them.

When, however, the situation is reversed and the market outruns the capacity of the plant, manufacturers standardize their product. They call in their salesmen and stylists to work in the factories. If buying power gives business a market, business is disposed to eliminate the wastes of distribution on its own initiative. During World War I, the big businessmen of the nation themselves, under the Council of National Defense, made up the committees in charge of eliminating duplication.

It is easy to understand how production increased, even though workers took it easy, when one pictures the economies that resulted when industries:

> cut the styles of stoves and heaters 75%, eliminated 5,500 styles in rubber footwear, cut tire varieties from 287 to 32, cut shoe colors from 81 to 6, cut trunks to 6 sizes, reduced washing machine styles from 446 to 18, and eliminated 90% of household wringer styles, cut pocket knives from 300 styles to 45, plows from 312 to 76, etc.

The explanation of increased production thus lay in a situation wherein monetary demand outran both supply and labor availability, and gave industry an incentive to standardize and to stop its wastes of elaboration. Self-interest itself, operating under an intensified monetary demand and labor scarcity, was explanation enough of the change that transpired.

Historically, economic competition has been regarded as a force which generates lower prices for industrial products—the force which drives prices down to the vicinity of the cost of production. It has done so in many industries, but in many others prices did not drop with a decline in manufacturing costs. Instead of prices dropping with each increase of efficiency, new investment and distribution expenses often crept in to eat up the difference which efficiency had made possible.

The reason this situation has not been understood has been because of an inadequate view of value, and an oversight of the new economic character which machine-made goods possess as distinct from that possessed by handmade goods. An explanation of how the process operates to permit and make necessary the injection of industrial wastes and excess plants, and how these can easily eat up the savings of efficiency, is discussed in detail in Chapter VI of my book, *Jobs, Machines, and Capitalism.*

Since the beginning of the industrial revolution, we have maintained our human exertions near a maximum during all the while that labor-saving machinery was being introduced. With the introduction of machinery, the percentage of "man-days" needed for the production of those necessary goods like food, shelter and clothing, which we spontaneously desire and demand, has rapidly decreased. As a result, an ever increasing portion of the practically constant amount of expended labor energy is *forced* to turn to the production of goods less necessary to those with money—goods for which demand must first be created.

These reluctantly wanted goods may be either consumption goods, such as new styles in dresses, hats and automobiles, or they may be capital goods, which the big income receivers purchase with their savings. The economic and social nature of commodities changes when invention makes available more labor hours than are urgently demanded and employed by the holders of buying power. At this point, consumption goods must then be high-pressured upon the people who have the income, since they already have their spontaneous needs satisfied. Their demand for reluctantly wanted goods affords a very limited market in comparison to that which the demand for spontaneous wants * provides.

---

* By "spontaneously wanted" and "nonspontaneously wanted" goods, I do not mean necessities and luxuries. The value of a want is not the essence of the case under our present system. Rather, the essence is whether goods are immediately wanted and purchased as soon as buying power is obtained. Spontaneously wanted goods may be valueless and useless; they may include perfumes, gin, and hired ostentation, but so long as they cause people with money to spend income as fast as they receive it, they facilitate the present operation of our system. Nonspontaneously wanted goods require for their introduction and continued production the persistent efforts of advertising. Most style elaborations, and many services and gadgets come under this classification.

It is in the new lack of spontaneity, in this new obstacle to the *prompt* completion of transactions, that trouble arises. John Stuart Mill—to take his example—taught that generally when machinery displaced a printer, more pressmen were needed. This was true; but today, when machinery permits even pressmen to be displaced, then designers, creators, footmen, advertisers, manicurists, and life insurance agents spring into being, workers who are not spontaneously wanted, but who must themselves create the demand which they seek to satisfy. This is a result with a far different social portent.

Not unless American consumers, including the wealthy, spend their income, either for consumption goods or investment, as fast as they receive it, can the economy function without unemployment. If human nature were such that people demanded their yachts and new styles as promptly and spontaneously as they demand their milk and meat, then the historic view that demand will always be adequate could be accepted without modification. The "economic man" of theory demands all goods in that way, but he is not like the rest of us. Economic theory errs in assuming that all goods—whether diamonds or bread—fit economic formulae in the same way.

Workers displaced by machinery are forced to try to create new wants for those with purchasing power as fast as they, as workers, are displaced. Thus the labor market contains (in addition to those workers who are engaged in ephemeral occupations) a residuum of unemployed which (until Congress gave the unions enough monopoly power to push employers to grant wage and salary increases far in excess of productivity increases) raises havoc with the bargaining power of workers during the initial slicing of the pie in the free market. (See Figure 3, page 15, for the size of the residuum of unemployed, and Figures 1, page 12 and 2, page 14 for the size of the initial slicing of the pie before Congress legislated monopoly powers to the unions, and for the size of the slicing after those powers were granted.)

As explained in earlier chapters, it was the use of a monetary instrument, the hoardable checkbook dollar, which gave money savers so much power to defer demand—so much of the available buying power that the economy was driven to produce nonspontaneously wanted goods in large quantity, and by this deferral to weaken the bargaining power of workers to such a high degree that in blind fury the workers induced the state to legislate to them the unreasonable coercive power they now possess. This turnaround in power does not, however, put a stop to the need to produce ever more trivial goods and services because we still: 1) maintain the forty hour long work week; 2) achieve about a three percent annual increase in man-hour productivity; and 3) use a postponable money which makes the stability of overall monetary demand so uncertain that no one personally dares not to build reserves for when recessions might again occur.

## A Materialistic Outlook

A materialistic outlook and culture is one of the apparent effects of a situation wherein an ever increasing part of the practically constant length of the working week is diverted into the production of less necessary goods, goods for which demand must first be created.

Laissez-faire production is more likely to produce socially desirable goods when it attempts to satisfy our bodily needs, but not when it attempts to satisfy our psychic needs. The first needs are prescribed by nature. They remain the same regardless of the motive to activity which seeks to satisfy them, whereas the latter needs are man-made. They are subject to creation, and when selfishness becomes the spur to this creation—as is necessarily the case when selfishness is made to work overtime by the retention of a long working week—they are as apt to be socially undesirable as to be socially desirable.

When selfish producers have satisfied the demand for necessities, they can find work for themselves with which to fill in the long working week only by creating and appealing to materialistic standards. Thus, by not releasing the selfish producer from the producing machine—by not shortening the working day appreciably when all the wood is in—we force the selfishness of the profits motive to become both the main creator and satisfier of psychic needs. *Here lies the root cause of our materialistic civilization.*

By being in a position where he must work overtime, and where he must determine what items shall be made in this overtime, the selfish producer becomes the most powerful director of human effort and aspiration. In self-defense, he is forced to direct these energies into materialistic channels—he is forced to stimulate standards which stress the desirability of a large consumption of new goods and services. Our long working week forces our producers to push us into a commercial religion and materialistic philosophy. Energetic salesmen, impelled by selfishness, try to determine the course of our spiritual expression. They impel us to desire wants and ends and methods which very well reflect the economic predicament in which our retention of long hours and uncertainty over the stability of monetary demand has placed us. When selfishness can turn nowhere else, it wraps our soap in pretty boxes and tries to convince us that that is solace to our souls. When hunger is satisfied, it appeals to snobbery.

With our Calvinistic worship of toil, we have had little concern with what might be most socially desirable, and have to an extravagant degree made of production an end and a world in itself. We have constructed a machine out of interest, wages, rent, and profit. Self-interest is the steam in the boiler. This machine turns out food, shelter, and clothing. But when all of these have been turned out and diamonds and pearls and platinum rings—and transient services and styles—flow out of the spout, we do not slow down the machine, but keep the whole force firing the boiler all day long. If a workman increases the efficiency of the unit turning out food, more men are then, as economists say, "released for other productive work" and are forced to shift to new diamond units. As economists, we worship production and do not bank the fires when several of the units begin turning out artificially maintained demands. As sociologists, we fuss over the distortion of values and behavior which diamond-ized fingers cause among the kneaders of bread, but we do not look at the boiler room to see whether the reading on the steam gauge is too high.

By forcing the selfishness of the profits motive to direct our industry long after the spontaneous wants of the people with money have been produced we force businessmen to seek new variations of our old products. With selfishness as their motive, they first aim their efforts at the people in the upper income group. But they hit us all. Soon even the poor wear white collars, cheap jewelry, and the latest styles. How does this come about? The producers first introduce a new item for the well-to-do, but it soon develops that cultural imitation, intensified by advertising, also drives the poor to seek a ranking on the basis of conspicuous consumption. Economics explains the stimulus; social psychology explains only the reaction. By being placed in a position where the businessman must seek and produce a new want every time a better tool is invented, he is driven to seek some human frailty which he can cultivate into a new demand. He is forced to inject materialistic standards to dispose of those products which the long working week compels him to make. We should not blame him because he has no alternative; it is the only way out of a predicament in which uncertainty of monetary demand and a long working week have placed him.

His technique of influencing human behavior has come to be an art of the highest refinement. Advertising agencies work with scientific zeal on the best presentation of some message like "The Rouge He Will Never Detect," or "Get Thin To Music." Hundreds of thousands of advertisers chant standard-forming statements in our ears. As we read the papers and magazines, our eyes must run the gauntlet of their impositions; on the highways, billboards pester us; on the streets, flashing signs arrest us; posters force us to read; in the mail, advertising literature comes to disturb us, until we suddenly discover that without conscious thought we have been hypnotized into believing that "clothes do make the man" or driving a Cadillac instead of a Ford confers social distinction. The most oily-tongued men in our midst devise the little phrases that mold our thoughts. Money comes to be the standard by which many of life's values are measured.

Salesgirls, with few talking points, describe the dresses that they sell as being fashionable or as being Parisian Creations; threadbare clerks stress the fact that an article is imported or "in style." We witness the strange paradox of men with twitching stomachs injecting wealth criteria into the milieu in which they must live. They are induced to do this in order to keep business activity going. Our poor as well as our rich have a powerful motive to foster wealth standards. Such standards produce more job and business opportunities.

The root of our materialism then, is not to be found in any mystical examination of man's spirit, but right here in an uncertain monetary demand, which causes the worried worker to produce reserves for a rainy day, and in the imposition of long hours of toil on the productive capacities of a modern industrial machine.

American youth rebels at the pattern of life which ever greater efficiency under a forty hour week brings forth. The youngsters see their fathers working strenuously at increasingly squirrel-cage work. They do not want that kind of a future for themselves. They rebel. They nurse a "counter culture," if one can call it that. Life, they reason, must have more meaning than their parents are able to extract from unreducible man-hours applied to machines.

### The Search for Adequate Markets that Will Justify Investing U.S. Hoardable Money Savings Leads to Unwise Public Programs and Policies

The combination of continuous three percent increases in man-hour productivity and forty hours of weekly input requires such an intense search for new products and expanded markets that public policy is driven into sponsoring programs of questionable wisdom.

Since 1960, an increasing portion of the released man-hour input of the U.S. has gone (see 19, 20 on chart following p. 346) into supporting nonworking claimants to the nation's output. Our laws increasingly arrange for such a diversion. And, as time goes on, it seems that ever larger portions will go to support the nonworkers.

The government institutes programs which tax the money claims of the well-to-do and then diverts them to the poor. By taxing the high income people (and divesting them of their potential leisure), and diverting the revenue by way of "transfer payments" to the nonworkers, government can successfully provide a market for the ever expanding output of the forty hour working week.

Already, during the booming 1960s, 14 percent of New York City's inhabitants were on relief. Inasmuch as the recipients of relief and other transfer payments are privileged to vote on how much of the producers' income shall be diverted to them, politicians will always cater to their votes and expand the diversion to the idle. In this way, a large portion of the potential leisure of the forty hour workers can be blotted up.

Because we do not stabilize the monetary demand for goods and thereby induce many workers to choose leisure, we inaugurate programs which give buying power, through long-term soft loans, etc., to our mortal eastern bloc enemies so that they can constitute a market for basic products such as wheat and computers. The real driving motive behind such foolishness is to create markets for all the things that our efficient economy can produce under our sacrosanct forty hour working week. By chanting that trade — even with totalitarian governments — promotes peace, we excuse our behavior in doing business with the enemy. Our urge for markets causes us to override U.S. security interests. We exchange our computers and atomic findings for hog bristles and long-term IOUs. Only by stabilizing monetary demand so well and so convincingly that workers will stampede into leisure, and in that way cancel our need to funnel buying power via gifts and IOUs to friends and enemies, will we cease undermining our own security.

With government sponsorship, both our savings and the fruits of our savings are now about to flow hellbent into Russia, China, North Vietnam, etc. The economic machines of socialism and communism produce so poorly that American investors, using quixotic logic, are even concluding that communist lands represent investment opportunity. Despite American experience in Cuba, Chile, and Canada, U.S. investment does not crumble the ideological walls. All of South America regards American corporations as exploiters, and rings with the cry of "Yankee go home."

The whole urge to invest abroad at any price represents still one more bit of evidence of the maldistribution of U.S. income which results through bargaining in a nominally free market when the monetary instrument in use is loaded against the worker and in favor of the saver. Today the savers, who are inundated with claims, do not know where to put them profitably in America. In desperation, they are building up the implacable enemy to our way of life by investing elsewhere.

## And if Private Monetary Demand Were Stabilized by the Use of a Nonloitering Money

The serious happiness of most men depends upon the satisfaction of both instinct and spirit. Both find their satisfaction in work and in human relations. The expression of spirit, of individuality, requires time—time in which to reflect and in which to freely and enthusiastically champion the practical furtherance of that work or those ideals which give meaning to one's life. But with uncertain stability of monetary demand, moonlighting and long working hours, our energies are so completely devoted to economic concerns which have little spiritual meaning to us, that we have no energy remaining for the time that is our own. The leisure that we do have is robbed of its sparkle. Forethought and fear for the morrow dull our thought. Spiritually poverty-stricken, we labor and die.

For poverty is far more than a matter of bread. Millions of workers are denied the opportunity of developing their personality, or of discovering and aligning themselves with vital social movements. Even the humblest unit might yearn to know and understand, to contribute his spirit freely to the promotion of what he believes to be the good, to add his bit to the world of creation. Instead, as things are now, millions are out to beat the system rather than to improve it. They are forced to live on a diet of frustration and despair. Certainty of stable spending and full employment plus leisure would change all this. Freed from worry for the future, and only required to work a short week, are not the possibilities for mankind encouraging?

What we need most urgently is a new attitude toward work and the working week. The age-old view, a product of centuries of niggardly productivity, that it is our predestined lot to labor from sunrise to sunset, must be revised in a time when iron slaves have come to do our bidding. Adoption of a nonloitering money would permit us personally to adjust our working hours to other values than just the wresting of food from the soil.

It is not selfishness, nor the profits motive, nor the institution of private property which constitute the root cause of our major socioeconomic evils. Rather, it is the fear and desperation growing out of inadequate monetary demand and unemployment, both superimposed upon selfishness, that is the cause. So often do we witness the honesty, generosity, considerateness, integrity, and kindliness — traits which generally characterize workers when they feel flush and secure in their future — shrink and shrivel into dishonesty, greed, untrustworthiness, and cruelty that it becomes easy to believe that desperation and uncertainty more than greed transform man into beast. Might not the social controls which grow out of human association be strong enough to hold selfishness within bearable limits if all men did not fear recession and unemployment?

How sad indeed it is to live with continuing uncertainty in monetary demand when we already have the plant which other nations have yet to build. How tragic when millions of adults have already seen, during two world wars, the milieu that blossoms under reduced but well-directed man-hour inputs. As explained earlier, it lies within our power — by using an improved monetary instrument — to eliminate unemployment and the fear of unemployment; to eliminate industrial wastes, inanities of consumption and corruption of values; to remove the brakes from our marvelous machine; to give engineers free rein to spin the wheels of industry, and to rekindle the American belief that the material world can be molded to our will.

We must sometime opt for leisure as efficiency is increased. We must sometime realize that labor-saving machinery does not of itself bring about a single moment of leisure when the working week is not shortened as a result of confidence that a stabilized monetary demand will be maintained; at best, it merely shifts our efforts from one task to another. Moreover, it is no rash guess that in another generation our present productive capacity will be doubled. What shall we do with it? Shall we use it to drive ourselves into more fears of recession, more moonlighting, more consumption of frills and tinsel, more industrial wastes, or shall we turn it into a hopeful, laughing leisure?

# Chapter 24

## Conclusion

ALL THE monies of history — sheep, cattle, furs, ivory, tea, grain, tobacco, silver, gold, warehouse receipts, bank notes, personal notes, government obligations — have consisted of three forms: commodities, warehouse receipts, and evidences of debt. For the last one hundred years, however, intangible debt obligations of one kind or another have served as our predominant form of money. The property content of these obligations is not satisfactory for our modern world. Fortunately it can be modified to advantage.

Having reviewed the evolutionary nature of money and the functional role that it seeks to play, we are in a position to consider "What should money do?" and "What should money be?" Among other things, money should clearly:

1. Provide a claim to the goods and services produced.
2. Constitute a gauge or standard of value.
3. Provide a store — but not an unlimited store — of value.
4. Be a form of property that facilitates the easy exchange of one property item for another.
5. Be available in a wide range of values — in small and large denominations — pennies, dimes, dollars, etc.
6. Be durable, compact, and easily portable.

7. Consist of identical units so that the time-consuming problem of appraisal does not arise at each transaction.
8. Help to speed up exchange and not help to slow it down.

As we have seen, modern money gives the holder complete
freedom in respect not only as to *what* he will take in payment, but also as to *when* he will take it. By using contractual debt obligations as money, producers of all kinds
are given the privilege either of taking their rewards in the
period during which they produce the goods and services, or
of suspending as long as they please the exercise of their
right to choose products in settlement of their claims. Inasmuch as undue suspension of choice means unemployment
and a piling up of unsold goods, we see where a poorly
designed money may help check economic growth and even
generate widespread unemployment.

During recent decades, people have been looking in a
floundering way for a new system of society which would
provide on the one hand for job security and rapid growth,
and on the other for freedom from bureaucratic control.

The Federal Reserve System, too, has overlooked the
curative possibilities of the approaches mentioned. The
System is a unique control mechanism which is designed to
govern a banking system that has thousands of independent
unit banks. It attempts to stabilize business with the few
tools that it possesses for controlling the reserves of those
member banks. Unfortunately, those tools are inadequate
for stabilizing overall private monetary demand, even when
the tools are wisely used. Basically, the whole Federal Reserve System is built upon an inadequate understanding of
the nature of money. Nowhere in its literature — nor in any
other economic literature for that matter — is there any
indication that our monetary authorities adequately understand the property content of money, particularly those
property attributes that both give money its excessive store

of value and the owners of that money excessive bargaining advantages in the markets.

Our present laws and rules simply do not constitute a well-integrated mechanism for insuring growth, full employment, continuity of monetary demand and job certainty. Sooner or later we must face up to the fact that society cannot function satisfactorily within limits that people will tolerate when it maintains a system of laws and rules which:

1. Enables savings to be made to too high a degree by those whose personal needs do not induce them to disburse their money savings steadily.
2. Concurrently grants them deferral opportunities so that they can postpone their disbursements indefinitely without loss; and then
3. Generates recessions automatically when money savings are not disbursed as rapidly as they are received.

Because of our failure to recognize that modern money possesses an excessive store of value, we have no adequate central bank control today for directly stimulating business activity whenever it sags. While our monetary controls are splendidly designed to check business booms when they begin to run away, we have only an inflationary tool—the monetization of government debt—for checking a business decline. When existing money is used tardily, the Federal Reserve can help to create a new, neutralizing batch of money. But the culprit money supply that has gone to sleep is not penalized or cancelled. In time it goes back to work and joins the new money in bidding for the current production. Price inflation naturally results.

Within the limits of the Federal Reserve System, the Federal Reserve authorities have historically been more conservative in their monetary behavior than has the Congress. On the analytical side, they have always stayed within the frame of reference of the existing Federal Reserve machine.

They could scarcely do otherwise. Their function has not been to pioneer the frontiers of monetary theory, but to operate an existing monetary machine conscientiously. They were not employed to design a new one. For that reason perhaps, their published material has historically been silent about several of the significant issues with which this book has dealt.

They have been silent about the nature of our money medium, which uniquely carries an excessive store of value. They have accepted this characteristic of money without criticism.

They have been silent over the irrationality of our government's paying $35 an ounce for gold — and for years drawing to itself most of the world's gold with its irrational price, a price which did not, and in logic could not, lift the price level.

They have worked with and have been silent about an interest rate structure that reflects to a large extent bribes to individual savers for not hoarding as well as rewards for saving.

Before 1970, they were silent regarding the extent to which Congress has empowered the labor unions in particular to increase business costs more rapidly than the nation could buffer the new costs with increases in man-hour productivity. They have also not dwelt on the manner and extent to which such a situation impairs the free enterprise system, when at the same time both they and Congress insist upon price stability.

Our examination of the nature of money and the processes of banking have revealed that society chronically faces four major monetary problems: (1) What should money be? (2) How much money should there be? (3) Who should have the power to create it? and (4) How should the prompt use of money be obtained?

Of the four problems, the two most difficult ones have been

to provide for the proper volume of money, the M, and for the prompt use of the money, the V. Great progress has been made in resolving the first problem, but practically nothing has been done about resolving the second.

It is the overabsorption of all central banks, including our own Federal Reserve Bank, with the money supply problem and their concurrent neglect of the prompt use problem that has made all central banks so ineffective at critical times in maintaining business activity that the State has felt it necessary to interfere even in the matter of influencing the money supply. At critical times during the past decade or two, it has not been the Federal Reserve's notions (of what is worthwhile spending and monetary need) that in the main have determined the actual level of the nation's money supply. In the zigzags of history, consequently, the power to create money and to decide on the quantity of it to be put into use is once again moving into the hands of the State and away from the central banks. That is quite a regressive and tragic reversal.

To me, it seems that the only way the Federal Reserve can regain its power and independence is to help with the design of a hot potato money to insure prompt reuse of money. In that way, it could remove the pressure that is periodically put on Congress to engage in compensatory spending and to enlarge the money supply via deficit bank borrowing.

The two questions of how much money there should be, and who should have the power to create it, are bound together. A few hundred years ago, irresponsible monarchs decided on how much commodity money should be put into use, and then used their own notions of need as their criteria for proper quantity — for high living or for war.

Later on, as society stabilized and the enforcement of contract could be taken for granted, people came to prefer for use as their medium of exchange the written and en-

forceable promises of reliable goldsmith-bankers. These
promises were private contracts reflecting private judgments.
As a result, money-making became a private affair, and it
became the private bankers who decided how much money
there should be.

For their criteria of proper quantity, they used their own
notions of what was a prudent and safe ratio between the
demand obligations that they lent and the reserves that they
had on hand.

Thus, after contracts had become acceptable as money,
private operators, instead of kings, became the determiners
of how much money there should be. They made it depend
mainly on the soundness of borrowers and the amount of
risk that they as bankers wanted to incur. By means of this
shift in power, the royal debasement of the currency was
avoided. But, on the other hand, overissue of bank notes
against inadequate reserves often occurred and brought on
new troubles such as runs on banks and business collapses.

In time, it became clear that the privilege of free note issue
by thousands of independent banks was not adequately
restrained by the bankers' own notions of prudence and risk.
Consequently, in an effort to obtain adequate restraint over
the total volume of money created, and yet retain the valuable help that the self-interest of lenders and borrowers
provide to the creation of "quality-money" through the
loan-making process, all large nations set up (nonprofit)
central banks. Under this arrangement, the governments
delegated to conscientious professional money managers
the power to control the aggregate money supply which the
independent bankers wanted selfishly to create.

This arrangement was a big improvement and worked
fairly well for several decades. But today it is beginning
to be circumvented more and more by lay politicians who
increasingly champion "growth" (of statist economic ac-

tivity) and deficit bank borrowing — if that should be needed to finance it.

Politicians would get little support for their proposals for statist activity and concurrent monetization of government debt if we were to so modify our money medium that it always insured the operation of our economy under a chronic scarcity of labor. Under such conditions, the desirable power and independence of the Federal Reserve authorities could be preserved. But if the Federal Reserve continues its unconcern over our use of sanctuary money, the characteristic which its own money possesses, it will probably be doomed to be — as it was during wartime — merely a subservient accomplice of the paternalistic state.

Unfortunately, it is the cancerous hoarding defect, now imbedded in the free market system, that helps to drive people from the market frying pan into the fanatical all-consuming statist fire. Even though the defect built into our money is devastating in its impact, it is very easy to remove it. And if our monetary system were to banish automatically the fear of unemployment and the practice of extending statism during recession; if it were to assure everyone a lifetime of job security and alternative job opportunity; if it were to assure us a labor and investment market wherein employers were always looking for workers instead of workers always looking for jobs, the virtues of the system would undoubtedly rekindle and refire that proselytizing fervor among Americans that once drove them to sing to the whole world the virtues of their system. There would be no need for, and little demand for, more bureaucracy, central planning, or statism in its many forms.

The major economic and social gains might come, not from the fact that we return to the use of hot potato money or to the full gold standard, but from the certainty that gold's gradually declining price will put continuous pressure on the owners of all kinds of money to disburse it more promptly, that the aggregate monetary demand for goods and services (and employees) will fluctuate at a higher level than before, and that the bargaining power of all employees will be so much higher in the wages market that their income will be lifted upward far enough to provide full blast activity for all the capital facilities that the slightly reduced percentage of savings can build.

In my opinion, the accidental removal of carrying charges from money has been the causal factor behind the historically unstable private demand for goods. It has been the recession and depression maker that has plagued the otherwise fine free enterprise system. Now that plague could be over.

Overcoming that plague is at best a long shot possibility. But the effort deserves the highest priority.

Until the free market mechanism is enveloped with working rules which insure a stable market demand for goods and services and the full employment that goes with it — something which has not been the case since demand deposit money became the dominant medium of exchange — the outlook for the survival of any free society is dim indeed. As is, it loses a little in position every day.

Unless the defect at the heart of the free market mechanism is corrected, it would behoove the anticommunist patriots of our society very little — even if they could achieve it — to elect their preferred candidates, obtain full hearing for their views and facts in the press, TV and schools, etc. They would still lose out over time in their "finger-in-the-dike" struggle with the relentless advance of the liberal-socialist-communist Juggernaut.

Let us assume that our libertarian patriots have miraculous luck, and that our press, our Congress, and our American milieu itself once again becomes proud of its fine industrial machine, patriotic in mood, against statist encroachment, awake to Russia's crafty war against us, alert to the sophistry of subversives, etc., so that the people actually learn to distinguish between good and evil.

Still, if the monopoly privilege to money savers of using society's exchange instrument out of phase with production is not destroyed, it would help the dedicated workers for a better world very little in maintaining their improved society. Their refurbished society would still periodically slide into recession, and the certain yammer for the government "to do something" would again bring on the freedom-killing improvisations of the New Deal economics.

# PART 5

## Supplements

# Supplement A
## Money, Government and Freedom

WHEN people organize themselves into communities, they pose for themselves the immense problem of effectively circumscribing power, of limiting its use and neutralizing its possible misuse. Only once or twice in history have people been wise enough to do this effectively. Fortunately, one such time was in colonial America when centralized power was circumscribed by an ingeniously written constitution. But even when centralized political power is ingeniously restrained by parceling it out wisely, and by continually investigating and checking its use and misuse, the additional task remains of restraining economic power by wisely parceling out that power too. History's most effective tool for diffusing and distributing economic power has been the invention of money and the marketplace.

It is, as we saw, the existence of money as an exchange instrument that makes it feasible to divert to political representatives only a limited amount of economic power. For money gives ordinary people a tight control over the economic direction of their lives and extends the range of their free behavior. To understand why this is so, one must examine the functional role of money in a free market economy. It is an exciting one, because money is the emancipating instrument by which the big consuming public guides the complex processes of production and distribution. Moreover, the use of money enables the people to direct economic activity by means of persuasion rather than by force. And force is the only other control instrument that people could use if they did not possess the guidance instrument of money.

Most people wish to release those productive forces which will make output ever larger and to install social institutions which will make distribution of the product ever more equitable. They know that income is very unevenly distributed, that some people are born to riches while others work and worry from childhood to the grave. Insofar as the laws and rules of our society, rather than innate abilities or unequal contributions account for the disparities in the rewards, they wish to improve the rules. They know that if poorly devised rules first unbalance the rewards for effort, and we then entrust officials with discretionary power to rectify the imbalance by skimming income from the rich and giving it to the poor, we court totalitarian government. For temptation and abuse of power follows the granting of discretionary power as surely as night follows day.

If democracy is government by the people and for the people in an atmosphere of liberty, it follows that government ceases to be democratic when the people lose control over it and it ceases to be responsible to the people. When that occurs, it is the unrepresentative officials of government—the kings, the czars, the fuehrers, the bureaucrats, the commissars—who utilize government power much as they please without submitting their plans and actions honestly for the approval of the people.

We are counseled from early childhood that eternal vigilance is the price of liberty. But vigilance against whom? The devil is seldom identified. Bewilderment stops us from pointing our finger at the usurping administrators of government. It is not often enough pointed out that the eternal enemy of government by and for the people is the executive group which—once entrusted with administrative and police power—tends to make itself the master and not the servant of the people.

Why is it that, in all ages and in all societies, this contest between the people and its officials is ever recurring? Why is it that the people can maintain a democratic society only through eternal vigilance?

The problem is eternal because when people live together and produce their goods as cooperating specialists, they must set up administrative agencies to which to delegate their collective control over contracts and property, and to whom they must delegate vast amounts of temptation, too. As a result, people always have the problem of protecting themselves against the misuse of the power that they have diverted to their officials. One of the best ways for people to protect themselves is to rely on private ownership, limited government, the market place, and on persuasion and the use of money.

Some ancient civilizations, like those of Egypt and Peru, got along awkwardly without money. But without it, people could exercise little choice in selecting the goods they produced and consumed. They could neither buy nor sell except through barter. They had no voice in deciding what was to be produced, what was to be exchanged, or what the values of the items were that were to be exchanged. Without money, they necessarily had to take orders from the men who planned the community's production in an authoritarian way. Without money, they were in a sense slaves. All highly organized and specialized societies of the past that did not use money had to use a large increment of slavery instead.

When moneyless societies consist merely of small primary groups, the gentle but powerful controls that normally grow out of familylike association—controls like considerateness, fairness, respect, banter, religion, and the like — can make the consumers' relation to the planners of production not seem to be slavery. But when the social group is large (and the controls of face-to-face association lose their potency) and production must be fitted to distant central plans, enforcement must be impersonal and rigorous, compulsion must be resorted to — and slavery must be practiced.

As money evolved from its primitive to its complex form, it moved through many stages. Time was when exchanges of product were few or were carried on entirely through barter. Money was used only for exchanging goods with groups outside the local community. But today in the United States, for example, everyone uses money. Eighty million Americans have checking accounts and use credit money extensively in their transactions. Without such widespread use of money, our high standards of living would be impossible. For money, even though it is not well-understood, is the instrument that facilitates exchange. It is the circulating medium that is used as an interim possession in jumping from the ownership of one asset to another.

Whatever changes have been made in money have represented evolutionary efforts to substitute one more efficient medium of exchange for another. Our historical shiftings — from barter to warehouse receipts, to gold, to certificates of indebtedness, to deposit credits, etc. — have all been made with a view to helping specialized producers exchange their surpluses more easily. But, as we have seen, we have at the same time inadvertently built a continuing imperfection into our money instrument, an imperfection which facilitates the disruption of exchange and, through exchange, both production and distribution.

Money is an instrument of freedom because it is the particular tool, the special means, that makes it possible for society's consumers (1) to determine the products that the community turns out, (2) to influence the relative size of the rewards that the many contributors to output shall receive, and (3) to provide for the whole operation via persuasion rather than by decree. With removal of the long-overlooked flaw in money, which facilitates the breakdown of demand and helps to bring on unemployment and distress, our money could instead be our most emancipating invention.

# Supplement B

## Note Regarding the Book's Diagrammatic Method

THE perspective diagrams made use of in this book represent an entirely new language of communication. Many years ago I realized that economists were peculiarly unlucky men in that they possessed no systematic symbolism for integrating and communicating their materials to others. Several fields of study, such as engineering and chemistry, possessed useful symbolisms, but economics was not one of them.

Music, for example, has had an integrating language of its own for hundreds of years. There was a time when musicians could play their tunes and sing their songs but had no means of recording or describing their music for others; no rigorous symbolism for communicating their melodies to future times and distant places. Today they have an integrating symbolism which can be used very effectively to convey their sound creations to others. Great musicians may have preceded Bach, Mozart, and Beethoven in the days when music could not be put into notes and bars and measures, but the world will never know. (Fig. 40, opp.)

Chemists, too, have invented an auxiliary symbolism for conveying their specialized knowledge. In dealing with the world of matter, they have a terse and rigorous means for

Figure 40

describing molecular structure and behavior. Complex though their world may be, they have a language tool by which to describe it effectively.

$$2Na + 2H_2O \rightarrow 2NaOH + H_2$$

Mathematicians can also effectively and objectively present and integrate their material. Concerned as they are with the relationships between the actions and balances in nature, they have over the centuries sought to measure and rigorously portray the static strains in beams and cables, the dynamic forces in whirling blades and plunging pistons and the measurable coordination that exists within circuits, engines, fluids, molecules and stars. Ever since the invention of the Cartesian coordinates, mathematicians have had a splendidly terse and nonsubjective language for measuring, summarizing and presenting the web of their concerns.

$$X^2 + Y^2 = R^2$$

Man has always been a builder, too. But until he could convey to others the detailed design of his contemplated work, his structures were relatively simple. In time, however, the engineers perfected a supplementary language of their own—the graphic conventions known as engineering drawing.

These conventions are superbly designed to portray both

## An Engineering Drawing
## Convention.

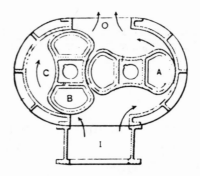

## Two Lobe Cycloidal Pump

Figure 41

structure and process. So engineers, too, can now first
describe their physical structures in words and phrases and
then supplement their verbal descriptions with graphic
means. (Fig. 41 above.)

Until this could be done, complex structures could not be
built. Mathematics could portray the interdependence of
many of the variables involved in design, but it could not
describe the structural frame of reference to which the
variables related. Engineering drawing alone could do this.
Happily, as of today, both engineering and mathematics
have a rigorous symbolism of their own and can now cooperate and design and build together.

Over the centuries, men have striven to equip themselves
with orderly aids to thought; hieroglyphics, alphabets,
number conventions and Cartesian coordinates. Men have
ever sought quick and vivid means for organizing knowledge
and communicating it to others. Nonetheless, after centuries
of effort, we are still handicapped in the complex fields of
government and economics by inadequate tools of communication. In the main, verbal means are still relied upon

for conveying our complex economic problems to the limitless seekers of understanding. In this book I submit and illustrate a new graphic technique for portraying economic complexities—a breakthrough analogous to engineering drawing—which I believe can greatly improve both economic analysis and communication.

The elements of that symbolism were illustrated in my *National Income Visualized* (New York: Columbia University Press, 1956) and discussed at some length in the conclusion of that book. A sample application of the symbolism is also shown in Supplement C of this book. There, the diagram "How Money Originates And Circulates" shows the processes by which "National Income Accounting" is related to the key processes of commercial banking.

*The Functional Characteristics of the New Means for Communicating Socioeconomic Relationships.*

The method consists of a set of symbols which help to make involved economic themes easier to understand. The symbolism has a certain logical construction. It is not random. It could be taught just as engineering drawing is taught.

Because economics deals with transactions between groups, the technique uses specific symbols for designating the major economic groups. It does this with its simulated houses, factories, and domed government buildings. Then, with flow through pipes and vats full of assets and liabilities, it symbolizes the exchanges between the groups. It shows both flows and levels concurrently and quantitatively. Thus the buildings and pipes together show the exchanges between the economic groups.

The technique's portrayals are made easy for laymen to understand by the exclusive use of perspective drawings. The portrayals are also subject to statistical check, just as engineering drawings are.

The symbolism can simultaneously present the two tabular

devices of corporate accounting, the income statement and the balance sheet, by presenting both rates and levels simultaneously.

Economics deals concurrently with two major aspects of social organization — the engineering world of physical production and distribution, and the financial world of ownership and indebtedness. So the symbolism portrays simultaneously the physical circuits of the engineering world and the financial circuits of the economic world — and keeps the two related.

When statistics are available, the symbolism can also show the relative importance of the component circuits. By using flow meters, it can show the quantities conveyed by the several pipes. Just as engineers, in portraying the flows in boiler rooms, use larger or smaller pipes depending on the average load carried by each pipe, and then use flow meters to record the wider ranges of variation, so we use pipes and flow meters in our portrayals.

Each portrayal is expansible or contractible at the portrayer's discretion. One can choose to highlight either the details of a situation or the overall picture. The methodology is like the Dewey Decimal System in that it is infinitely expansible or contractible, and still retains its integration. One can drop one portion of a sketch while adding another and still retain the frame of reference. One can go from simple component sketches to larger integrations just by adding a bit here and dropping a bit there.

Integrated visualizations of economics might even induce students to think of themselves as problem solvers, and not merely as learners. Visualization makes it easier to view knowledge as knowing how best to act, instead of merely as the accumulating of accepted truths. It inclines one both to express knowledge in relatives and not in absolutes, and to check whether one's ideas are philosophically complete.

It necessarily reveals relations and data that test hypotheses for their solutions. It also makes it difficult to premise that abstract clichés and concepts alone constitute something definite in themselves apart from the portrayable relationships associated with the terms.

In the world of business, I have thoroughly tested my graphic symbolism as a clarifying means. As founder and president of the U.S. Economics Corporation, an economic consulting and research firm, I made extensive use — over three decades — of my graphic technique for aiding the group discussion of problems and policies with a multitude of America's very largest corporations regarding the outlook for business.

Such corporations usually have on their staffs top-flight economists trained in theory and extremely aware of current reality. Unwittingly, I was probably lucky in having my academic propensities pushed into a disciplined exploration of socioeconomic reality. As time went on, I diagrammed my observations in scores of flow charts for discussion purposes.

And in handling the structural economic problems and relationships dealt with in this book, I first wheeled them into my graphic Mayo clinic. Its diagnostic methodology enabled me, I believe, to uncover a veritable cancer in our otherwise fine free market system, and also discover a simple means for removing it.

Because of the effectiveness of my technique as a teaching tool, Columbia University, with the financial support of the Alfred P. Sloan Foundation, established the Visual Economics Laboratory in 1951. I was made the director. In 1956, the Columbia University Press published my *National Income Visualized* and my *How U.S. Output Is Measured*. This book, like my former book, *Money In Motion* (a graphic portrayal of the nature of money and the American monetary system) are also products of the Laboratory. In my work, I have had complete independence of thought and action. Consequently, if I have stumbled here and there with some analysis, mishandled some statistic or bobbled some contentious issue, I alone am to blame for the slippage.

# Supplement C

## How Money Originates and Circulates

THE large fold-out diagram mounted inside of the back cover of this publication (Fig. 42.) was electrically animated and shown at the New York World's Fair in 1964–65 by the American Economic Foundation in its Hall of Free Enterprise. The diagram shows the major monetary circuits which enter into the Department of Commerce's National Income Accounts. It also shows how money creation is related to the major U.S. monetary flows for the year 1962.

The role of money is an exciting one. For, as I have tried to make clear, money gives to ordinary people a control over the economic direction of their lives and extends the range of their free behavior. Money is the emancipating instrument by which the big consuming public induces people by persuasion rather than by force to produce the goods and services that it wants. Money also coordinates the efforts of all those who contribute to production without invoking the discretionary judgments of government officials.

This fold-out diagram's use, therefore, is as a functional and statistical combination of many stories about money and its movement through the economy. In particular, it contains very important information about spending, income, investment, saving and money creation.

The five buildings through which the money flows — reading from left to right of the diagram — are Government, Business Enterprise, Commercial Banks, Savings Banks and Institutions and, finally, the People themselves who receive the personal income.

## What Consumers Spend Their Money For

The diagram shows how the American people in 1962, by spending their money for selected goods and services, guided the U.S. economy into producing the things they wanted.

The high building on the right labeled "Persons" represents the American people as both Workers and Consumers. The stream of income that flowed to them in 1962 was, as shown, $442 billion (1). After paying Personal Income Taxes of $58 billion (2) and saving $29 billion (3), the people disbursed $355 billion of their income for consumption (4).

Persons constitute the single biggest block of buyers for the nation's output. There were 186.7 million people in the U.S. in 1962. Collectively, they spent $355 billion (4) for goods and services.

Most of the $355 billion spent by Persons for goods and services was used to buy nondurable goods (5) such as clothing, food, gasoline, oil and other items which wear out rather quickly.

Persons spent another $146 billion for services (6) such as rent, electric and telephone service, medical care, auto repairs, interest on personal debt and other services which U.S. consumers feel they want. Shelter takes a large portion of this total. In 1962 consumers spent $98 billion (partly on an imputed rent basis) to provide shelter for themselves and their families. Spending for utilities took another $15 billion, while medical services took $16 billion. The money that consumers borrowed in 1962 and in earlier years cost them $7 billion in interest in 1962 alone, or about 1.6% of their total income.

The smallest and yet the most volatile outlet for personal spending is for durable goods. Durable goods are items which last longer than two years. They include automobiles, furniture, appliances, tires, radios and TV. In 1962 consumers spent $48 billion (7) for these items.

## What Business Spends Its Money For

A second group of buyers for the nation's final output is the Business Community itself, represented by the low flat building in the center of Figure 42. In total, business spent $79 billion (8) in 1962 in the end markets for the finished equipment (9) and structures (10) that it needed to carry on its business. Its total outpayments during that year were several times the $79 billion, but these other payments were made to obtain parts and components along with the services and contributions of people who contributed to the total production.

In any given year, business produces more or less than is used up by the nation's consumers. In the process, its inventories change. To accommodate the consumers' needs efficiently, business maintains a bin of inventory. Each year goods are either added to stocks or withdrawn. In 1962, business in total added $6 billion (11) to its inventories.

Business must be constantly alert to new processes and products which affect its operations. In its drive to increase efficiency, to replace worn-out equipment, and to add to its ability to produce, business carefully reviews and monitors the scientific developments of the nation. Each year, business invests billions of dollars to equip workers with the most efficient and modern machines that it can find. As of today, each American worker is being helped with $28,000 worth of facilities.

*How Government Disburses Its Revenues*

In 1962, all governments—federal, state, and local, represented by the building on the left, disbursed $162 billion
(12). This big green flow (12), pouring out of the front of the
Government building, divides to show that $53 billion was
used for National Security expenditures (13) and $109 billion
(14) for all other purposes.

The $109 billion (14) not spent for National Security in
1962 were used by the federal, state and local governments
as follows: $16 billion for the construction of highways and
other community facilities; $44 billion for the pay of govern-
ment employees who were not directly concerned with
defense; about $4 billion for subsidies to farmers, and $45
billion for transfer payments and interest on government
debt.

Collectively, Government, Business and Persons spent
$555 billion in 1962 for goods and services. This sum, shown
at the meter on the large horizontal pipe, is called "Gross
National Expenditures." (The counterflow of actual goods
and services—not shown in the diagram—which was purchased with those expenditures is called "Gross National
Product.")

*Some Business Revenues Do Not Become*
*Part of National Income*

The $555 billion expenditures stream which flowed as
Gross National Expenditures (18), partly into the cash bin
of the Business Enterprise Building and partly (31), into the
cash bin of Government, all flowed out again. The sums
which Business disbursed out of its cash bin to those who
helped to produce its goods—when added to the wages and
salaries (35) which the government paid out to its employees
—also added up to $555 billion. The two outpayments
streams when added together are called "Gross National

Income Produced." Except for discrepancies, the sum of these two major outpayments always equals the "Gross National Expenditures" figure.

In 1962 Business, in turning out its produce, wore out tools and facilities worth an estimated $49 billion. This was called "Allowances for Depreciation" (23). So part of the $555 billion Gross National Expenditures figure was not entirely a payment for new products but a payment for replacing the old facilities that wore out in turning out the new product. What was left was called "Net National Product." In 1962, this totaled $506 billion.

In collecting payments for its new products, Business also acted as a tax collector for the Government. Business collects the sales taxes, excise taxes, and other taxes which the Government levies on the products that Business sells. In 1962, such taxes amounted to $53 billion. They are shown (24) to the left of the Business Enterprise building flowing downward into the Government "Taxes" stream. After the Government collected this slice of receipts, the remainder was called "National Income" produced. That widely publicized figure amounted to $454 billion in 1962. It is shown as a meter reading (25) to the left of the Business building.

The Government taps the "National Income" stream before it is distributed as "Personal Income" to those who helped to produce it. In 1962, by means of corporate profits taxes of $22 billion (26) and Social Security taxes of $24 billion (27), Government collected $46 billion of National Income before the balance was distributed to Persons as part of "Personal Income."

Personal Income amounted to $442 billion in 1962. It was made up of two major portions. One portion, $397 billion, was generated by the efforts of the employees of Business and Government. It is shown by the big long horizontal stream (29) at the top of the diagram. The Second portion

(19), on the far lower right of the diagram, represented a pocket-to-pocket flow of government Transfer Payments and Interest Payments to selected citizens. That sum amounted to $45 billion in 1962.

In 1962, $499 billion of the total Gross National Expenditures of $555 billion flowed over the counter (30) to Business in payment for the goods and services that it turned out, while $56 billion went (31) to Government for the services that it provided.

Business generated $397 billion of the total generated National Income of $454 billion (25). It disbursed the income generated as follows: $297 billion for Wages and Salaries (32); $26 billion for "Supplements to Wages and Salaries"; $50 billion to Unincorporated Businesses (such as farmers and store owners); $22 billion to Net Interest; $12 billion to Rents and Royalties; and $47 billion to Profits Before Taxes (33). The Government took to itself as Corporate Profits Taxes, $22 billion (33) of these $47 billion Profits Before Taxes. The remainder, Profits After Taxes (34), amounted to $25 billion in 1962.

## How People Save a Part of Their Personal Income

The upper righthand corner of the fold-out diagram shows what people do with the money that they save out of their current income. In 1962, when people had a personal income of $442 billion (1), they paid Personal Taxes of $58 billion (2) and spent $355 billion (4) for consumption goods. The remainder, $29 billion (3)—not spent for consumption goods—is regarded by the Department of Commerce as "Personal Savings," a residual item.

Personal savings can also be calculated by adding all the additions to the assets of Persons and subtracting the additions to their liabilities. Thus personal savings equals the net change in the assets and liabilities of Persons.

The total increase in assets of Persons in 1962 amounted to $61 billion, of which $39 billion (36) were financial assets in the form of bank deposits, insurance reserves, and purchases of securities. The remaining $22 billion represented investment in tangible assets (37) by Farmers, Unincorporated Business, and Nonprofit Institutions, who are among the groups called "Persons" by the Department of Commerce.

The $39 billion in additional financial savings sought profitable investment outlets. Part of the savings went to federal and state and local governments and part to Business in return for securities. The outflow of savings ("Personal Savings Invested") is shown in the diagram coming out (39) into either business investment or into the deficit financing operations (41) of the federal, state and local governments.

When people do not pour all of their current income into the big "Consumption Expenditure" stream (4), shown to the left of the Persons building, they divert most of it to institutions like "Savings Banks, Savings and Loan Associations, Pension Funds, Insurance Companies, etc." These institutions appear as a single building at the top of the diagram. The diverted stream of personal savings is shown flowing upward (3) from the big "Consumption Expenditure" stream and then to the left into a bin (42)—in the Savings Institution building—labeled "Income Delegated For Investment." For these diverted savings, the people who delegate the money are shown receiving, by way of a red stream (43), the debt obligations of the Savings Institutions. These obligations consist of such things as time deposits, savings deposits, and claims against insurance companies. The red stream is shown flowing to the right out of a bin labeled "Claims Against Intermediaries" down into the asset bin of the "Persons" building labeled "Time Deposits And Insurance Claims." By exchanging some of their money for claims in an effort to earn interest on it, people delegate to Savings Institutions the responsibility of keeping a part of their current income invested. They also place on the Savings Institutions the responsibility of moving the money savings into investment at least as rapidly as they divert it from their big expenditure stream (4).

The Savings Institutions have three major outlets for the funds delegated to them. One is to meet Business's demand for money (40) for use in buying equipment, construction, and inventory. A second is to meet the Government demand for borrowed money (41) for schools, subsidies, foreign aid, highways, defense, etc., a demand which exists whenever governments decide to spend more money than they can raise in taxes. A third is to meet the Consumer demand for borrowed money.

The stream of "Personal Income Invested" (39) shown at the top of the diagram flowing to the left of the "Savings Institutions" moves on into the cash bins of either Business or Government in exchange for Stocks and Bonds, Government securities, Mortgages, or other paper. The diagram shows this counterflow of securities by means of the several red streams (44) that flow horizontally just below the top green "Personal Income Invested" stream (39) just referred to.

Even though the growth of private debt is often disapproved of, and the act of saving often regarded with approval, this diagram makes clear that the two actions are counterparts of one another. It shows that money income not used for "Consumption Expenditures" (4), but delegated to "Savings Institutions" for investment, can get back into the markets again — as a demand (8 and 12) for plant, equipment and goods — only if Business, Government and "Persons" create a matching volume of debt obligations and give these to the Savers and Savings Institutions for the delegated funds. Thus, to the extent that debt is created and exchanged

as the counterpart to currently saved income, debt is as commendable as savings. One is not possible without the other.

## Governments Obtain Their Incomes By Taxing and Borrowing

The Federal Government gets its spending money in
three different ways: (1) by levying taxes; (2) by exchanging
its bonds, notes and other debt obligations for some of the
public's dollar savings, and (3) by exchanging its dated
obligations at the Federal Reserve Banks and Commercial
Banks for demand obligations against these banks. Inasmuch
as demand claims on these banks constitute our modern
money, the Federal Government's third recourse consists
essentially of minting new money for itself whenever it has
difficulty in obtaining it from the first two mentioned sources.

During the five years, 1957–1962, the Federal Government made average annual cash disbursements of $104.8
billion, and had average annual cash receipts of $100.5
billion. This five year deficit was met by borrowings. The
Federal debt rose by about $4 billion annually during the
five year period.

State and local governments raise their revenue in only
two ways: either by levying taxes or by borrowing it from
nonbank savers in exchange for government obligations.

In 1962 the federal, state and local governments collectively raised $162 billion. The large fold-out diagram shows
that of this sum, $157 billion (46), was obtained through
taxes, and $5 billion (47) met through borrowing.

Personal taxes (2), which are shown flowing to the Government building from the Persons building, provided $58
billion of Government revenue in 1962. Indirect business
taxes (24) — such as sales and excise taxes — provided $53
billion; corporate income taxes (26) $22 billion, and Social
Security taxes $24 billion (27).

*The Debt Obligations of Banks Constitute*
*Our Medium of Exchange*

The fold-out diagram illustrates vividly how borrowers'
debts are exchanged for bank debt and how *bank debt*
becomes the nation's medium of exchange. The diagram
illustrates how a Person located at the extreme right of the
diagram — sitting at a desk (48) toward the front of his building — in the process of "borrowing" sends (via the red line)
an obligation like a note or a mortgage (49) into the bin of
the Commercial Bank labeled "Consumer Notes & Mortgages." In doing so, the diagram shows that this person gives
himself at the same time a liability (50). That liability is
also depicted by a red line flowing into the bin labeled
"Notes & Mortgages" on the right-hand side of the house.

Two more flows or simultaneous entries are involved: The
money that the banker — shown at his desk — gives to the
borrowing consumer becomes an asset for the borrower. It
is shown (51) flowing into the consumer's "Demand Deposit" bin near the top of the "Persons" building. That sum
simultaneously becomes a liability (52) to the banker who
now owes the money to the borrower. This liability is shown
going into the "Demand Deposit" bin (52) on the right side
of the bank. Such bank obligations — given in return for borrowers' notes, mortgages, securities, etc. — constitute our
modern checkbook money. (As the borrower writes checks
on his account, he puts the checkbook money into circulation
via the streams (4) and (3).)

Both Private Businesses and Governments borrow from the
Commercial Banks and help to create new money by doing
so. The diagram shows a red stream labeled "Obligations
Exchanged for New Bank Money" flowing out (53) of the
Business building into one of the bank's asset bins labeled
"Commercial And Industrial Notes and Bonds."

As a counterflow to this red stream is shown a stream of

new money (54) labeled "Money Created Against Business Property" flowing from the desk of the bank into an asset bin in the Business Enterprise building labeled "New Money Borrowings." The diagram illustrates vividly that in Credit Banking, borrowers give their collateralized obligations in exchange for bank debt obligations. Collateralized borrowers' debt is exchanged for bankers' debt.

The diagram also illustrates with a red stream the Federal Government sending its debt obligations (55) labeled "Pledged Future Tax Receipts" into the bank's portfolio bin, labeled "Government Securities," and in return receiving from the Bank new money (56) into its "New Money" bin.

These promises, which bankers give to borrowers in exchange for collateralized obligations, constitute the major part of our money today. Realistically, this checkbook money consists of transferable claims against that whole stew of assets in the bank's portfolio which the borrowers had put up as collateral. Once upon a time, these assets consisted partly of gold, but since 1933 they have consisted entirely of miscellaneous assets like notes, bonds and mortgages — assorted commitments to repay reserve currency at specified future dates. The repayments are made, but seldom in currency. They are almost always made by collecting other people's claims against the bank and transferring these back to the bank.

# Index

346

This comprehensive diagram presents graphically the logic of GNP accounting, and shows how U.S. output is measured in dollar terms. In an overall way, this diagram shows how the banking system is related to GNP accounting. It does more than that, however.

GNP accounting is only one-legged accounting. It ignores balance sheet changes among Consumers, Business Enterprise groups, the Banks, and Federal, State and Local Governments. Consequently, the Gross National Expenditure figure for any one year may be reported as being, say, $1,000 billion and then as being $1,050 billion for the next year. All the component spending figures for each year seem to be accounted for accurately. But where did the $50 billion increase for the one year come from? One must—among other things—look into the changes in the banking system and the spenders' balance sheets for the explanations.